The
Democratic Muse

Folk Music Revival in Scotland

First edition 1984 by Kahn & Averill, London

This revised and updated edition published 1996
Scottish Cultural Press
PO Box 106, Aberdeen AB9 8ZE
Tel: 01224 583777
Fax: 01224 575337

British Library Cataloguing in Publication Data
A catalogue record for this book is available from the British Library

ISBN: 1 898218 10 2

The publisher acknowledges subsidies from the Scottish Arts Council, the Carnegie Trust
and the Russell Trust towards the publication of this volume

THE SCOTTISH ARTS COUNCIL

A tape (ref. SSC 076) featuring many of the songs
transcribed in this book is available from
Scotsoun, 13 Ashton Road, Glasgow, G12 8SP

Printed and bound by BPC-AUP Aberdeen Ltd

The Democratic Muse

Folk Music Revival in Scotland

Ailie Munro

Including *Folk Revival in Gaelic Song*
by Morag MacLeod

Foreword by Hamish Henderson

SCOTTISH CULTURAL PRESS

To Sandra and Robin

Contents

Background to the present revival: the earlier English revival; Sharp, Greig and Duncan. 1945: appeal of songs celebrating lives of ordinary people. Folk or traditional; collectors; comments on folk music in 17th, 18th and 19th centuries. The folk scene today: ceilidhs and their model; a folk club evening; pub sessions, Sandy Bell's, festivals.

Beginnings in the USA

Importance of topical songs; the IWW (Wobblies); Joe Hill and the songs. The Almanacs, People's Songs, *Sing Out!* Robeson, Seeger, The Weavers, Woody Guthrie – his songs and his singing. Jazz: American left, and folk music.

Development in Scotland

Historical background: 1603–1707; art music renaissances; Scottish 'popular' music; the kailyard; twentieth-century literary renaissance. American influence and collecting; seminal broadcasts; first signs of revival in late 1940s. Post War climate, search for a people's art. MacColl, Henderson. 'The Red Flag' to the original tune. (Allan) Lomax's visit. Protest Songs: (1) *Sangs o' the Stane*, 1950; (2) *EIIR*, on Queen's accession, 1952. Edinburgh People's Festivals 1951–55; Buchan; School of Scottish Studies, first folk clubs; Blythman. Travellers 'discovered'; Jeannie Robertson. Jazz, skiffle, American influence still. Folk clubs proliferate. *Tonight* on television: Hall and Macgregor. Protest songs: (3) *anti-Polaris*, 1961. Trend towards native tradition, and away from American. Festivals. Beginnings of instrumental 'explosion'.

Songs heard in the Seventies

Forty songs presented as 'facts and experiences' of revival story; reasons for choice of songs. Groups based on themes. Revival and Source singers. The transcriptions: descriptive, compromise; ornaments, idioms. The songs, and comments from the singers, 1981–82.

V Folk Revival in Gaelic Song
by Morag MacLeod

Some details of historical origins and older types of song; words can often be traced to written sources but melodies depend on oral sources; the way knowledge of songs has lasted or changed; collectors; solo and group performance today; the Celtic music bandwagon.

VI The Travelling People

Origins, history, persecution of; important tradition-bearers; their culture, part of Scotland's; their life-style, singing style, problems and special gifts; contributions from travellers. Two way Revival influence. Storytelling: an example given as told by Duncan Williamson. Developments over last decade: New Age Travellers; traveller culture declining.

VII Signposts to the Millennium

'Revival'? Dispersal of folk music, in for example the theatre, the media, literary circles and country dance resurgence. Five primary areas of development during the last 12–15 years: 1. Song; 2. Storytelling; 3. Instrumental music; 4. Protest songs; 5. Influence on education and the wider community. Notes on other topics: the TMSA; world music and *Folk Roots*; clubs, festivals and magazines; art music; the School of Scottish Studies.

Concluding thoughts: whither? The social descent of Scots language and folk music; startling statistics; the democratic contradiction. Difficulties of music composition for folk composers. Models for singers. Reflections on tradition now: the ubiquitous beat, new songs on the outer fringes of folk 'idiom'. Caveats for the future. Paradox: the democratic singer.

Appendix

Four songs, with four related versions of each; plus comments from the singers, 1981–82.

List of Plates

Acknowledgements

for the first edition, *The Folk Music Revival in Scotland*

Grateful thanks to Angus Russell, Sheila Douglas, Andrew Douglas, Hilary Cusker, Patrick Shuldham-Shaw, Jean Redpath, John Watt, Andrew Hunter, Pete Shepheard, Adam McNaughtan, Jane Turriff, Ian MacDonald, Lizzie Higgins, Peter Hall, Josh MacRae, Hamish Henderson, Morris Blythman and Norman Buchan; to Betsy and Bryce Whyte, Jane Turriff and Danny Stewart, Belle Stewart, Sheila MacGregor, Ian MacGregor, Bella and Willie MacPhee, and to Duncan and Linda Williamson: for permission to record and for hospitality.

To Sheila Douglas, Archie Fisher and Bobby Campbell, Ewan MacColl, Janette McGinn for Matt McGinn, and Belle Stewart, for permission to print their songs. To the singers and recorders of songs transcribed in Chapters 3, 4 and 5; and to John MacQueen, then Director of the School of Scottish Studies, for permission to use material from the School's archives.

To John Blacking, Derek Bowman, Alan Bruford, Morag Bruford, Ian Campbell, Eric Cregeen, Jan Fairley, Hugh Gentleman, Daphne Hamilton, Hamish Henderson, Rhodri Jeffreys-Jones, Emily Lyle, Hugh MacDonald, Charles K Maisels, Jack Rutherford, Anne Dhu Shapiro, Pete Shepheard, JAC Stevenson and Ronald Stevenson for advice and comments.

To Angus McIntosh and Margaret MacKay for information. To Allan Palmer for copies of his tapes. To Barry Ould for printing the music. To the BBC for information. To Morris Blythman for permission to use the Ding Dong Dollar disc. To the Music Corporation of America for permission to print 'Joe Hill', and to Harmony Music Ltd., London and Stormking Music Inc., New York, for permission to print 'The Moving on Song'. To all those who sent written contributions (acknowledged where quoted). To Sheila Somerville for cheerfulness and skill in typing the manuscript. To Hamish Henderson for his unfailing helpfulness and wit in answering queries. Morag MacLeod thanks Donald A MacDonald who read and commented on her chapter.

for the second edition, *The Democratic Muse*

I would like to thank the following: Vic Smith, Ian Campbell and John Barrow who read sections of the book and wrote comments; Vic Smith also for his inestimable help in making two tapes of extracts; Sandy Fenton for encouragement and for help in finding grants; Morag MacLeod for her wide-ranging update of Chapter V and for her tireless help in discussions; Rhodri Jeffreys-Jones for further help with Chapter II; Jane Fraser, former National Secretary of the TMSA, for information; Eileen Penman for written memories relevant to the women's section, Chapter VII, and for her general interest; Sheila Stewart and Stanley Robertson for updated information on the travellers; Geordie McIntyre for his brainchild: the new title for the book; Ian Green who trustfully lent me his tapes (and from whom I bought many); Sheila Somerville who processed the whole book and provided laughter and chat; Hamish Henderson for discussion, and above all for his uniquely pertinent foreword; Jean Bechofer, Margaret Bennett, Sheila Douglas, Jan Fairley, Rita McAllister, Margaret MacKay, John MacInnes, Danny Kyle, Allan Morris, Sheena Wellington and others for discussion and information; the Music Sales Group Ltd, London, for permission to reprint *Joe Hill* by Alfred Hayes and Earl Robinson; Stormking Music Inc., sub-publishers for Harmony Music Inc., London, for permission to reprint *The Moving On Song* by Ewan MacColl; and Jill Dick for her careful editing and for publishing the book. Written contributors are acknowledged where quoted.

Morag MacLeod would like to thank Arthur Cormack for information on the Feisean movement.

Finally, special thanks to my friend Ronald Stevenson, the *fons et origo* who first thought of the book and suggested it to Morris Kahn.

Foreword

The inception of the present 'folk revival' – as far as Scotland is concerned – can be dated, with fair confidence, to the halfway house of this century, for it was in 1950 that the celebrated American folklorist Alan Lomax arrived in Britain on the first stage of what was to become a world tour. Like many other intellectuals in the USA during Franklin D Roosevelt's 'New Deal' presidency, Alan was well known as a 'liberal'; indeed, as his noble book *The Land where the Blues began* testifies, he was an intrepid pioneer in the opening up to the world of black American culture. However, it did not take long after the end of World War II for what later became known as McCarthyism to begin making itself felt. Consequently, when Columbia Records invited Alan to superintend the production of 'World Albums of Folk and Primitive Music' he readily accepted, and his first port of call was London.

I was alerted to his presence by the brilliant left-wing actor-playwright and singer-songwriter Ewan MacColl, who knew that Alan would need help from 'resident collectors' in the various countries he was going to visit, and thought that I might fulfil this role in Scotland. I had collaborated with Ewan, and Joan Littlewood, in helping to organise the various 'fringe shows' that Theatre Workshop laid on in the Epworth Hall during the first Edinburgh Festivals, and these had included one or two poetry and folksong events – affectionately satirised by Robert Garioch in his poem 'Embro to the Ploy'. The 'folksong' consisted, incidentally, mainly of items from my own book (*Ballads of World War II*, which was published for the Lili Marlene Club of Glasgow in 1948) such as 'Banks of Sicily' and 'The D-Day Dodgers'.

The timing of this initiative of Ewan's could not have come at a better time for me, because I had just finished my translation of Antonio Gramsci's *Letters from Prison* and was unsure of my next move. I knew that the creation of a School of Scottish Studies was on the cards, but at that time it existed only on paper, and I was by no means sure that I would land a job with it. However, the very productive tour I did with Alan in the summer of 1951 enabled me to secure on tape a large amount of the folk material I knew was waiting to be collected in the North-East, and copies of these reels naturally found their way without delay on to the still bare shelves of the fledgling School, then housed in a modest corner of the Phonetics Department. (I was even hired by the University to transcribe them, and this enabled me to play hours of brand-new material to enthusiastic Edinburgh students.)

If I have begun this foreword on an unashamedly personal note, I do feel that this is one of the occasions when a direct personal testimony is not out of place. It also affords me an opportunity to pay tribute to the unique work of Ewan MacColl in laying the foundations of what on any reckoning can be seen as a quite extraordinary socio-cultural exploit.

Ailie Munro, in this masterly 'update' of her already celebrated account of the Scottish Revival, rightly gives due credit to the important American influence – Woody Guthrie, Pete Seeger, The Almanacs, the Lomaxes – on cultural developments in Europe during the 1950s. This influence was, of course, by no means a new phenomenon. In the nineteenth century the work of Francis James Child in surveying the entire field – as known at that time – of the *English and Scottish Popular Ballads* ensured for America an honoured place on the academic side of folklore scholarship which gifted researchers have sustained right up to the present day. And thanks to radio, the collecting work of John A Lomax and his equally gifted son Alan had a huge influence on young folksong aficionados in Britain in the 1930s, because songs from the aluminium discs deposited in the Library of Congress were used by Alistair Cooke in his thrilling broadcast series *I heard America Singing.*

In this book, Ailie has given due coverage to the importance of the 'protest' element in folksong, and anyone even vaguely familiar with the bountiful heritage of radical poetry in our tradition will readily comprehend what wonderful fallow ground Scotland was – and is – for this invigorating demotic influence.

It has been suggested, and not without demonstrable plausibility, that the Scottish folk tradition – at any rate since the early eighteenth century – has been nothing other than the sum total of a succession of revivals. From Allan Ramsay's *Evergreen* and *Tea-table Miscellany* through William Thomson's *Orpheus Caledonius* to Robert Burns's editorship of much of James Johnson's *Scots Musical Museum* – not to mention his enthusiastic work on the bawdry enshrined in the *Merry Muses of Caledonia* – it can be shown that interest in our folk culture was never livelier than in the eighteenth century. Moving into the nineteenth century, we encounter the massive contribution of Sir Walter Scott, and grouped around him we find James Hogg, Charles Kirkpatrick Sharpe and – in the North-East – Peter Buchan, collector of that rival to Burns's *Merry Muses,* 'The Secret Songs of Silence'. The Victorian period seems to have been in the main one of consolidation, but before it ended we come across Dean Christie's work in Aberdeenshire – like Scott's, an inimitable blend of devoted ear-to-ground folk 'scavenging', and sophisticated literary expertise.

This century has witnessed – again in the North-East – the monumental labours of two sterling collectors: Gavin Greig, the modest New Deer dominie, and the Rev James Duncan of Lynturk. Together, they amassed one of the biggest folksong collections the world has ever seen. Greig used a country newspaper, the *Buchan Observer* (alias 'The Buchanie'), to spread knowledge of their work far and wide in the fructuous North-East, using his column in it as a very effective collecting tool.

The effects 'on the ground' of the labours of Greig and Duncan were clearly visible to a schoolboy, rambling on a pushbike through Aberdeenshire in the 1930s. I still have a ticket (price 6d.) for an event organised by the Aberdeen Scottish Literature and Song Association. It reads as follows:

BOTHY NICHT
to be held in
THE IMPERIAL HOTEL, ABERDEEN
on
Tuesday, 19th October, 1937, at 8pm

AN ATTRACTIVE PROGRAMME

x

And a few years later, invited into a farmhouse near Ellon to hear a singer that had been recommended to me, I caught sight – behind the piano – of two piles of newspapers: one consisted of three or four dozen copies of the *Financial Times,* and the other – considerably larger – of yellowing copies of the *Buchan Observer* lovingly preserved since before World War I, and containing many of Gavin Greig's seminal articles on the 'Folk-Song of the North-East'.

Gatherings like the one mentioned above had plenty of professional 'bothy' singers to call on: men, for example, like the redoubtable old farmer John Strachan (who was still around to be recorded by Alan Lomax and myself on our 1951 tour); George Morris of Old Meldrum, the author of *Nicky Tams;* John Mearns, popular for decades on the Aberdeen BBC; and – most nostalgically remembered of all, perhaps – the late Willie Kemp, whom Francis Dillon thought 'the greatest of them all'.

Further south, in Perthshire and Angus especially, the popularity of 'diddling' contests had never waned; in many places they are still going strong to this day. And as for piping competitions...

In view of all of this, you may well ask – why revival? The reason is surely implicit in all I have written above. In the sphere we are discussing, no national tradition can ever afford to 'mark time' – to regard itself as unassailable: there are always possibilities of decline, or even extinction. Happily, in Scotland, we have usually been lucky in having champions never sweir to enter the lists in defence of something they valued – in this case, a central part of the country's culture. Burns, Scott, Greig and Duncan are only some of the most conspicuous on the Scots side – and Alexander Carmichael, Campbell of Islay and Calum I Maclean on the Gaelic side.

Also, we have now begun to understand that the learners, the apprentices are as important as the source singers and champion storytellers – they too have embarked on the carrying stream of tradition.

I hope that I may be pardoned one further anecdote. In the mid 1950s, when I was drawing up a list of guests to be invited to a ceilidh which Alan Lomax wanted to record, I told him that I intended to invite one or two enthusiasts who had spent hours listening to tapes in the School of Scottish Studies, and who were making quite a creditable job of singing songs from the North-East, employing a near authentic singing style. His first reaction was: 'I thought you were just going to invite real people.' I didn't know what to say in reply to this, but I know now what I should have said: 'Alan, these are the real people we'll be recording soon.' And indeed these very folk turned out to be the source singers that even younger apprentices were learning from before too long.

Hamish Henderson

Preface

to the first edition, *The Folk Music Revival in Scotland*

This book is a collection of facts and opinions, of thoughts and memories, of story and song.

The first step in collecting was to record a number of representative people talking about the Revival in Scotland. The next step involved listening to, and selecting from, many existing music recordings on tape and disc, with particular reference to those more directly connected with the Revival process. Collecting extended to the written word and the written note: ephemera of various kinds, newspapers, folk journals, books, song-books, scrap-books, and replies to questionnaires from singers and from teachers. Objectivity became progressively more difficult and indeed less desirable as an aim... in the end I became my own informant, as it were.

I hope that the results may suggest lines for further research to students in related disciplines. The subject is vast and would require a whole battery of books to do it justice: history, sociology, folklore, politics, literature... the musical aspects alone cover a wide area. Here I have chosen to focus attention on the songs, but have tried to keep the instrumental side in the picture.

I am grateful to my colleague Morag MacLeod, a native Gaelic speaker, for her contribution of Chapter 5.

It is impossible to mention all the fine singers, players, writers, organisers, and even pioneers in the Scottish field, but fortunately folk enthusiasts pay more than lip-service to the concept of anonymity. The friendly and patient co-operation of all those whom I pestered for information is deeply appreciated.

August 1982

to the second edition, *The Democratic Muse*

This book is an updated version of *The Folk Music Revival in Scotland*, commissioned by Kahn and Averill, London, and published in 1984; Chapter VII is entirely new. Morris Kahn asked for the update in 1990 when the first edition sold out, but because of the recession he had later to withdraw from this project.

The new title reduces to more manageable proportions the alarmingly vast scope of the subject, as does the removal of 'the' from the subtitle. This is a contribution, it is *about* the subject, it does not pretend to be a detailed account of the whole; such an account would require several volumes by different authors. The preface to the first edition defined it as 'a collection'.

My hope that further studies would appear has begun to be realised. Douglas's *The Sang's the Thing* portrays Lowland memories and songs, McVicar's *One Singer One Song* the Glasgow revival scene, while Henderson's *Alias MacAlias* covers a 50-year span of wide-ranging essays on related topics and gives an invaluable all-round picture.

Angus Calder's introduction to the latter book conjures up a most felicitous imagery for what we have called the democratic muse: '...a continuous strong flow of language and music in which labourers and scholars have swum together.'

Ailie Edmunds Munro, March 1996

In 1932 the great American democrat Franklin D Roosevelt spoke of his concern for 'the forgotten man at the bottom of the economic pyramid'. Since then, other democrats have worked to disinter the forgotten music at the bottom of the cultural pyramid.

Morris Blythman

Norman Buchan

Jeannie Robertson

Hamish Henderson

1 Setting the Scene

Once you accept that the model of literature is based on universal equality of human existence, past and present, then you can travel in literature, as a writer or a reader, wherever you like... No caste has the right to possess, or even imagine it has the right to possess, bills of exchange on the dialogue between one human being and another. And such a dialogue is all that literature is.[1]

Tom Leonard

That the above comments are true for music, as well as for literature, is the assumption on which the present book is based. Tom Leonard really means it when he says 'you can travel...wherever you like', for he claims the freedom to talk about Anton Bruckner (not one of the more accessible of nineteenth-century composers) 'without being called "élitist": I happen to like his music a lot'. This proves Leonard's truly democratic, all-embracing approach to the arts, for the poems in his book have all been rescued from the nether regions of Renfrewshire public libraries – and most of them have been out of print for over a hundred years: they had not been considered part of the *canon* or *code* of literature. A broadly similar attitude has obtained in the world of music, especially in the oral tradition.

The musical renaissance in Scotland since 1945 is usually taken to mean certain major developments in the world of art music. These include the establishment of the annual Edinburgh International Festival; the continually growing reputation of the Scottish National Orchestra, now the Royal SNO;[2] the birth of Scottish Opera and its rise to such excellence that audiences are drawn from London and farther afield; and lastly the increasing number of composers who have chosen to live and work in Scotland, and the quality of the music they have created here during this period.[3]

There is, however, another equally important phenomenon in this musical renaissance: part of a movement embracing the whole world, yet with deeper native associations than any of the four mentioned above. This is the folk music revival.

'Traditional' is sometimes a better word for this music than 'folk'. Although neither is completely satisfactory, and both will be used here *faute de mieux*, the latter is still the most widely used term; it was also used by the predominantly English revivalists of some 50 years earlier and by their supporters.

The forerunner of our revival was the folk song collecting of S Baring-Gould, Cecil Sharp, the Broadwoods, and others during the late nineteenth century and the early twentieth. Although Lucy Broadwood made a fine contribution to Scottish Gaelic song,[4] Sharp and his associates were concerned with collecting English folk songs from rural districts; but their influence was felt throughout Britain. Hundreds of these songs were published, the music consisting of the basic shape of the verse tune. The melodies were to have an enormous influence on the new English school of art music composition led by Vaughan Williams (himself a collector), Gustav Holst and later Alan Bush. A much-needed, definitive account of this first revival can now be found in *The imagined village,*

1

subtitled 'Culture, ideology and the English Folk Revival', by Georgina Boyes.[5] As the title indicates, this author's approach is critical and myth-debunking, setting the movement firmly in its social/historical context and charting, by the thirties, its declining hold on public imagination.

In Scotland at the turn of the century, Gavin Greig and James Duncan, contemporaries of Sharp, collected over three thousand song versions in Aberdeenshire and the surrounding counties. Most of these songs were not published: those that did appear were among the chief printed sources for enthusiasts several decades later, but publication of the entire Greig-Duncan collection did not start until 1981.[6]

With the basic shifts in opinion which occurred after the Second World War, the time was ripe for a major revival of this music:

> The 1945 election saw a massive Labour victory...the heroic struggle of the Soviet Union gave the left a tremendous credibility among working people. In this moment, songs...which celebrated ordinary people in all aspects of their lives spoke to the hopes and fears of a generation.[7]

The idea of folk music as a separate category is a concept found chiefly in Europe and America – it does not exist in many other parts of the world.[8] The only attempt at a definition by the International Folk Music Council was made in 1954,[9] whilst after 1980, when the IFMC changed its name to the International Council for Traditional Music, it was recognised that a universal, single definition would be difficult to sustain. But *'traditional music* hardly seems more precise than *folk music.* Yes, folk music forms traditions, but so do other genres of music.'[10] To oral transmission had been added transmission by print, both of words and music, and also transmission by disc and tape. The print factor is especially important here because folk or traditional music in Scotland has been assiduously collected and printed for over 300 years: by Allan Ramsay, James Oswald, James Johnson, Robert Burns, William Dauney, Patrick Macdonald and many others.[11] This exceptional richness of collection and publication is connected with the loss of nationhood experienced by many Scots after the unions with England; they felt preserving their native music in this way might help to preserve their national identity.[12] This applied more to the literate urban-dwellers, who had been cut off from the living tradition still continuing in the countryside. How important were these collections in keeping the music alive? And was this music *heard* by the people who studied the collections?

There is some evidence that nobles of the seventeenth century included grass-roots as well as courtly musicians in their country house music making. 'The *Mar Account Book,* to take only one of several such, records within a few months gifts to "a blind singer at dinner", "a Highland singing woman", "Blind Wat the piper" and "ane woman harper".'[13] In the eighteenth century, when public concerts first started in Edinburgh, Glasgow and Aberdeen, traditional Scots songs and fiddle music were often included alongside Italian and German art music. As regards fiddle music, a supreme exponent, Niel Gow, was often asked to play at these events, and the craze for dancing ensured its continued hearing. But the songs were sung by singers with trained voices, so that, in the towns at any rate, traditional singing styles were seldom heard. As for drawingroom music making, folk enthusiasts, such as Walter Scott's daughter Sophia[14] in the early nineteenth century, although singing in a simpler manner, would still be far from traditional in style; they probably sang in a style midway between traditional and art. And the folk-based songs of Robert Burns were, and still are, adapted in style when performed in the drawingroom or concert situation. Bagpipe music, played by the town piper or pipers, was heard at ceremonial occasions of various kinds.

The nineteenth century saw a veritable explosion of amateur music societies, at first mainly choral but soon extending to orchestras and chamber music groups; these practised and performed church music, glees and madrigals, and classics by Handel, Beethoven, Mozart, Spohr, J C Bach and others. Members of these societies, and those who attended the growing number of public concerts following the breakdown of the old system of aristocratic patronage, were not only the middle classes: 'the masses also became largely the inheritors of what had hitherto been the possession of the privileged few.'[15] After the Industrial Revolution these masses were mainly in urban areas. Some of them would still sing 'the auld sangs' in their homes, and in rural areas these songs still flourished, especially in the Gaelic North-West and in the rich ballad and bothy-song parts of the North-East. Even as early as 1826 this difference between the industrialised South-West and the North-East had been remarked on by the ballad collector and editor, William Motherwell, writing from Paisley to Peter Buchan in Aberdeenshire:

> I sincerely rejoice in your good luck in being so fortunate as every other day to meet with venerable sybils who can and are willing to impart to your thirsting soul the metrical riches of 'the days of other years'. I wish I were at your elbow to assist in the task of transcription. I cannot boast the like good fortune. This part of the country if it ever did abound in this *Song of the people* is now to all intents utterly ruined by every 3 miles of it either having some large town or public work or manufactory within its bounds which absorbs the rustic population and attracts strangers – corrupts ancient manners – and introduces habits of thinking and of living altogether hostile to the preservation and cultivation of traditionary song.[16]

The members of amateur societies in towns did not meet to sing traditional songs or to play traditional music: the desire to better themselves culturally led quite naturally to music of the upper sections of society, to 'music of learned origin'.[17] Traditional song and the style of singing it came to be despised as lower class and uncouth. (Although class divisions in Scotland were never as rigid as, for instance, in England, they certainly existed.)

For several hundred years the singers and players who had inherited this music orally from generations of their forebears, the grassroots tradition bearers, were rarely heard in those centres where only one kind of music flourished. Although a great and highly developed form, this music of concert hall, salon and conservatoire is just one of the many kinds of world music. Only as the value and beauty of these other musics come to be recognised are 'educated folk' realising that on their very doorstep they have their own other kind: unvarnished rather than rough, unfamiliar (to ears used to learned music) rather than unsophisticated, stoical rather than harsh, with different assumptions of form and of timing, and with melody far more important than harmony. Music of a different genre, yet still within Western tradition.

Where can this different genre, folk or traditional music, be heard? You can hear various forms of it in any large concert hall: Scottish groups such as Runrig and Capercaillie; Gordeanna MacCulloch with the Eurydice women's choir; Dick Gaughan; Jean Redpath; English – Martin Carthy; Irish – Mary Black or Christy Moore; the Reel and Strathspey Societies – these and many more can fill such a hall. But the best places to hear it are smaller, and more intimate – certain folk clubs, especially in the smaller towns; certain folk pubs and festivals; and, in some ways best of all, gatherings of friends in each other's houses, where you will find something nearer the original ceilidh situation.

The Gaelic word *ceilidh* means literally 'a visiting', a group of friends in a room. Originally such gatherings do not include music, but gradually the new kind develop at certain houses or occasions. No-one is a star, although some can sing or play better and some can tell stories well, while others may be gifted conversationalists or simply agreeable companions whose presence enlarges and helps to knit the pattern of the evening together. For these were essentially evening, and winter, events, often extending into the small hours of the morning. Originating in rural parts of the country, after the day's darg was over, the housewife, shepherd, fisherman, ploughman, laird, factor, village teacher and sometimes the local minister or priest, foregathered for company and for an extension of this fellowship. The old songs and ballads, with their images and archetypes of human behaviour and their melodies shaped by generations of singers long since dead; the wordlessness of instrumental music, as the fiddler played a slow air or march and then broke into a strathspey and reel which set feet tapping and often started an impromptu dance session; the symbolism of the stories too, the age-old art of suspension of disbelief – all these would inform the unconscious by stretching tentacles far back into the past and bringing it forward, making it relevant to the fleeting and ever stressful present. These sounds fed mind and spirit, refreshing them anew from the wellsprings of human existence with its joy and its pain, bringing order out of chaos and beauty out of ugliness.

A E Housman once said that when he was shaving, if he thought of certain lines of poetry, he could feel the bristles stiffen. Then there is Sydney Carter's criterion for recognising the traditional: 'What alerts me is a sort of shiver.'[18] You could say that both these psycho-physical reactions describe human response to all great art, and I would agree; but with folk poetry, music and story one's reaction seems somehow more immediate, almost more…atavistic. This is chiefly due to the content of what one hears, but it is also due to the more intimate and unified nature of a situation where the singer, player and storyteller *are* the audience and vice versa.

A more public approximation to this can be found in the folk clubs which have appeared over the last 30 years or so. There are close on 40 of these in Scotland at the present time, meeting weekly, fortnightly or in some cases monthly. Clubs tend to be in cities and large towns, with only a few in small country towns. Predictably there is much diversity in content and style, ranging from clubs with a strong bias towards the traditional, through those which encourage newer songs and other music in the folk style (a significant development), to those which present a kind of folk-pop.

The following is a description of a folk club evening in the late seventies, typical of many during that period and still the model for the more informal kind of club – The Edinburgh Folk Club was founded in 1973 by a journalist, a policeman, a technician and a physicist.

People sit facing a part of the room where the soloist or group will be performing. This modification of the true ceilidh situation is dictated by the pressure of numbers (between sixty and a hundred) and by the need for good acoustics.

So what is different here from the ordinary concert, with its 'them' and 'us' separation of performers and audience? First, the audience always contains a considerable proportion of performers, called floor singers or players. These are club members who contribute to the evening's music making, more particularly when there is no guest singer or group. Second, when guest performers are present (usually professional or semi-professional artists, professionalism being bound to appear within this mainly amateur movement) they invariably mingle with the rest of the company, not only during the interval and at the close of the evening, but often during breaks between their own items, to chat and to listen to the other singers or players. Last, and most basic, is the music itself.

Members of a recently established folk club in a country town are the non-professional guests tonight. The compère welcomes the company, and announces the artists as they appear. Irish jigs, on fiddle and guitar, are followed by two American songs: in the second of these, Tom Rush's 'Honey I'm a jazz-man, tryin' a trick or two', the fiddler weaves a beautiful obbligato round the voice line. An expatriate Highlander gives a spirited unaccompanied version of 'The Muskerry Sportsmen', but his second, Gaelic, song about Loch Leven, with its tender lyricism and delicate ornamentation, shows where his true roots lie. Next comes concertina music, and more songs: an Ulster march, 'O'Neill', followed by two jigs; a haunting ancestral folk version of 'Down by the Sally Gardens'; and two mining songs, 'The old miner' ('me hair's turning grey') and an account of a mine closure. Two young women provide some fine two-part unaccompanied singing, with lots of lovely bare fourths and fifths, and with every word audible: two songs on a similar theme – a girl follows her sailor to 'the watery main' – with a modern song, plus guitar accompaniment, sandwiched between.

Then appears the most consistently traditional singer as yet, again with guitar. His songs include 'Corachree',[19] as learned from the Aberdeenshire itinerant singer Jimmy Macbeath, and Jeannie Robertson's 'The twa recruitin' serjeants' with a chorus which everyone joins in. The last of his group of songs is on a familiar theme in Western folk tradition: that of the deserted woman. A Shetland woman sings an exquisitely sad song to an Irish tune, explaining first that it enshrines the belief 'if you mourn too long for the dead, they can't lie easy', and concludes with a version of the much-loved 'She moved through the fair'.

During the interval, over drinks, people meet and talk – no formal introductions are needed – and you find visitors from England, Ireland, the Continent and farther afield.

The second half of the programme presents more instrumental music, with a tin whistler from Somerset plus a famous Border fiddler, the winner of the Kinross Festival's men's singing class in a group of songs with guitar, and two more Border singers to end with, one giving a particularly fine version of 'The rigs o' rye'.

An evening well spent, you feel as you go home or on to a friend's house for more company or music. There are always some bits, both words and

music, which give you that 'sort of shiver', which go on singing in your head
and seem to illumine the next day.

An even more informal setting for different kinds of folk music can be found
in the folk pubs. It would be difficult to assess how many exist throughout
Scotland; Edinburgh alone has around 40, the uncrowned king among them
being Sandy Bell's Bar (officially, the Forrest Hill Bar – Bell was the name of a
former owner). It is situated little more than a stone's throw from the Royal
Infirmary, from various centres of Edinburgh University, from Moray House
Institute of Education, the College of Art and the Dental Hospital. Some thirty
years ago, before many old tenement blocks were knocked down to make way
for new academic buildings, this was still a residential area with a largely working class community. Members of this community still return to Sandy Bell's,
and you find a fair cross-section of society there.

According to several authorities with long memories of the Scottish Revival,
Sandy's was 'where it all started', way back in the late forties; through music,
discussion and the making of plans, it became in one sense the first unofficial
folk club of Scotland. It is still a centre for information and for meeting other enthusiasts, whether from Edinburgh and outlying districts or simply passing
through.

What is it that draws people like a magnet to Sandy's, to crowd into the single
room with its Edwardian decor and its awkward shape – long and narrow? The
friendly atmosphere, of course, and the social drinking, but one of the chief at-
tractions over the last 40 years has been the hope of hearing some music,
spasmodic and extempore though it may be: the exciting possibility that a good
music session may erupt, like a volcano from the seething, molten flow of that
'submerged world'.[20] You may be having an engrossing conversation (and these
four old walls seem to encourage, to draw out good talk) with a miner, a tapestry
weaver from an old town studio, a doctor from the nearby infirmary, an Irish
traveller, a university lecturer escaping from academia, a mother relegating for a
while the awesome responsibility of young children, a labourer, an unemployed
teacher, a visiting world-famous authority on some esoteric subject, or a well-
known alcoholic on whom the management keeps a watchful eye, when suddenly, right beside your ear or at the farthest corner of the room, you hear it. At
first only just audible in the hubbub: a jig, hornpipe or reel on the fiddle or
penny whistle, or from a group of players; a voice raised in an old familiar ballad or a song written last week; a rollicking, ranting ditty belted out by a trio of
young men; the dancing irresistible lilt of an accordion, or the moan of the concertina now enjoying renewed popularity. But what happens after those first
strains percolate depends on two things: the quality of the music, both content
and performance, and the kind of people who happen to be present, for without
the right mixture and vibrations nothing worthwhile will happen.

If both these factors are right then you are in luck. The babble of talk will
gradually or with miraculous speed die down, movement will be stilled, the next
drink ignored or unordered, and while the music lasts the varied company will
be united in its thrall. On the other hand if you are unlucky, if voices rise in pitch
and volume to compete with the music, the result can be cacophony.

A more spacious establishment, in the Royal Mile nearby, is gradually
overtaking Sandy Bell's as the city's leading folk-bar centre. Cy Laurie had

already initiated the ceilidh dance upsurge at Glasgow's Riverside Club; in 1991 he looked Edinburgh-wards and took over what has become the Tron Bar and Ceilidh House. It has several rooms – in particular the lowest basement room, the 'dunny', is sacred to music on Fridays and Saturdays. It is one of the main regular clubs for the city's jazzers; poetry and stories are also creeping in.

At a festival you experience a distillation of the folk clubs and the folk pubs scenes, with several added ingredients. Usually a weekend event, lasting from Friday to Sunday evening (with the quieter Monday aftermath if you have sufficient stamina and do not have to be at work), there is more time to enjoy the familiar and to absorb the new. Impromptu ceilidhs spring up everywhere – in hotel lounges and bedrooms, in the streets, on the steps of a hall, in pubs, in fields, in tents and caravans – from morning to midnight and long past. There is often the drama of competition classes on the Saturday. Classes include such sections as: women's singing and men's singing, usually unaccompanied (and at some festivals combined in one class); solo folk instruments such as fiddle, accordion, melodeon, tin whistle, concertina, jew's or jaw's harp, and mouth organ; ceilidh bands (combinations of three or more instruments – sometimes including piano, guitar or pipes) playing traditional music for dancing; oral whistling; diddling, (singing to nonsense syllables) which has connections with *canntaireachd;*[21] and lastly storytelling, a more recent development at several festivals. There is an opening concert on the Friday evening, a prize winners' concert on Saturday, and several more official ceilidhs with a compère and invited artists. Many local residents take part.

If there is a local pipe band, it may pipe in the festival with a march, strathspey and reel; but both solo pipers and pipe bands have their own festivals and competitions which flourish separately from folk events.[22] Accordion and fiddle clubs also run separate festivals.[23]

There are around 60 folk festivals in Scotland now, most of them held annually, with locales ranging from Shetland in the far north to Newcastleton near the English border. Emphasis and organisation vary from place to place, but those affiliated to the TMSA (Traditional Music and Song Association) lay special emphasis on the traditional. Several longer festivals include those at Edinburgh (ten days) and Glasgow (a week).

The supreme value of festivals is that enthusiasts from widely distant parts can meet, listen to each other and exchange news and views. The atmosphere is one of relaxed celebration.

Footnotes

1. Tom Leonard, 1990, pp. xxx–xxxi
2. 'Royal' was conferred by the Queen in January 1992, in recognition of the SNO's centenary.
3. These have been documented in what was the Scottish Music Archive in Glasgow; relaunched in 1985 as the Scottish Music Information Centre, its activities were extended to include folk as well as art music.
4. *Journal of the Folk Song Society*, no. 35, 1931; *Journal of the English Folk Dance and Song Society*, vol. 1, nos. 1, 2 and 3, 1932. See also Bassin, 1977.
5. Boyes, 1993. This also covers the post-1945 movement, mainly up to the late sixties.
6. Greig, 1909, 1914; Keith, 1925. Shuldham-Shaw and Lyle, 1981 onwards.
7. Alun Howkins, review, *WMA (Workers' Music Association) Bulletin,* no. 19,

February 1985.
8. Klaus P. Wachsman, *The New Grove Dictionary of Music and Musicians*, 1980, vol. 6, p. 693.
9. *Bulletin of the IFMC*, 1954.
10. Bohlman, 1988, p. xiii.
11. See Farmer, 1947 and Collinson, 1970, regarding collections.
12. See Aitken and McArthur, 1979.
13. K. N. Colvile, 'Scottish culture in the 17th century (1603–1660)', University of Edinburgh Ph.D. thesis, 1932, p. 28. I am grateful to Pat Jackson for this reference.
14. *See* Ailie Munro, '"Abbotsford collection of Border Ballads": Sophia Scott's Manuscript Book with Airs', *Scottish Studies 20* (1976), pp. 155–88.
15. Farmer, 1947, pp. 456–8.
16. Letter of 5 September 1826, Glasgow University Library, Robertson MS 9. See also Motherwell, 1827, and Lyle, 1975.
17. Lloyd, 1969, p. 15: Bartok, researching in the Balkans, '…discovered there a submerged world of vigorous music essentially different in many respects from music of learned origin'.
18. Sidney Carter, 'Where you find it', *Folk Review*, August 1973, p. 9.
19. See Chapter IV for a version of this song.
20. See note 17.
21. *Canntaireachd* – chanting. Now used to denote the vocal method used in teaching bagpipes. See C. K. Chambers, 'Non-lexical vocables in Scottish Traditional Music', University of Edinburgh Ph.D. thesis, 1980.
22. See *The Piping Times*.
23. See *Box and Fiddle* published by the National Association of Accordion and Fiddle Clubs.

Ewan MacColl

II   The Story of the Revival
Beginnings in the USA

Very few of us were singing Scottish songs – mostly American songs. Jeannie Robertson complained bitterly about Aberdeen Folk Club [in the sixties], 'You don't get in there unless you are wearing a cowboy hat and spurs…' Scottish material was devalued.[1]

Andy Hunter

The initial interest was in the American greats, you know, Guthrie and Leadbelly and these sort of people – they were the role models of that generation, people identified with them, *as Americans*…in a way that seems to indicate the hegemony of American culture…it's global in a sense…[2]

Robin Munro

Let me be known as the man who told you something you already know.[3]

Woody Guthrie

It is in the topical songs of the USA from the early years of this century, in the events and movements which sparked them off and in the social response which they evoked, that we find the beginnings of this revival, and of present-day songs within its context. They form as it were the chief wellspring of the most significant recent tributary to the North American mainstream of traditional music, and in particular traditional song. The springs from which this main-stream flows lie far distant, hidden in the mists of centuries of traditions, from different countries and different classes. The old ballads found in the eastern states by Cecil Sharp, Maud Karpeles, Phillips Barry and many others during these early years, were to come into their own much later: it needed the impetus provided by the topical song movement, and the social consciousness which it both reflected and further aroused, before these traditional songs could be de-submerged and become meaningful to a wider public.

The sense of 'topical', as used here to describe a certain genre of songs, has come to include dealing with especially current or local topics. The fact that these songs are sometimes – though not always – ephemeral does not detract from their importance: they record the reactions of people to what happens at a certain time or in a certain place (and they are sometimes protest songs). Many topical songs must therefore be included under the umbrella term of folk song (see also p. 11).

The mass of the colonists were poor country folk, carriers of traditional melodies. Many were rebels, fleeing from political persecution and longing to express their feelings openly. Thus a note of social protest rang through native American balladry, and the lives and problems of the common people became its main concern.[4]

There were other, more distant wellsprings from which contributory influences flowed towards the post-Second World War revival in the States. These include black music, representing the largest oppressed group in the country;[5] hymns, and perhaps especially revivalist hymns – religion was a powerful influence among the settlers and their descendants; Civil War songs, from both sides and still within living memory by the turn of the last century; hobo songs, from the vast army of migrant workers spawned by the American expansion; and Robin Hood-type ballads, songs of the Western highwayman. Signs of these influences will also become apparent during the course of this chapter. (For a much wider-ranging study see Dunaway 1987.)

The Industrial Workers of the World (IWW, or 'Wobblies'), founded in 1905 with the aim of forming One Big Union (OBU), free from hierarchical craft divisions and with branches all over the world, provided inspiration for many topical and political songs. The words were usually written to already existing tunes of popular song hits, hymns or migrant workers' songs. Members of the IWW had learned many of the hymns from the Salvation Army, the organisation with which they frequently found themselves in competition on street corners and which sometimes tried to break up IWW meetings 'with blare of trumpet and banging of drum'.[6] Since these melodies were often very appealing, both spirited and moving, the Wobbly song maker would simply pick a suitable one for his own words.[7] Alternatively he would rewrite or parody the existing words, in a satiric vein often employed with devastating effect to expose shallow or misleading sentiments. For example, in 'Onward Christian Soldiers', an unsigned parody of the hymn, the chorus is:

> Onward Christian Soldiers,
> March into the War,
> Slay your Christian Brothers,
> As you've done before.

and the closing lines –

> Onward Christian Soldiers,
> Shoot your brothers through,
> While your chaplain's praying,
> They do the same to you.[8]

The borrowing of tunes reminds one of a remark ascribed to Rowland Hill but quoted by General Booth himself: 'Why should the Devil have all the good tunes?' At first it might appear that ironically the wheel had come full circle here – but second thoughts suggest rather that it was the same process at work, with the Wobblies representing true religion as defined in the New Testament parable of the sheep and the goats: '…I was hungry and you gave me meat…naked and you clothed me…in prison and you came to me'. The Salvation Army *et al* got the immediate message of this parable but were on the whole blind to its deeper implications; for instance that charity, like patriotism, is not enough, and that finding jobs and organising the Labour movement was an essential way, ultimately, of feeding the hungry and clothing the naked.

In many ways the Wobblies were half a century ahead of their times. They could be seen as foreshadowing in the USA – '…the land *par excellence* of revivalism…' – the 1960s protest movements which Ahlstrom has portrayed as examples of secular revivalism.[9] The word 'revival' has a common denominator in whatever context it may appear; in particular, the rediscovery of old truths and arts, including the restatement and reshaping of these in modern terms plus commitment to the new movement.

Not all the IWW songs were parodies, and not all used existing tunes. One of the most popular was Ralph Chaplin's 'Solidarity Forever'; the words are in a vigorous, rallying vein, with a chorus consisting of the title words repeated thrice and ending 'For the Union makes us strong'. This calls to mind – though it hardly measures up to – William Morris's 'The March of the Workers' ('What is this the sound and rumour? What is this that all men hear?'), which was also written to the much used yet ever-powerful and faintly menacing tune of 'John Brown's Body', a Civil War song. And the Swedish immigrant Joe Hill or Hillstrom, the best known and most prolific of these songwriters, created the tune as well as the words of 'The Rebel Girl', inspired by the noted Wobbly orator Elizabeth Gurley Flynn. She herself wrote, 'Joe writes songs that sing, that lilt and laugh and sparkle, that kindle the fires of revolt in the most crushed spirit and quicken the desire for fuller life in the most humble slave... He has crystallised the organisation's spirit into imperishable forms, songs of the people – *folk songs...*'[10] (my italics).

But the laughter and the sparkle are most evident in the hard-hitting parodies and rewritings, many of which appeared in the IWW's 'little red songbook',[11] including a dozen or so by Joe Hill. (This combination of humour and biting satire seems to point prophetically forward, to Scotland's anti-Polaris songs of 50 years later. It may also help to explain the strong influence of the IWW in Scotland.[12]) In place of the hero of the original song, we find 'Casey Jones, the Union Scab' (union scabs were skilled or craft workers who broke the strikes of unskilled workers and thereby broke the solidarity of the OBU/IWW). 'Nearer my God to thee' is transformed into 'Nearer my job to thee'. The religious song 'In the sweet bye and bye' becomes 'You will eat bye and bye', from 'Pie in the Sky' or 'the Preacher and the Slave'; the crunch line from this song, 'You'll get pie in the sky when you die', has since entered English-speaking usage – just as a later remark of Hill's, 'I don't want to be found dead in Utah', has become an American catch-phrase. The Salvation Army becomes 'the starvation army'; this is spelt out further in verse three of 'The Tramp', to the tune 'Tramp, tramp, tramp the boys are marching':

> Cross the road a sign he read –
> 'Work for Jesus' so it said,
> And he said 'Here is my chance; I'll surely try';
> So he kneeled upon the floor
> Till his knees got rather sore,
> But at eating-time he heard the preacher cry:
>
> (*Chorus*)
> Tramp, tramp, tramp, keep on a-tramping,
> Nothing doing here for you;
> If I catch you 'round again
> You will wear the ball and chain,
> Keep on tramping, that's the best thing you can do.

The bias of the Salvation Army, in the North American Rockies district early this century, is shown up here. In Britain this organisation has consistently worked to feed, clothe and shelter down-and-outs; but in the situation in question the Salvation Army was envisaged as having sold out to the mine-owners.[13]

There can be little doubt that the life of Joe Hill showed a selfless dedication to this cause. At first a rather marginal figure in the IWW struggles, he was known chiefly for his songs which came to be sung across the world and were linked with working-class agitation as far afield as Australia. In 1914 he was arrested in Salt Lake City, Utah, on a murder charge, convicted on highly circumstantial evidence, and executed after 22 months in prison – despite an international defence movement, and petitions which included two pleas from President Wilson and one from the Swedish minister for further consideration of his case. The story of his trial by a hostile court, and the outcome, can be read in Barry Stavis's *The Man Who Never Died*; written after five years of research into the facts, it fully endorses Hill's claim that he was framed as an anti-union, anti-IWW move. This claim is also supported by the Labour historian Foner.[14]

Joe Hill's last message to his friends was 'Don't mourn for me – organise.' And his last will, written in the death cell the night before he was shot:

> My will is easy to decide,
> For there is nothing to divide.
> My kin don't need to fuss and moan –
> 'Moss does not cling to rolling stone'.
>
> My body? – Oh! – if I could choose,
> I would to ashes it reduce,
> And let the merry breezes blow
> My dust to where some flowers grow.
>
> Perhaps some fading flower then
> Would come to life and bloom again.
> This is my last and final will.
> Good luck to all of you,
>
> Joe Hill

His body *was* reduced to ashes, which were placed in many small envelopes: 'These were sent to IWW…sympathisers in all forty-eight states of the US except…Utah'[15] and to many other countries throughout the world, to be scattered over the earth on 1 May 1916. But the Harvard-educated revolutionary John Reed wrote, 'I have met men carrying next their hearts, in the pockets of their working clothes, little bottles with some of Joe Hill's ashes in them.'[16] His funeral in Chicago was attended by an estimated 30,000 sympathisers, who marched through the streets to the cemetery.[17]

Some twenty years later, Alfred Hayes and Earl Robinson wrote this song:

Joe Hill

1. I dreamt I saw Joe Hill last night, A - live as you or

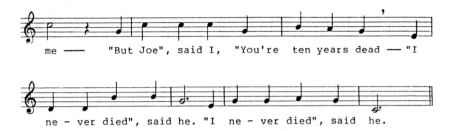

me —— "But Joe", said I, "You're ten years dead —— "I

ne - ver died", said he. "I ne - ver died", said he.

(Note: the tunes of this song and of the political songs in the next chapter are given in skeletal form only – but they are sung generally with rhythmic freedom, lengths of notes being adapted to fit speech rhythms and individual interpretations. 'Joe Hill' for instance, is often sung in a free declamatory style.)

1. I dreamt I saw Joe Hill last night,
    Alive as you or me –
    'But Joe,' said I,
    'You're ten years dead' –
    'I never died,' said he,
    'I never died,' said he.

2. 'The copper bosses shot you, Joe,
    They filled you full of lead.'
    'Takes more than guns to kill a man,'
    Says Joe, 'But I ain't dead,'
    Says Joe, 'But I ain't dead.'

3. And standing there as large as life,
    And smiling with his eyes,
    Says Joe, 'What they forgot to kill
    Went on to organise,
    Went on to organise.'

4. 'From San Diego up to Maine
    In every mine and mill
    Where working men defend their rights,
    It's there you'll find Joe Hill,
    It's there you'll find Joe Hill.'

5. I dreamt I saw Joe Hill last night,
    Alive as you or me –
    'But Joe,' said I, 'You're ten years dead' –
    'I never died,' said he,
    'I never died,' said he.[18]

Robinson's fine tune[19] is in the hymn-like style already mentioned which was popular among Labour songs up to the 1940s and the 1950s.

In the 1960s, the English composer Alan Bush based his fourth opera on the life and death of Joe Hill as told by Barry Stavis. *Joe Hill: the Man Who Never*

Died was first performed at the German State Opera House, East Berlin, in September 1970 and ran for the whole winter season.

Contrary to popular assumption the IWW were against violence, although they defended the use of violence by workers when attacked. At the 1913 convention a resolution was adopted which described their programme as offering 'the only possible solution of the wage question whereby violence can be avoided, or at the very worst, reduced to a minimum'.[20] Many of their leaders were arrested for opposing the First World War, and their anti-war songs pioneered a new genre, for few songs carrying this direct message had appeared in the USA before the early years of the twentieth century. Even after 1924, which marked the end of the IWW as a substantially influential organisation, the songs continued to be sung by ex-Wobblies and others during industrial struggles of the twenties and thirties. The 1960s saw a resurgence of interest in the IWW: students worshipped them, sang their songs and attended university courses on Wobbly history. And in the seventies there were still IWW offices in Detroit and Chicago.

The Almanacs was the best-known group of singers who followed on in this tradition during the thirties and who supported the Congress of Industrial Organisations (CIO).[21] This group included the outstanding singer and banjo player Pete Seeger, and the Lomaxes (Alan and Bess) – their roots were as much in academia as in the Labour movement, and their families were among the early collectors and publishers of folk song; Woody Guthrie, once described by Alan Lomax as 'America's greatest living ballad writer'; Huddie Ledbetter ('Leadbelly'), the black 'King of the Twelve-stringed Guitar' and a singer of powerful emotional appeal; Lee Hayes from the Southern Labour college tradition, with a religious background; Sis Cunningham from Oklahoma, who had taught at Commonwealth Labour College, Arkansas; Burl Ives, actor, singer, song writer and radio presenter, whose records were influential in Scotland; their musical director Earl Robinson, a trained composer; the writer Millard Lampell; Cisco Huston, itinerant actor; and the black singers Sonny Terry and Brownie McGhee, close friends of Leadbelly.

The Almanacs sang union songs but also anti-war and anti-fascist songs. When they broke up in 1942, their very considerable influence continued to be felt; they were an integral part of what has been called the proletarian renaissance, circa 1935–39, which included artists, dramatists, novelists and some musicians. 'Not only the Almanacs, but many traditional singers in those years identified themselves, intellectually as well as musically, with the broad Left movements... The hard-won victories of the union drives of the 1930s and the anti-fascist crusades of that decade and the 1940s had a great and moving influence on the thinking and action of topical song writers after the war.'[22]

Song collections published regularly included the *Bulletin* of the organisation People's Songs (this had articles as well as traditional and topical songs), its continuation *Sing Out!* – at first a monthly periodical which started in 1950 – and later *Broadside* (1962). *Sing Out!* published a widely varied collection which included traditional songs from America and elsewhere, popular songs, union songs, soldiers' songs, anti-war songs and children's songs. Amongst these were new songs (and some rewritings) by Woody Guthrie, Ewan MacColl, Pete Seeger, Hamish Henderson, Earl Robinson and many others, and there were more than 800 songs during its first decade. This periodical was supported by

People's Artists (the inheritors of People's Songs). The Hootenannies, originally a nickname for concerts sponsored by People's Songs, included good traditional singing, both solo and in groups, theatre turns, Southern protest songs, and songs from many foreign countries. Paul Robeson, of the unique, magnificent bass voice, supported the broad movement for people's songs; in 1949 he also sang at a special concert given for him by the Scottish Miners' Union in Edinburgh, where he formed lasting ties.[23] And in the late fifties Pete Seeger and The Weavers toured Scotland, thereby confirming the deep impression their recordings had already made here.

Reverting to the question whether songs such as those sung by the IWW, and those sung by the Almanacs, can be described as folk songs: Elizabeth Gurley Flynn certainly considered that IWW songs, as exemplified by Joe Hill, came into this category (see p. 11), and one of the Almanac Singers declared: 'We think this is the *first time* there has ever been an organised attempt of this kind actually to sing the folk songs of America... We are trying to give back to the people the songs of the workers.'[24] Denisoff states that 'The IWW evidently disclaimed folk music and rarely used it in their organisational efforts.' He explains this apparent contradiction by suggesting that after the First World War the American Left rejected 'popular' music, and incorporated 'folk music' style as a propaganda vehicle to create folk consciousness. Be that as it may, the answer would seem to depend on whether the songs were accepted by the rest of that section of society by whom (Joe Hill, Woody Guthrie etc.) and for whom they were written, and on whether they were absorbed – partially or wholly, but at least temporarily – into oral tradition. If these two conditions are satisfied, they can be described as folk songs. Periods of conflict and social change produce songs which reflect struggle, and which reflect different points of view in that struggle. For example, 134 songs by Southern US writers have been discovered, which were favourable to the Ku Klux Klan during the period 1922–27.[25] Conversely, during times of comparative stability, or times when issues are less clear-cut, people tend to sing about more personal matters and also to be more introverted in their thoughts and hence in their songs: the influential Bob Dylan's career illustrates this process.[26]

The most influential figure of the 1930s and 1940s – a period which led directly into the revival of more traditional music and cast long shadows over several decades – was the singer-songwriter Woodrow Wilson Guthrie, know as Woody Guthrie.[27] Born in Oklahoma State in 1912, by the time he reached adolescence he had to fend for himself and was forced to wander all over the country in search of work. His autobiography *Bound for Glory* gives an intensely vivid account of life in an Okie oil boom town, the subsequent Depression, the terrible dust-storms, and the grinding struggle for existence which he shared with so many others of his time.

Most of Guthrie's best songs were forged out of his own experience; those mentioned here may be found in his collection of nearly 200 songs,[28] and he has recorded several on his disc *Dust Bowl Ballads.*[29]

'The Great Dust Storm' starts in the time-honoured style of disaster songs – 'On the fourteenth day of April of Nineteen Thirty Five' – and describes the devastation of a huge area of countryside by a flood, not of water but of dust.

'Talking Dust Blues' is one of his most famous and dryly humorous ditties: the title indicates the sort of parlando tone he uses.[30] 'Dust Pneumonia Blues', based on the twelve-bar blues musical structure, ends on a note of stoically ironic laughter:

> Down in Texas my gal fainted in the rain
> Down in Texas my gal fainted in the rain,
> I throwed a bucket o' dirt in her face just to bring her back again.

'Pretty Boy Floyd' is a Robin Hood-type ballad based on the story of a real-life Oklahoma outlaw of Guthrie's own time; the highwayman-with-the-heart-of-gold is a familiar figure in balladry on both sides of the Atlantic.

> So long, it's been good to know ya [thrice]
> What a long time since I've been home,
> And I gotta be driftin' along

is the chorus of one of his best-known wanderers' songs, and as with many good choruses it follows on the meaning of each succeeding verse. 'Tom Joad' is a long heroic ballad which tells the story from John Steinbeck's famous novel of the dustbowl, *The Grapes of Wrath*, and which Guthrie wrote after seeing the film version.

> Dear Mrs Roosevelt, don't hang your head to cry
> His mortal clay is laid away but his good work fills the sky.
> (*Refrain*)
> This world was lucky to see him born

is the first verse of a long elegiac ballad which tells the story of Franklin Roosevelt's life and achievements. 'Woman at Home' is another twelve-bar blues. 'The Union Maid' and 'Union Feeling' are very different, in words and melody, from the older type of labour songs. His 'Joe Hillstrom', to a fine tune in the Dorian mode, is a tribute paid in a fitting style. Lastly, he wrote some delightful songs for children, which have been translated into many different languages.

Most of the airs for these songs were borrowed from other sources; he chose good tunes, and often added good refrains, using elements of the tune in a musicianly fashion. The main source for these tunes was country and western songs, which are related to the 'white blues' (the tunes of many hobo songs also come from country and western). The blues are a central part of the jazz tradition and are almost certainly of black, and ultimately African, derivation.[31] Guthrie and other whites used blues forms, but their expressive style is very different from the black blues style in which the voice is allowed expressive freedom. By contrast, the white blues tend to sound laconic, 'flat', especially when couched in the Oklahoma and mid-Western speech style, and part of Guthrie's genius lay in translating this speech style into song. Blue notes – which became part and parcel of the whole southern/southwestern singing style – are those which have been flattened by approximately a semitone at some point or points in the music: the most common are the third and the seventh of the scale, but other notes of the scale are sometimes flattened, by white as well as by black musicians.

Of at least equal importance to the verbal and musical content of these songs was Guthrie's performance of them. I would go further and say that his recorded singing is the finest and the most memorable of all his legacies to us. The first impression of his singing is that of vitality and a kind of simple magic. But the careful listener will notice that his voice combines a certain edge, or bite, with a liquid, warm, rounded quality; there is also a very exact pitching of notes, and some sliding, with leaning notes or appoggiature which provide the only ornamentation in his style. There is no break between different ranges of his voice, and an astonishingly complete absence of vibrato. He bends and varies the tune with great skill to fit the words, pausing on this word or that. His verbal articulation is outstanding, with good vowel sounds and clear though not over-emphasised consonants. Occasional unexpected rests serve to highlight the word or words at that point. Even where the words depict hardship or cruelty, there is no passion, no anger, in his delivery: it is matter of fact, but with an occasional chuckle – and not always at the obviously humorous bits. His 'Talking Blues' are among his best known and most frequently imitated numbers.

Guthrie's instrumental accompaniment to his singing is very effective. Self-taught, he invariably used the guitar and between verses often added a mouth-organ, fixed around his neck – no mean feat. His guitar playing is unobtrusive though skilful, when used as accompaniment, with a good bass line and much rhythmic interest: when played alone, as in the introduction or ending of a song, or in occasional playing of the verse tune without words, it introduces more blue notes and more ornamentation of the melodic line. In his harmonica interludes – but always with the guitar continuing – he allows an emotional intensity to appear which is carefully barred from his singing. The wailing, windy sound of this often under-estimated little instrument, with its chirpy melodic ornamentation and with the harmonic concentration – which often sounds like overlapping chords and which thus includes not only sevenths but ninths, elevenths and thirteenths – can be quite heart-rending in its effect. It is as if Guthrie allows his instruments, especially the mouthorgan, to express the overt poignancy which he denies himself in his singing style.

To hammer home his desire to be down to earth – realistic – he himself said he did not want to sound 'like dew dripping off the petals of the morning violet', but 'rather…like the ashcans of the early morning, like the cab drivers cursing at one another, like the long-shore men yelling, like the cowhands whooping, and like the lone wolf barking'.[32] Of some folks in a New York street who joined in singing his 'Normandie' song, he said '…their voices sounded good, like coal being dumped down into a cellar'.[33] My favourite comment comes from a Paisley schoolboy of fourteen, in an essay on various kinds of music he had heard in my music class: 'Woody Guthrie, a folk singer, was very good – although his voice was terrible the noise he made was good, and it was the rotten voice which held your interest in the music. Some singers with excellent voices very well trained were outshone by Woody's voice.'[34]

This last quotation sums up beautifully the initial impact of good traditional singing on the open-minded listener who has been conditioned to think that the only 'good singing' can come from a voice developed and trained for Western art song, '…although his voice was terrible the noise he made was good'. The reaction of the listener with a closed mind is exemplified by the comment I overheard from a distinguished Scottish art musician and scholar after first hearing Jeannie Robertson: 'Of course that's not really singing at all.' This rivals Sir Thomas Beecham's ethnocentric remark, 'I suppose in my lifetime I've conducted all the world's great music.'[35]

On the cover of one of Woody Guthrie's early records were the words 'Folk song builds up man' and on his guitar case was written 'This machine kills fascists'.[36] Was this empty rhetoric? How far, in particular, did Guthrie and his inheritors influence the young folk of the post-war decades, the mature people and leaders of today and tomorrow? Dunson again: '...so far as I can see, no poet, no novelist, no speaker, no academic spokesman, has moved so many young people as has the topical songwriter in the north and the freedom singer in the south,'[37] and Guthrie was the daddy of them all. He has been compared with Robert Burns, and has been described as America's Homer; his songs became enormously popular and many were absorbed into oral tradition.

In 1966 Guthrie was awarded the US Department of the Interior's Conservation Award. The Guthrie Trust Fund for Children was also set up in his memory, with its headquarters in New York City.

Woody's close friend, travelling companion and singing partner for many years was Cisco Huston; in 1943 they joined the Merchant Marines, and after the war they made many recordings together. Cisco died in 1961, and it was chiefly Pete Seeger and Jack Elliott who continued Guthrie's tradition and made his songs known to the new generation in America and far beyond.

Little mention has as yet been made of jazz. Since this kind of music, with all the varied forms it has developed, originated among black people in the United States and has had an increasingly worldwide impact during the twentieth century, it is clearly of paramount importance in any consideration of music of the people. One possible point of contact between jazz and the folk music revival is found in the hypothesis advanced by Esman and Margolis that 'Jazz is essentially a protest music'.[38] The influence of jazz on folk song in Britain was strong in the brief skiffle period of the mid-1950s, and reappeared later towards the 1980s; while jazz influence on instrumental folk music began much earlier and has lasted into the 1990s.

By 1950, the American Left was under heavy fire from the McCarthyite inquisition, and with the Korean war these attacks grew sharper and more frenzied. In this connection, Gordon Friesen, journalist and critic, noted a curious example of what might be seen as good – in the sense of freedom to diversify, to experiment – coming out of evil: 'The Almanacs, obviously, had committed themselves irrevocably to certain causes. The Weavers,' – the group, with Seeger, which took over from the Almanacs after the war – 'on the other hand, could branch out. They went down the road of traditional folk music where they enjoyed their greatest success. (By traditional I mean the old classics like "Old Smokey", the old songs, without, at least, an immediate message).'[39]

The last two sentences parallel so closely what later happened in Scotland, as well as in other European countries, that it is time to return to this side of the Atlantic and consider the developments here.

Footnotes

1. Andy Hunter, 7 June 1988, Edinburgh.
2. Robin Munro, 9 August 1988, Beckenham, Kent (with Ewan MacColl and Ailie Munro).
3. Quoted by Peter J. Welding on the disc-sleeve of Guthrie's *Dust Bowl Ballads,* RCA

Victor Series, RD 7642.
4. Lomax, 1960, p. xvi.
5. The American Indians were even more oppressed, but because they were isolated their music had little opportunity to influence the mainstream.
6. Denisoff and Peterson, 1972, p. 62.
7. Foner, 1965 (B), vol. 4, p. 153.
8. Kornbluh, 1964, p. 327.
9. Ahlstrom, 1972, p. 1090.
10. Foner, 1965 (B), p. 154.
11. *IWW Songs*, 1980. 'Songs of the Workers to fan the flames of discontent…Songs of the Miseries That Are. Songs of the Happiness To Be.' *The Little Red Songbook.*
12. See Edinburgh and Glasgow editions of *The Socialist Newspaper* in 1910.
13. Dubofsky, 1969, pp. 177, 197.
14. Foner, 1965 (A).
15. Stavis, 1954, p. 115.
16. Waters and Murray-Smith, 1947, p. 46.
17. Foner, 1965 (A), p. 155.
18. Waters and Murray-Smith, 1947, p. 46. Verses 2, 3 and 4 conflated from memory.
19. *Pocket Song Book*, 1949, p. 96.
20. Thompson and Murfin, 1955, p. 85, pp. 80–9. See also Kornbluh, 1964, p. 352, for instructions to strikers: '…no rough stuff. If anyone is going to be killed let it be one of our men first.'
21. The American Federation of Labor (AFL), representing the skilled workers, was started in 1886, and the CIO in the 1930s.
22. Dunson, 1965, p. 17–18.
23. Arnot, 1955, p. 420.
24. *Daily Worker*, 14 August 1941, p. 7; quoted by Denisoff and Peterson, 1972, p. 106.
25. Denisoff and Peterson, 1972, p. 85.
26. See *Playboy*, March 1966 and March 1978; also *Folk News*, May 1978.
27. See Richard A. Reuss, 'Woody Guthrie and his Folk Tradition', *Journal of American Folklore* 83 (1970), pp. 273–303; also Klein, 1981.
28. Seeger, Pete, 1958.
29. See n. 3.
30. See Lomax, 1960, pp. 432–3.
31. See Stearns, 1977, pp. 8, 99, 105, 277–80.
32. Lampell, [1960].
33. Guthrie, 1974, p. 299.
34. Also quoted in Leach and Palmer, 1978, p. 70.
35. Quoted by Lloyd, 1969, p. 37.
36. Cf. two variants: Josh MacRae recorded 11 February 1977, 'This machine disarms people'; and Pete Seeger, *Folk News*, April 1978, 'This machine surrounds hate and forces it to surrender.'
37. Dunson, 1965, p. 114.
38. Stearns, 1977, p. 297.
39. Quoted by Dunson, 1965, p. 50.

III   *The Story of the Revival*
Development in Scotland

The opinion that art should have nothing to do with politics is in itself a
political attitude.[1]

George Orwell

Good culture was becoming infinitely more complex, and simple culture
becoming commercialised.[2]

Norman Buchan

For over 300 years the demotic vocal music of Scotland consisted of two principal strands, the sacred and the secular. After the Reformation of 1560 the metrical Psalms of David were sung in church services by the whole congregation; so
powerful was the appeal of these ancient meditations and prayers, set to their
dignified, soul-stirring tunes, that for many Scots psalmody took the place of
secular song for recreational purposes. This tendency was greatly strengthened
by the censorious attitude of the reformed church towards secular, and especially
dance, music. A parallel, alternative tradition thus arose which continued up to
the close of the nineteenth century and even after (for instance it can be traced in
the writings of James Hogg and George MacDonald). But both words and tunes
of the Psalms were written down; even though not everyone could read them
they were fixed, unchangeable. We are concerned here with song which has been
for the most part orally transmitted and subject to variation – that is, secular traditional song, or folk song.

In examining the background to the folk revival, we must be concerned with
art music as well. (I prefer the term *art music* to *classical music*; there are objec-
tions to both, but 'classical' has a separate and more particular meaning which
should be recognised, while 'art' is a broader term and has a certain indefinable
'feel' about it which seems to make it more suitable here. The terminology is not
of great importance, however, and need have no pejorative implications.)
'Musick fyne', both secular and sacred, was also regarded with hostility by the
reformed national church of the sixteenth century, and a further blow fell when
the court, the chief patron of the arts, moved to London in 1603. While it could
be argued that the political union of a century later opened up fresh cultural
vistas, the eighteenth-century musical renaissance, though intense while it lasted,
was comparatively short-lived.[3]

A longer renaissance was achieved by composers of the Scottish National
Group in the late nineteenth – early twentieth century. Inspired by the work of
Alexander Mackenzie, this group included William Wallace, Hamish MacCunn,
Learmont Drysdale and John B McEwen, all born in the 1860s. Their search for
a national music was part of a wider movement which swept through Europe
around this time. Since there was as yet no music conservatoire in Scotland, all
five of these gifted composers had to go to London or to the Continent for their
higher musical education, and all lived for most of their working lives in
London.

As regards the 'National' epithet: none of these composers seems to have devoted any time to collecting or listening to his own traditional music *in the field*, as for instance Vaughan Williams and Bartok did with theirs. Many printed *collections* of their country's folk music were available then; but although this group of Scots made affectionate use of beautiful melodies, of musical idioms and of literary and historical themes, they did not achieve the lasting international reputation of other contemporary nationalist composers such as the Norwegian Grieg, the Czechs Smetana and Dvorak and the Finlander Sibelius. Why was this so? And why has their music, with few exceptions, been so seldom performed in Scotland during the last half-century?

Their '…valiant attempt…to demonstrate wholehearted allegiance to their country of origin'[4] did help to prepare the ground for twentieth-century developments in Scottish music. Of three later composers – F G Scott, Ian Whyte and Eric Chisholm – Scott wrote some breathtakingly lovely songs, showing careful attention to speech-rhythms of the Scots language.

There were of course economic reasons for Scotland's failure to develop its art music, whether national or more international in content. This music, requiring professional and highly trained composers, '…will flourish best in affluent communities'.[5] Scotland was for long a poor country, overshadowed in certain ways by England, its larger and more powerful southern neighbour. Material difficulties included the lack – except in mid-eighteenth-century Edinburgh – of music publishing firms.

Perhaps most interesting, in the context of this study, is the opinion that because their folk music was so good, the Scots had no need to develop their art music. In 1847, Robert Chambers commented: 'It is to be feared that the beauty of the melodies [i.e. popular, or folk] is itself partly to be blamed for the indifference to higher music.'[6] I have occasionally heard this view expressed by folk musicians. But I suspect the answers are more complex, and I hope to indicate some clues when we come to consider the 1980s and 1990s.

A significant factor in the musical background to the revival was a reaction against Scottish 'popular' music. Comedian Will Fyffe's act, 60 years ago, included a few music hall songs; there was also the pawky Scotsman Harry Lauder whose songs are almost never performed today. More recently Jimmy Shand has been the chief exponent of the popular country dance band repertoire, which has traditional roots. Robert Wilson was an example of the trained singer whose range covered Burns songs sung in a drawing-room style with piano accompaniment, and 'ballads' such as 'The northern lights of old Aberdeen'; his successors in this genre included Kenneth MacKellar, Moira Anderson and Peter Morrison. Calum Kennedy specialised in popular Gaelic song; Andy Stewart and the Alexander Brothers also had a large following. Pipe-bands and 78rpm transfers of Orpheus Choir recordings formed two more ingredients of this mixture, aimed partly at the tourist market. In most record shops this was found under 'Scottish'. Some of it is good stuff (Will Fyffe's songs have lasted well, and piano accompaniments are coming back into fashion). But one cannot ignore the mawkish, kitsch element in it; what has been described as 'cultural sub-nationalism',[7] and as 'the persistent curse of Scottish music at the international cultural level'.[8]

After 1707, the shrinking and the gradual desuetude of the Scots tongue, first in writing and then in speech, had a numbing, debilitating effect on Scottish literature. This was exacerabated by emigration, by the creaming off of much of the nation's talents in every field, which was in full flood by the mid-nineteenth century. A hundred years later, statistics showed that '...whereas at the Union, Scotland had about one-fifth the population of England and Wales, she now has about one-ninth.'[9] Walter Scott's novels had been soaked in Scottish tradition, including song, and in some ways he portrayed well the life and speech of the common people, but he wrote about the past, and chiefly from the point of view of an antiquarian rather than a student of and participator in contemporary events. And nostalgia was a significant element in the work of Robert Louis Stevenson, for personal as well as historical reasons. Later émigré writers (no less than émigré engineers, farmers, labourers, surgeons, etc.) also became a prey to nostalgia: this affected their own creative work and provided a market for home-based Scottish literature, which allowed it to develop into the so-called 'kailyard' school. In defence of this group of writers, which included S R Crockett, James Barrie and Ian Maclaren, it should be said that their work preserved some seeds of a languishing Scottish culture and helped to prepare the ground for more fruitful later developments. One could go further and predict that this much-maligned trio are ripe for rehabilitation.[10] With these reservations, one can hardly dismiss the view that '...Scotland was figured to the world at the turn of last century through *Punch's* jokes about golf caddies, ministers and gawky housemaids, the soft-headed ruralising fiction of the Barrie-Maclaren school, and the century-old genius of Burns...'[11]

Into this backward-looking, nostalgic, almost never-never land, came the precursors of the Scottish literary renaissance: novelists like J MacDougall Hay, and George Douglas Brown with his now over-harsh realism, and poets such as Violet Jacob with her authentic humanism. Lewis Grassic Gibbon developed a musically idiomatic style, with dialect words an essential part of that idiom. In his trilogy *A Scots Quair*, set in Kincardineshire and Aberdeenshire in the first third of this century, he introduces both traditional song (the wedding, in *Sunset Song*) and protest song (events of Armistice Day, in *Cloud Howe*). But the most wide-ranging of all the Renaissance literary figures was Hugh MacDiarmid, the nationalist with a world outlook.

Most first-class minds possess a certain humility, a sympathy with the whole human condition, and although MacDiarmid was not without this quality he was also, paradoxically, an uncompromising élitist, and his attitude to folk song embodies in true Marxist fashion these two diametrically opposed extremes, the unity of opposites. But it was not Marx who first gave utterance to the ever-new cliché that truths can only be expressed in paradoxes. The New Testament is full of this, as are many other religious writings. 'Do I contradict myself?' said Whitman. 'Very well then I contradict myself (I am large, I contain multitudes).'[12]

In 1964 MacDiarmid referred to traditional folk song as 'the simple outpourings of illiterates and backward peasants...,'[13] but in one of a series of articles which he contributed to the *Scottish Educational Journal* 60 years ago, he states: 'We hear a great deal about the Scots being a musical people... If [this] has any reality it would make it all the more inexplicable...that a people possessed of *a Folk-Song that has probably no equal in the world*...should have become so completely disorientated and precluded from the natural exploitation of it'[14] (my italics). The last phrase reveals one possible aspect of his apparently inconsistent position here: this folk song with no equal in the world should be exploited as material for art music, but has, it would seem, no value in itself. And yet, as we shall see, MacDiarmid attended the Edinburgh Peoples' Festival Ceilidhs of 1951–52 and was moved and impressed by what he heard there. In addition to this musical experience, he must surely have realised by then that the submerged world of folk song, and especially the ballads, had been one of the most powerful influences in keeping the Scots language alive. The famous 'flyting' on this subject between MacDiarmid and Hamish Henderson is described in the magazine *Cencrastus*, issue no. 49, Autumn 1994.

By the 1930s the literary scene was a kind of matrix in which new structures and elements, as well as evocative old Scots words, struggled to be born (or reborn, for it is often hard to distinguish between birth and rebirth). It is possible that the first vague stirrings of a dual need were felt at that time, throughout the Western world but perhaps more especially in smaller countries which needed to regain their sense of identity: stirrings which were to become stronger, more conscious and more articulate after the Second World War. On the one hand, people were groping towards a more 'democratic' and realistic art, towards a people's art, towards their cultural roots. On the other hand (and the two are not unrelated) many people yearned for melody in music, finding little inspiration in atonal, and especially dodecaphonic, art music. One answer to both these needs could be found in folk song, in the synthesis of traditional words with traditional melodies, which is largely sung unaccompanied.

In the mid-thirties the young Alistair Cooke's series of broadcasts, *I heard America Singing*, which used many of the John A Lomax recordings from the Library of Congress, made a powerful impact. Cooke drew, not on the Cecil Sharp, Appalachian, Child ballad tradition, but rather on songs about what was actually happening; work songs of all kinds, from those about lumberjacks and railroad construction workers to chain-gang and prison songs – the face of contemporary America. Hamish Henderson recalls how thrilled people here were who listened to them: 'It was absolutely the first time that a lot of people had heard this kind of thing.'[15] And owing to the great prestige already attaching to popular culture in the USA, this present-day folk material had an added kudos in that it came from the States.

As well as records from across the Atlantic, five series of broadcasts during the next three decades helped to build up interest in this 'other' kind of music. Donald MacCullough, of the Ministry of Agriculture, started a series on country music, to project the role of the farmer and the wartime 'grow your own food' campaign: *Country Magazine* ran intermittently from 1942 to 1954. The Scottish composer and conductor Francis Collinson joined the search, led by Peter Kennedy, for folk tunes and songs from various regions. There were 35 Scottish programmes in all, mostly arranged and performed in art music style. Francis Collinson explained, 'Many of the powers-that-be were strongly opposed to the idea of folk songs and so we had to dress them up to fit in with these ideas.'[16] By the end of this series it was presenting much more traditional styles of performance.

In 1955 traditional music from different parts of the British Isles was heard in *As I Roved Out*, twelve programmes presented by Peter Kennedy and Seamus Ennis which included songs from Galloway, Skye and Barra. Two years later came eight broadcasts entitled *A Ballad Hunter looks at Britain*, only two of which were heard in Scotland, and in these Alan Lomax and Hamish Henderson introduced Scots and Gaelic music, including recordings from the School of Scottish Studies. In 1960 a series of six programmes on folk collectors, *As They Roved Out,* was transmitted on the London Home Service only.

The fifth and most impressive series was *Radio Ballads,* devised and presented nation-wide by Ewan MacColl, Charles Parker and Peggy Seeger (for a full account see the *Folk Review* articles referred to below). These broke entirely new ground. They presented both traditional and new songs, they dealt mainly with industrial rather than rural subjects, and they introduced the singers and the workers – miners, road builders, fishermen, lorry drivers etc. – as commentators, so that vernacular and local speech was heard for probably the first time in such broadcasts. Of these, *Singing the Fishing* (1960) which won the Press Association's Documentary award of the Italia prize, and *The Travelling People* (1964) each had about a third of the material drawn from Scotland.

An important new name has just been mentioned. In the hungry years of the Depression, maturing amid the unemployment, strikes and hunger marches of North England, there had appeared a young man who was to become a leading figure in the Revival: the actor-singer-songwriter Jimmy Miller, better known as Ewan MacColl. Born of Scottish parents, and absorbing from them a vast amount of Scottish traditional culture, he grew up in Salford, and by the age of fourteen he had inherited his father's militancy and become active politically. A detailed account of MacColl's career can be found in four issues of *Folk Review* (May to September 1973); these include contributions from, Peggy Seeger (sister of Pete Seeger), the brilliant American singer, instrumentalist and songwriter who lived and worked with him for some 35 years, in London. MacColl's relationship to the Scottish revival was of necessity different from that of people living and working in Scotland, but he made frequent visits to Scotland, including a period from 1948 when Theatre Workshop, the company originally set up by Joan Littlewood and himself in Manchester, performed in Glasgow and Edinburgh. His pioneer work in unearthing Scots songs and ballads, together with his fine voice and unashamedly dramatic as well as authentic style of singing them; his fieldwork in Scotland at various times;[17] and the many industrial and lyrical songs from his own pen – all these have had a powerful and seminal influence on the whole Scottish scene.

But what of Scotland's Labour and Trade Union songs? – for we have noted the importance of such songs in the American experience. I have found little specifically Scottish from the period between the two World Wars;[18] in fact, few protest songs have survived in Scotland from the two and a half centuries which followed 1707.[19] Nationalism within the Scottish Labour movement was probably stronger in the days of John MacLean and Jimmy Maxton than it is today, yet until 1950 music seems to have played a smaller part in the nationalist movement here (in sharp contrast to that of Ireland) than might have been expected. In songs of the Labour movement the enemy was not England but capitalism, and the same songs (for example, 'The Red Flag', Blake's 'Jerusalem') were sung both north and south of the border. A Socialist Sunday School songbook of 1925, printed in Glasgow, includes in its preface a note that in the case of a certain song, 'the word "England" is to be broadly interpreted.' However, 'there was quite a lot of borrowing from America in Clydeside in the twenties and thirties. American tunes and Wobbly songs were sung at climbing clubs, cy-cling clubs and such.'[20] The decline in home music making of this time was partly compensated for by organisations such as the Girl Guides and Boy Scouts, the Co-operative Movement and church groups.

There were several Socialist choirs, including, between the Wars, The Scottish Socialist Choristers, whose conductor Tom Kerr became Lord Provost of Glasgow. But perhaps the best known were the Glasgow Socialist Singers and the Glasgow Young Communist League Choir; under their conductors James Callan and James Service they won many prizes in music festivals, and in the early 1960s, under guest conductor Alan Bush, they made a recording of 'The Red Flag' to the tune for which James Connell actually wrote the words – 'The White Cockade' (WMA 101).

The Red Flag

This Scottish dance tune provides a more fitting drive and impetus than the hymn-like, triple-time 'Maryland' – the same tune as the German 'Der Tannenbaum' – to which the words are usually sung.[21] The change of tune is reported to have taken place after the song had crossed to America – a band due to play it did not have the parts for the right tune, so they substituted 'Maryland', and it stuck. It is also said that Jim Connell was angered by this change of tune, saying he had written a song to storm the barricades and not to bring bourgeois Protestant Germans and Dutch Catholics to their knees in prayer.

The Glasgow Orpheus Choir during the first half of this century became internationally famous under the conductorship of Sir Hugh Roberton. It is less widely known that it was cold-shouldered by the BBC for a time, almost certainly because of Roberton's personal political convictions. Although he never allowed politics to touch his choir, he himself was known to have supported the ILP leader James Maxton, and the Republicans in the Spanish Civil War. He was also a pacifist during the First World War. Superb as was the performance standard of this choir, it must be said that some of the arrangements which Roberton made of Scottish songs cannot be justified: the modal character of a tune is destroyed by the introduction of notes which are foreign to its scale.

In 1947 *Ballads of World War II* appeared, collected by Hamish Henderson. Although all these songs were presented anonymously, three are from Henderson's own pen, and in his foreword he pin-points the difference between these and the more official 'straight' patriotic songs put out by radio in wartime: 'For the Army balladeer comes of a rebellious house. His characteristic tone is one of cynicism...Shakespeare...knew him well and called him Thersites.' 'The Ballad of the D-Day Dodgers', to the tune of 'Lili Marlene', started as a composite, soldiers' creation; Henderson's version is one of the wittiest, most ironic and most moving of army songs.

In November 1948 an event was organised in Glasgow to commemorate the twenty-fifth anniversary of John MacLean's death. A teacher and communist propagandist of courage and integrity whose death was hastened by years of imprisonment, MacLean had commanded wide support and affection throughout Scotland, particularly in the West. The speech by pioneer suffragette Helen Crawfurd Anderson was one of the best at this MacLean Memorial meeting. Then came the poems, two of which demand special mention: Sorley MacLean read his marvellously succinct eight-line 'Clan MacLean', first in Gaelic and then in his own English translation; and Morris Blythman read his moving 'Til the Citie o John MacLean', which contains this:

> They've rieved the live rose frae the leaf
> An bluidit aa hir snawy bosom;
> Bit rose-buds laved wi rievers' bluid
> Wull lowe wi loe, come simmer seasoun.

The lines just before –

> An rowed aside that muckle rock
> Thit stappit the mou o her makars

– express in a single image the ineluctable connection between politics in its widest sense and the arts. (Blythman's pen name was Thurso Berwick, the names of the most northerly town and, formerly, the most southerly in Scotland.) William Noble gave the first performance of Hamish Henderson's 'The John MacLean March'; written for the occasion, it has been described as the first (new) song in the Revival.[22] A special issue of the magazine *Conflict*, edited then by Norman Buchan, printed the poems read at the concert.

Two years later Alan Lomax came from the USA to collect material for the disc series *World Library of Folk and Primitive Music*. As editor of these albums he used some of his father John Lomax's material, which Alistair Cooke had drawn on some fifteen years earlier. He met Ewan MacColl and Hamish Henderson, and with the latter made two collecting tours the following summer. From this material Lomax produced *I heard Scotland sing,* one of his broadcast series of music from many countries. Henderson also introduced Lomax to Gaelic poet Sorley MacLean, to master-piper John Burgess, to singer and piper Calum Johnston and to Gaelic singer Flora MacNeil. In order to get contemporary as well as traditional songs, Lomax recorded Morris Blythman singing three *Sangs o' the Stane.* In the best tradition of Scots satire, these appeared soon after the Stone of Destiny had been taken, or retrieved, from Westminster by four young Scots.

The ancient Scottish Coronation Stone was alleged to have been brought from Ireland not later than the ninth century. It found a home in Scone, near Perth, and the central act in the inauguration ceremony was the placing or seating of the new king on the Stone.[23] It had been removed (or, to use Dunbar's word in *The Flyting of Dunbar and Kennedy,* 'spulyeit') to Westminster in 1296 by Edward I, the Hammer of the Scots. Its cleverly executed 'theft' on Christmas Day 1950 and its speedy return to Scottish soil (in the abbey of Arbroath eventually) was regarded by many Scots as the righting of an ancient wrong, as a symbol of their re-emerging national identity. This bold act inspired a spate of poems and songs, most of them written to Scottish tunes; the best known of all became John McEvoy's 'The Wee Magic Stane',[24] to the tune of 'The Ould Orange Flute' (also known as 'Villikens and his Dinah'). This clever and attractive song is in Scots dialect but the second half of verse 5 is sung with a pukka English accent:

> 'Now its no use you sending your statues down heah,'
> Said the Dean, 'but you've given me a jolly good ideah.'

Reference is made later in the song to strong rumours that replicas of the Stone of Destiny had been made, and to the morale-raising idea that possibly the wrong stone was returned to Westminster.[25] In 1951 there occurred several demonstrations at Glasgow's Central Station, and the idea of demonstration songs was then renewed.

The Queen's accession to the throne in 1952 inspired a new flow of songs. 'Coronation Coronach', to the Orange tune 'The Sash', is in some ways the archetype of the folk-rebel song: it is both Republican and Nationalist, springing from the not unreasonable reaction of many Scots to the Queen's title of Elizabeth II. Elizabeth I was queen only of England, not of Scotland –

> For ye cannae hae the second Liz
> When the first yin's never been.

This seems to have been the first time a similar objection had been raised since the Union of the Crowns (though some murmurings were heard at the time of Edward VII)[26] – an indication no doubt of raised national consciousness. A later Republican song by Jim MacLean is 'NAB for Royalty', to the tune 'The De'il's awa wi' the Exciseman'. Both these songs were later included in the *Ding Dong Dollar* disc.

Sandwiched between the Stane and the Coronation there occurred two other events which were important in the story of the Revival: the first Edinburgh People's Festival,[27] and the founding of the School of Scottish Studies.

Since the start of the Edinburgh Festival in 1947 various people had felt that traditional Scottish culture should be represented in it, and many informal ceilidhs had sprouted in private houses and flats. These were very different from the more official 'folk' events which took place under the Festival umbrella. The official attitude can be assessed by the notes on a play performed in 1947 which included 'folksong *arrangements* of great felicity...and sung with natural charm by *an octet of fine voices*'[28] (my italics). Such well-meaning attempts were soon shown to be travesties of the genuine article as revealed by the late-night ceilidhs, especially those occurring after Joan Littlewood and Ewan MacColl's Theatre Workshop performances (1948–53). Many citizens welcomed to their homes not only local enthusiasts but also visiting folk musicians, singers, actors, poets, artists and – a constant ingredient of this mixture – those who were predominantly listeners, all hungrily absorbing this 'new' musical experience.

In 1951 the Edinburgh Labour Festival Commitee was set up, with representatives from the Labour Party, the Edinburgh Trades Council, various Trade Unions (especially the Musicians' Union), the Co-operative Movement, and a few Scottish members of the Workers' Music Association including Janey Buchan. They had two specific ends in view: firstly to try and modify the élitist nature of the Festival, which meant arguing about the high prices of tickets, and secondly to include working-class culture as well as high art under the same Festival aegis. Norman Buchan recalls how he went round Trade Union branches talking on the importance of cultural activities, and spoke to dockers from the back of a horse-drawn lorry in Leith Docks as well as to workers on a building site. He found an enthusiastic response from all labour organisations.[29]

Hamish Henderson was asked to arrange a People's Festival Ceilidh; Martin Milligan was the organiser, assisted by Mary Black, wife of the Rev. Calum Black from Iona. They booked Theatre Workshop to return, this time with the famous peace play *Uranium 235*.

The first People's Festival Ceilidh took place in the Oddfellows Hall, on 31 August 1951. Alan Lomax was there and recorded nearly all the evening's items. The Ceilidh 'had the explicit aim of entering the lists, as far as the official Festival was concerned, by saying, "Look, we have here in Scotland – and up to now it hasn't received any attention from the big Festival – this fantastic tradition of popular culture, both Gaelic and Scots...and here it is!"'[30] There were Gaelic singers Flora MacNeil and Calum Johnston from Barra, Jimmy MacBeath from the North-East, piper John Burgess, and prosperous Fyvie farmer John Strachan who knew some of the big ballads, the muckle sangs.

Norman Buchan was one of those for whom this was an entirely new experience, a revelation: 'I was indeed "bowled over"[31], in fact that's an understatement.' His most memorable impression was of Jessie Murray from Buckie: '...a little old lady dressed in black, sang a song I've never forgotten...it was the most fragile and delicate and beautiful tune I'd ever heard... "Skippin' barfit through the heather" ...it seemed to dissolve, to vaporise in the air with an indescribable effect...marvellous.'

Jessie Murray: *Skippin Barfit through the Heather*
First People's Festival, Edinburgh 1951; rec. H.H. SA/1951/20

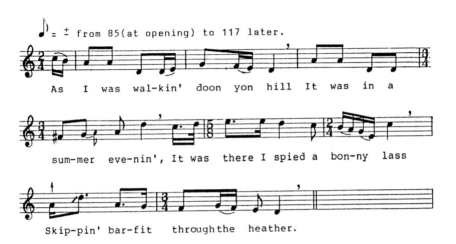

1. As I was walkin' doon yon hill
   It was in a summer evenin',
   It was there I spied a bonny lass
   Skippin' barfit through* the heather.

2. Eh but she was neatly dressed,
   She neither needed hat nor feather;
   She was the queen among them a',
   Skippin' barfit through the heather.

3. 'Will ye come wi' me, my bonny lass,
   Will ye come wi' me and leave the heather?
   It's silks an' satins ye will wear
   If ye come wi' me and leave the heather.'

4. She wore a goon o' bonnie blue,
   Her petticoats were a pheasant colour,
   And in between the stripes were seen
   Shinin' bells o' bloomin' heather.

5. 'Oh young man your offer's good,
   But sae weel I ken ye will deceive me:
   But gin ye tak my hert awa'
   Better if I had never seen ye.'

6. Oh but she was neatly dressed,
   She neither needed hat nor feather;
   She was the queen among them a',
   Skippin' barfit through the heather.[32]

*'Through' here rhymes with 'bough'.

But the People's Festivals did not present only popular culture and topical drama. The 1952 Guide to Events announces concerts of piano and violin music by Beethoven, with an introductory lecture; also poetry readings, art exhibitions and film shows.

The establishment of a centre for the study of native traditional culture had concerned many people within and without Scotland, and in 1949 an advisory board on postgraduate Scottish Studies was set up within Edinburgh University. Amongst press material then appearing was a seminal article in *The Scots Review*, February 1950, by Angus MacIntosh, Professor of English Language. He was a prime mover both in launching the university's Linguistic Survey of Gaelic and Scots dialects and in setting up the proposed traditional studies institute. Two other leading Edinburgh figures should be mentioned in the *fons et origo* of the School of Scottish Studies: Sidney Newman, Professor of Music, and Stuart Piggott, Professor of Archaeology, who stressed the importance of Material Culture. A powerful influence was also exerted by Professor J H Delargy, Director of the Irish Folklore Commission, an Antrim man with a personal knowledge of Scottish traditional life.

Calum MacLean, brother of Sorley and at that time working with the Irish Folklore Commission, was 'despatched' from Dublin to Edinburgh and in January 1951 became the first Research Fellow in Celtic. Directed by a University Court committee which included heads of principal departments concerned, the School received its official name in October 1951. Other early research appointments included Francis Collinson in Music and Hamish Henderson in Scots Folk Song, and in 1952 Stewart Sanderson became the first Secretary-Archivist. In May of that year a conference on Scottish Studies was attended by those in related disciplines such as Scottish history, Scottish literature, social anthropology and archaeology.

The School's first office consisted of converted cubicles in an old warehouse, where the early researchers transcribed and annotated the tapes they had recorded. Fieldwork then was mainly in the Gaelic-speaking North-West and in the rich ballad areas around Aberdeenshire. In spring 1954 the School moved to George Square, eventually occupying three of the few remaining eighteenth-century houses there. Fieldwork and research covered traditional Scots and Gaelic music, material culture, social history and organisation, social anthropology, archaeology, a folk-tale archive, and a place names survey separately housed nearby. An up-to-date laboratory dealt with the work of copying tapes, for preservation, and making example tapes for lectures; and the academic journal *Scottish Studies* started in 1957. At first dealing directly with Edinburgh University Court, in October 1965 the School became a department within the Faculty of Arts.

More will be heard later of the School's development and activities, but a brief statement of its beginnings is necessary in any chronological account of events, because this institution played an important part in the revival. A two-way process was at work here. For the very first time the actual sound of Scottish folk music was made available not only to posterity but to present-day research workers, to visiting scholars and to folk singers and players themselves. Later this was extended to undergraduate as well as postgraduate students, and to the general public by way of discs and cassettes. The School will always be deeply grateful to its 'informants' – that rather clinical name for people who have freely given time to record music, stories, reminiscences and other oral information, now in the huge archive of tapes and still being added to. But the other side of the coin should also be looked at. The work of recording has been a source of encouragement to many tradition-bearers (who in not a few cases – at any rate in the Scots sector – have been unaware of the value of what they had to give) as well as to revival musicians; both could listen to themselves and to each other, and so draw mutual inspiration.

A good example of this encouraging influence may be found in the story of the first folk song club in Scotland. This was at Allan Glen's secondary school for boys, in Glasgow, and was started in 1953 by Morris Blythman, who taught French and German there and who felt that more emphasis on the Arts side was needed. He hit on the idea of doing folk song with a rather turbulent form class (he had already tried this out on a German class which included Robin Hall). He told them, 'Turn up at four if you're interested', expecting perhaps three or four – but the whole class came. Supplied with notebooks, they took down the words of songs Blythman sang to them. He had complete freedom of scope since the music teacher was not interested in this venture. In contrast to later pioneer clubs, they began straight away with Scottish songs.

'The kids picked up song after song... I used to take them to all sorts of places: the Gas Board, Ladies' Guilds, Co-operative organisations...anyone who would listen. It was always best at a women's organisation, because they were nice boys and the women took a motherly interest in them.' They found that starting with Glasgow songs, for example, 'My Maw's a millionaire', broke the ice and made other Scots songs more acceptable. At a Medical Association meeting, after a just politely nodding reception for 'The barnyards o' Delgaty and 'Johnnie lad', the boys pitched in with local songs – '...and the audience accepted this because they...had come to know Glasgow people in their work as doctors. It made us realise the Glasgow patois was a weapon to be used.'[33]

Morris Blythman stressed how 'the thing picked up tremendously' when Hamish Henderson started visiting and recording them. As well as school concerts there were evening ceilidhs at Morris and Marion Blythman's home; the bothy song 'McGinty's meal and ale when the pig gaed on the spree' was once performed by a boy 'with no sense of rhythm or tempo, but he was the hit that evening' – notwithstanding Lonnie Donegan's presence. A school pipe-band was formed, and Glasgow Corporation appointed their first guitar teacher, Josh MacRae, an art student with a remarkable flair for American songs and blues.

Christened Ian, his nickname resulted from a partiality for Josh White's songs. 'I never think of myself as an ethnic Scottish singer, yet oddly enough I can sing in Gaelic and I feel my Gaelic heritage' (his parents came from Skye and Lewis). '...*I was much more of a cowboy than a ploughboy*...there's more in common between a Celt and a cowboy than between a Celt and an Englishman.'[34] The 'tartan cowboys' (a term often used pejoratively, in the breaking away from American influence) represent an important stage in the Scottish story. Another Scottish singer who started off as a 'cowboy' was the versatile and influential Alex Campbell, who lived for many years on the Continent.

Glasgow folk concerts in the mid-fifties also brought in jazz – for example, Jim MacHarg and his band – and piping.

By 1955 Morris Blythman and Josh MacRae had started inviting guests to the school concerts: Moyna Flanigan, Enoch Kent, Jimmy MacGregor, Rena Swankey...with Jeannie Robertson the brightest star of all. An Aberdeenshire traveller described by Alan Lomax as 'a monumental figure of the world's folk song', she had been discovered by Hamish Henderson in 1953. 'Jeannie...was tremendously popular with the boys,' said Blythman. 'She would tell stories as well. The headmaster, an Aberdonian, treated Jeannie with the utmost courtesy... She had a sort of duchess nobility but at the same time a popular warmth, that got the boys both ways, and got everybody else.'

Jeannie Robertson had already appeared at the third Edinburgh Festival People's Ceilidh in 1953, only a few months after her discovery. She was at the top of her form then and her extensive repertoire included many classical ballads, lyric songs, riddles, bairn-sangs, and a wealth of stories.[35] Many recordings are available of Jeannie's singing and these provide a constant source of delight: her magnificent voice, her shaping of phrases so that words and music become an inseparable whole, her versatility of style matching her wide-ranging repertoire, her subtly expressive use of rubato and ornamentation – above all the paradox of a traditional timeless objectivity combined with dramatic, consciously histrionic power. A L Lloyd has summed it up best: 'A singer sweet and heroic.'

In 1952 the second Edinburgh People's Festival had been the only organisation to honour Hugh MacDiarmid's sixtieth birthday. MacDiarmid was again present at the ceilidh, as he had been the year before, and some of his poems were again read at the ceilidh social, as the late-night sessions following the official events came to be called.

The same year saw the first production of Ewan MacColl's play *The Travellers*, a political thriller which was baldly – in both the English and the Scots sense of the word – anti-US imperialism. But McCarthyism was then at its height and reverberations were heard across the Atlantic. This might explain possible over-simplications within the play, but it would also explain the scared over-reaction which it produced from sections of the Labour movement including the Edinburgh Trades Council. The Scottish Trades Union Congress proceeded to ban the People's Festival and called on trade unions to cease giving it financial support. This proscription did not stop it from continuing, although on a decreasing scale, but debts accumulated and 1955 saw the last of these festivals as such.

But the music which some four years earlier had been heard for the first time on a city concert platform – and which came with all the force of a revelation to audiences of questing intellectuals, industrial workers, students, douce city folk and cosmopolitan culture seekers – could not be re-submerged, and the Edinburgh Festival would never be the same again. For these people the bones of the copious collections of traditional music had at last been given flesh and blood by actual sound, by the authentic style of performance. Before long the folk music of Scotland and beyond, put on chiefly by the gradually appearing folk clubs, became an integral part of the Edinburgh Festival Fringe.[36]

So far this authentic sound had been heard by relatively few people. The broadcast programmes have already been mentioned; a few records had percolated across the Atlantic, plus pioneering discs from the Workers' Music Association (WMA). But a mass audience had not yet been reached. The jazz revival, starting pre-war, was now well established, and jazz enthusiasts were also seeing an 'alternative music', something different from art music or the dance band music of that period. Like folk music, jazz was also more anti-Establishment, an important element in most revivals (the jazz revival was particularly strong in Scotland).[37] It was not surprising therefore that folk and jazz should come together. The surprise was that this should happen so suddenly, that what resulted should spring up almost overnight like Jack's beanstalk. This phenomenon became known as skiffle.

Skiffle has been described as 'a virtually universal musical vogue among young Britons...a modification of revivalist jazz to suit an even more completely unqualified and lay public.'[38] And although Francis Newton describes the term itself as 'dug up from the obscurer recesses of American jazz history, and virtually without meaning for anyone in the USA',[39] there is no doubt that skiffle was based on American music[40] – from different work fronts...steel workers...chain-gang songs...and perhaps especially songs about trains. The catalytic agent of this new movement was a record by Lonnie Donegan of Glasgow called 'Rock Island Line': riveting in its powerful, ongoing drive, it is totally American, delivered in a rich southern states accent quite amazing to hear from a Glaswegian. The instruments are double bass (Barber), guitar (Donegan) and wash board (Deryl Bryden). Donegan sang with Chris Barber's jazz band, and their album 'New Orleans Joy' (1954) included two skiffle songs – 'Rock Island Line' and 'John Henry' – which were later put out by Decca as a single, the first British record to get into the American top ten. The accompaniment of 'Rock Island Line' consists of regular tonic chords during the spoken parts and during all of the singing except the chorus, where it expands into three chords: tonic, dominant and subdominant.

This harmonic and instrumental simplicity, plus the jazzy syncopation and rhythmic drive, formed the basis of skiffle. Its success was part of the rejection of canned music – which was nearing the end of the smooth, cheaply romantic 'moon and June' period – and part of people wanting to make their own music. There were usually several singers as well as instrumentalists, and group singing gave confidence to early efforts. The necessary equipment was cheap: galvanised zinc washing-boards gave forth a kind of rattle which took the place of drums, plywood tea chests, with a pole and stout string, made rudimentary double basses, and a ukulele, banjo or guitar could be bought for 30 bob. The thing caught on like wildfire. Norman Buchan recalls speaking to Ewan MacColl in London – 'he said with eyes aglow, "There are about 300 different skiffle groups going now, all within a few months".' This was to double by mid-1956 in Greater London alone.[41]

Remember that this was the first time in Britain that teenagers had money to spend and were recognised as a section of the public with their own needs and even their own *mores*. This arose from the improved job and pay situation for them in the fifties, and the fact that students could supplement their grants by holiday jobs. Without this market record companies would hardly have taken the calculated risk of making 'Rock Island Line' and other discs in the skiffle genre. The net result was that a particular kind of folk music was for the first time available to a truly mass audience, extending into millions, and this music stemmed from America. Here we have yet another facet of the American connection, immensely influential because of its mass appeal.

I have not found any estimate of how many skiffle groups arose in Scotland, but people I have recorded who were in that age group at that time testified to the widespread influence of skiffle during its short but exciting life. In Rutherglen Academy alone there were six groups, another concrete example of the way the revival worked at this stage.

In the mid-fifties Norman Buchan was teaching English at Rutherglen Academy, a mixed senior secondary school near Glasgow. (Morris Blythman left Allan Glen's in 1957 for a period abroad, and in his absence the school club gradually folded up.) Buchan had been collecting records: some by HMV featuring Ewan MacColl, and some by WMA which later became Topic, the first British company to issue folk music discs. Burl Ives was another influence from across the Atlantic: 'I realised there was a lot of relationship between these American songs and the Scottish songs – we could learn from these, they were still being sung, you still had an indigenous thriving folk musical culture in the form of jazz, negro song and negro worksongs, on a much more overt level than was our own traditional song which was still being excluded into the countryside by and large...' During these years he arranged various folk events in Glasgow, including a Ballads and Blues concert in 1958 in aid of the Christian Action fund for political prisoners in South Africa.[42] The Weavers, now revived after some years in limbo during the McCarthy era, were a strong influence at that time. When Norman Buchan was approached by Scottish Television for a programme, he christened the group which he then worked with 'The Reivers'.[43] 'It sounded like the Weavers, and had the right idea of raiding for Scotland.' Around this time the talented Fisher family, who have Gaelic connections, appeared on the scene: Archie, Ray, and later Cilla, Cindy and Joyce.

Glaswegians Jimmie Macgregor and Robin Hall were among those most strongly influenced by Blythman and Buchan at that time (Hall had been at Allan Glen's School). After hearing MacColl, Lloyd and others at the Glasgow Ballads and Blues concert, Macgregor set his face towards London, first for weekends and eventually for good; Hall moved to London in 1959. This was just before the growth of folk clubs in Scotland, and there were far more folk music activities of all kinds in London. These moves were to have important consequences for the whole British revival.

When skiffle came, Norman Buchan saw it as a means of getting Scottish material through to his pupils, but it was 1958 before he finally took the plunge. 'I took my nerve in both hands – I'm a nervous singer and tend to go off pitch – and sang "The Dowie Dens of Yarrow" to an English class. One kid said "That sounds like an Arab..." – I said, "Well you're not far wrong" – I knew it was pentatonic or modal or whatever...' He pinned on to the school notice-board, 'Do you want to learn about skiffle and other songs?' The Ballads Club quickly proliferated, and skiffle groups plus solo singers were soon giving regular concerts attended by several hundred parents, pupils, and other interested people. A number of boys from Allan Glen's helped at the beginning. They also performed to outside bodies, including Old Age Pensioners Associations. A third-year Rutherglen boy taught guitar, and two ceilidh bands started, which included fiddlers. Some excellent singers emerged from this school club, notably Gordeanna MacCulloch who later became a leading member of the Clutha group, Allan Morris (see Chapter IV for further mention of these two singers), Fraser and Ian Bruce, John Craig, Alan Knox, Mary Stewart, Ian Young and Anne Neilson. 'The interesting thing was that starting thus, within months they were wanting to sing the big ballads...they began to like them, partly because they found other people were thrilled by them.'

However, skiffle soon died out, killed ironically by its own success; for although it had begun as a spontaneous, grassroots – city rather than rural – answer to Tin Pan Alley, its very popularity caused its take-over by commercial recording companies. In this process it split into folk on the one hand and rock on the other.[44] Rock'n'roll had come to Britain in 1956, heralded by Bill Haley's singing of 'Rock Around the Clock', the title first of a song and then of the film.[45] Rock, with the varied offshoots which sprang from it, was to become in some ways an even more anti-Establishment voice, acclaimed in particular by young working-class people, and especially by the male sector.[46] Young folk enthusiasts felt that there was no point in doing themselves what they could hear professionals doing much better. But getting to know music which was rooted in the indigenous culture of another country – America – made people aware that they had their own tradition, just as rich and exciting, and on their very doorstep. (This pattern was later repeated elsewhere – in Denmark and other Continental countries, including Germany where folk music was suspect after the war because of its Hitler movement connections – with the difference that it was often Scottish traditional material which gave the impetus and turned people towards the search for their own roots).[47] The revival was thus left at a very much higher and more creative level than before.

In support of this statement one need only look at the number of clubs which started to snowball, chiefly in cities and towns at first. The Edinburgh University Folk Song Society, started in 1958 with Stuart MacGregor and Hamish Henderson as leading spirits.[48] In the following year a similar club opened at Glasgow University. Among its leaders were Adam McNaughtan, then a student and noted later for his collections of Glasgow children's street songs as well as for his own songs, and Ian Davison, another teacher at Rutherglen Academy. (McNaughtan later joined the staff when Buchan became an MP.) In Aberdeen the New Left movement had become active around 1958 and 1959, with influence also from Arnold Wesker's Centre 42; concerts were held with poetry, jazz, and traditional revival singers, and Arthur Argo started the Aberdeen Folk Club.

In 1959 a club called The Sporranslitters took over premises in Edinburgh's High Street and expanded into a folk club, The Howff. During the three weeks of the Edinburgh Festival they put on a late show every night and this attracted many visitors, especially those going to and from The Tattoo at Edinburgh Castle, just up the road.

It was around 1959 that Jean Redpath, then a student, met Hamish Henderson, who helped to foster her shining talent and who directed her towards the University Folk Song Society. St Andrews started a general folk club in 1960–61, led by an English student, Pete Shepheard, who identified himself both as singer and collector with the folk revival in Scotland and Ireland. Shepheard and Jim Craig were instrumental in organising the first Traditional Music and Song festival at Blairgowrie, in 1966: later that year the TMS Association of Scotland was formed. St Andrews also had a jazz club. In Dunfermline, a folk club was started in a cellar in 1961 by John Watt, another pioneering singer, songwriter and lecturer; it was also called The Howff.

'In 1959 Norman and Janey Buchan felt there could be a folk club in Glasgow.'[49] These words open an eye-witness account of the Glasgow activities which brought forth the first Scottish folk club open to the general public. Orchestrating this build-up were Buchan's group 'The Reivers', Archie and Ray Fisher, Drew Moyes and influential visitors such as Ewan MacColl and guitarist-banjoist Ralph Rinzler. Performers at the club soon included Jimmy MacBeath, Hamish Imlach, Jacky O'Connor, Bobby Campbell, Josh MacRae, Sheila MacRae and Ewan McVicar, with Martin Carthy another influence. As in other clubs, the early taste was for American music. When Drew Moyes took over it became the Glasgow Folk Centre, with workshops in the Iona Community cellar. Among other city clubs were the Grand Hotel which had 'feature evenings', Celtic nights with Irish artists and the unique singer, box player and storyteller 'old' Davie Stewart; organisers were Ron Clark, Carl McDougall, Geordie McIntyre and Ian Philip. On national television at the time were Hall and Macgregor, with Rory and Alex McEwan.

In 1961 a successful club was launched in Perth by a group which included John Young, George Craigie and John Thomson, and they were joined in the mid-sixties by Sheila Douglas, singer and songwriter. Andrew Douglas has become known as a witty versifier whose more serious ballads are extraordinarily traditional in style.

Ross Paterson was a founder member of Dundee Folk Club in 1962, and Kirkcaldy folk club was started the same year by a group of teachers from Templehall junior secondary school; Jack Stuart, the headmaster, was president of the club. As a weekly event he started inviting singers and players to the school, on the morning after a ceilidh-concert, to perform, talk and answer questions, as part of the day's teaching. This was for pupils to listen and discuss rather than to sing, and to perceive traditional music as part of their Scottish heritage. Concerts were held in schools in different parts of Fife, at which both visiting artists and school pupils performed. Stuart also initiated the part-time appointment of Archie Fisher and Josh MacRae as guitar (and song) teachers in Fife schools. A concert was held after Jack Stewart's death in 1972, to inaugurate a memorial fund with the aim of helping young people in Fife.

The following list includes a few names of other singers and players invited to Glasgow's Grand Hotel club in particular, as well as to other Scottish clubs during the sixties. *From Scotland*: Arthur Argo; Norman Kennedy; Donald Higgins (piper and singer, husband of Jeannie Robertson); the Stewarts of Blairgowrie; Pat McNulty (Uileann or Irish pipes); the noted Shetland collector, composer and player Tom Anderson, his pupil Aly Bain, and Simpson Pirie (fiddlers); and the influential guitarist Davey Graham. Gaelic singers Flora MacNeil; Joan MacKenzie; Willie Matheson (later Reader in Celtic, Edinburgh University); and Norman MacLean (piper and singer). *From England*: Bert (A L) Lloyd; Cyril Tawney; Frankie Armstrong; Sandra Kerr; John Faulkner; Jack Warshaw; Martin Carthy; the Watersons; and Colin Ross (Northumbrian pipes). *From Ireland*: the popular Clancy brothers; Joe Heaney; Paddy Tunney; the Furey brothers; Festy Conlin; the Dubliners, and Dominic Behan.

Folk clubs continued to sprout in other centres, including Inverness in 1965.

Matt McGinn (1928–77), singer and songwriter, was a Glaswegian in whose work all the varied strands of the revival were interwoven. The eighth child in a family whose home was a small room and kitchen, his harsh childhood experiences turned him into a rebel; but this rebellion was channelled into political commitment, partly by his father's socialism and partly by the influence of the socialist 'University' near the Trongate, where Sunday afternoon crowds gathered to hear speakers. Matt followed in the footsteps of Woody Guthrie, Pete Seeger and the Almanacs, and wrote many hard-hitting and often very funny topical songs. His humour was irreverent and he lampooned anyone he saw as a *poseur*, even among his own ilk. A thumbprint of his style, especially when putting over his own songs or verses, was to pinpoint any irony by affecting a 'posh' (English upper-class) quasi-genteel accent. He could move his listeners deeply, by his delivery no less than by the content of his songs; his voice had an edge to it, effective whether he was shouting out a chorus or almost whispering as at the end of his 'Miner's lullaby'.

Matt McGinn: A *Miner's Lullaby*
Glasgow Weekend School, 1962; rec. H.H. SA 1962/13

(Chorus) Coo-rie doon, coo-rie doon, coo-rie doon ma daur - lin',

Coo-rie doon the day doon the day (V.1) Lie

doon ma dear and in yer ear, tae help ye close your eye,

I'll sing a song, a slum-ber song, a mi-ner's lu - la -

- by. Yer dad-dy's doon the mine, ma daurlin', doon in the

Cur -[ə]l-by Main, Your dad-dy's how-kin'coal, ma

daur-lin', for his ain wee wean.

(Chorus)
Coorie doon, coorie doon, coorie doon ma daurlin',
Coorie doon the day. (repeat these two lines)

1.   Lie doon ma dear and in your ear, tae help ye close your eye,
      I'll sing a song, a slumber song, a miner's lullaby.
      Yer daddy's doon the mine, ma daurlin', doon in the Curlby Main:
      Your daddy's howkin' coal, ma daurlin', for his ain wee wean.

2.   There's daurkness doon the mine, ma daurlin', daurkness, dust and damp,
      But we must hae oor heat, oor light, oor fire and oor lamp.
      Your daddy coories doon, ma daurlin', doon in a three-fit seam,
      So you can coorie doon, ma daurlin', coorie doon and dream.

In addition to the words, Matt McGinn created this deceptively simple tune, which hugs the tonic closely at every cadence and has a dream like, near-hypnotic quality. 'Coorie doon' means 'snuggle down' as well as 'crouch down', and so applies to both the child in bed and the miner in the pit.

One of his finest songs is 'Just a magic shadow-show', with its overtones of Omar Khayyám. Like Woody Guthrie, Matt also wrote children's songs: two of the best known are 'The Kirkcudbright centipede' and 'Stop the world I've lost my yo-yo' (or 'The wee red yo-yo').

Meanwhile, Jimmie Macgregor had been hearing and performing a wide variety of material in London, both solo and with various duos and groups. While working with The City Ramblers he met and started singing with Robin Hall. Soon they were on BBC Television's immensely popular *Tonight* programme, five nights a week from 1959 to 1964. With an audience of millions, they became household names; they toured the world, and they were the first artists who had the opportunity to sing Scottish and other folk songs to a mass audience. Their repertoire included urban songs and Glasgow street songs. Their influence was immense.

In 1961 an event occurred which induced an immediate reaction and which spawned some of the best protest songs of this century – the American submarine depot ship, *Proteus,* along with smaller ships, sailed into the Holy Loch near Dunoon. 'Polaris' was the name of the submarine-launched ballistic missile (A-2) which it carried. Public hostility came from a wide cross-section of thought: the Peace Movement, spearheaded by the CND (Campaign for Nuclear Disarmament), the Committee for Non-Violent Disarmament, church people, Quakers, the Committee of 100 and members of at least three political parties – Labour, Communist and Scottish National.

The Scotsman, 22 May 1961, reported fully on the first of the larger demonstrations. About a thousand people marched from Dunoon to the Holy Loch where they split into two groups, one to take part in the seaborne attack on the *Proteus* and the other to demonstrate on shore. A bonfire was lit on the beach and members of the Scottish CND stayed for an all-night vigil. Those arrested were later released, but many were fined.

Songs had already been pouring forth from anti-Polaris pens, and the theme song of the protesters, as well as of the commandos of the Holy Loch, was 'I shall not be moved'. It is based on an American trade unionist song which was connected with the Shellback Fundamentalists, a religious sect whose name has obvious 'not to be moved' connotations. Versions of it have appeared in other protest situations throughout the English-speaking world.

The following three songs are on the disc *Ding Dong Dollar*, and in its accompanying booklet.[50]

'The polis are fascinated by every reference to themselves... They don't know whether they're folk-friends, folk-villains, folk-comedians or folk-crowd scenes. But they do know that they're accepted as folk-somethings and relax. They're quite photogenic as they tap out time to the old banjo, and join in the chorus singing...'[51] Morris Blythman, one of the chief anti-Polaris organisers and songwriters, also commented, 'The police received a bad press for their handling of demonstrators...they reassessed the situation and next time they sent Glasgow policeman Detective Inspector Runcie, famous for his expertise in crowd control. We made up a special song for Runcie...when the police heard it, they tried to look serious!'

Ye'll no sit here

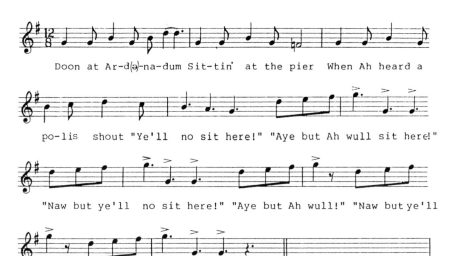

Doon at Ar-d(a)-na-dum Sit-tin' at the pier When Ah heard a

po-lis shout "Ye'll no sit here!" "Aye but Ah wull sit here!"

"Naw but ye'll no sit here!" "Aye but Ah wull!" "Naw but ye'll

no!" "Aye but Ah wull sit here!"

1.   Doon at Ardnadam, sittin' at the pier
      When Ah heard a polis shout, 'Ye'll no sit here!'

      (Chorus)
      'Aye but Ah wull sit here!'
      'Naw, but ye'll no sit here!'
      'Aye, but Ah wull!' 'Naw but ye'll no!'
      'Aye, but Ah wull sit here!'

2.   'Twas Chief Inspector Runcie, enhancing his career,
      Prancing up an' doon the road like Yogi Bear.

3.　He caa'd for help tae Glesca, they nearly chowed his ear:
We've got the G'ers an' Celtic demonstrators here.

4.　He telephoned the sodgers, but didnae mak it clear,
The sodgers sent doon Andy Stewart tae volunteer.

5.　He radioed the White Hoose, but a' that he could hear,
Wis...two...one...zero – an' the set went queer.

6.　For Jack had drapt an H-bomb an' gied his-sel a shroud,
An' he met wi' Billy Graham on a wee white cloud.

The tune derives from 'Hey Jock, ma Cuddy', but was more appreciated popularly as 'Ye'll no shite here'; a variant has been collected in Arkansas. This song is seriously funny and is of the rebel-burlesque genre. Runcie it seems was flattered at thus being immortalised in song.

After the first year or so the trade unions joined in. On at least one occasion, the demonstrators walked through Dunoon belting out 'The Cooncil o' Dunoon, they want their hauf-a-croon':

We dinna want Polaris

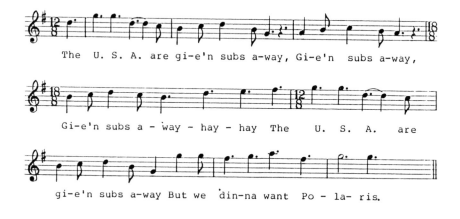

1.　The USA are gie'n subs away,
Gie'n subs away,
Gie'n subs away – hay – hay
The USA are gie'n subs away
But we dinna want Polaris.

2.　Tell the Yanks tae drap them doon the stanks,
Drap them doon the stanks, etc.

3.　The Cooncil o Dunoon, they want their hauf-a-croon,
Want their hauf-a-croon, etc.

4.   The hairies o' the toon are sailin' tae Dunoon,
     Sailin' tae Dunoon, etc.

5.   It's suicide tae hae them on the Clyde,
     Hae them on the Clyde, etc.

6.   Tak the haill dam show up the River Alamo,
     River Alamo, etc.

7.   Anchors aweigh for Poppa Kennedy,
     Poppa Kennedy, Poppa Kennedy, hay-hay,
     Anchors aweigh for Poppa Kennedy,
     An' ta-ta tae Polaris.

The tune is 'Three craws sat upon a wa'' and the words are by Jim MacLean who wrote many other uncompromising and sometimes witty songs. (See Chapter IV for a very different version of 'Three Craws'.) Blythman said: 'There was extreme opposition to us from some of the people of Dunoon because they knew we were getting at them, but they could see we were fanatical at them betraying Scotland...they were making a lot from the trade, the girls had Yanks, etc... But this was international...there were hundreds of English demonstrators, very troubled people.'
Several *Ding Dong Dollar* collections of songs had been printed and sold widely at the modest price of 6d. They were also translated by the Russian Sam Marschak, well known for his children's stories as well as for his translations of Shakespeare and Burns. The title song, with words by John Mack, was one of the most humorous as well as hard hitting; the tune was taken from a Glasgow children's street song, 'Oh ye canny shove yer Granny aff a bus'. It is also the tune of 'She'll be coming round the mountain when she comes'.

Ding Dong Dollar

(Chorus)
O ye canny spend a dollar when ye're deid,
O ye canny spend a dollar when ye're deid:
Singin' Ding...Dong...Dollar; Everybody holler
Ye canny spend a dollar when ye're deid.

1.   O the Yanks have juist drapt anchor in Dunoon
      An' they've had their civic welcome fae the toon,
      As they cam' up the measured mile
      Bonny Mary o' Argyll
      Wis wearin' spangled drawers ablow her goun.

2.   An' the publicans will a' be daein swell,
      For it's juist the thing that's sure tae ring the bell,
      O the dollars they will jingle,
      There'll be no a lassie single,
      Even though they maybe blaw us a' tae hell.

3.   But the Glesca Moderator disnae mind;
      In fact, he thinks the Yanks are awfy kind,
      For if it's heaven that ye're goin'
      It's a quicker way than rowin',
      An' there's sure tae be naebody left behind.

      (Final Chorus)
      O ye canny spend a dollar when ye're deid
      Sae tell Kennedy he's got tae keep the heid,
      Singin' Ding...Dong...Dollar; Everybody holler,
      Ye canny spend a dollar when ye're deid.

Other children's song tunes were also borrowed, for example 'Bee Baw Babbity', which became 'K-K-Kennedy'.

A big Labour Party open-air rally at Ayr was the occasion for what was probably the sharpest confrontation of all. The anti-Polaris singers group had been invited to come and lead the singing and Josh MacRae had the crowd enthralled listening to 'Joe Hill'. It was a rainy day, and about 200 yards from the platform were some open shelters. 'When the singers were on, the crowd came out from the shelters...as soon as the speakers got up to speak, they all went back to their shelters. We had the same sort of experience at all the demos...people were getting something from the songs that none of the speakers could give them,' said Morris Blythman. Since it is unlikely that many of the words would have been audible to the crowd in this open-air demo situation, the influence exerted by the songs is evidence of the power of non-verbal communication.

Josh MacRae stated: 'There was a very good spirit abroad at that time...it was a vital force...the important thing was a strong togetherness and a political certainty about things. If we'd had the numbers, we could have done it then.'[52]

'10,000 peaceful demonstrators at this critical time would have sorted the Americans out,' said Blythman. 'They were just on the verge of deciding whether to stay or not...'

Whatever argument there may be about this attitude, there can be no doubt that most of the songs were brilliantly on-the-ball, even though not all were equally good. They proved a nice change too from the Aldermaston 'Ban the Bomb' type of songs, hymns like 'Stand to Ban the Bomb', and the apocalyptic 'Little man, where're you going to run to?', which though sincere and moving lacked the humour and edge of the anti-Polaris lyrics, including the Republican ones. Pete Seeger took the songs to America where they were enormously successful. At Berkeley, California, he started with 'The USA are gie'n subs away', and one can hear on the tape made of it that the whole student audience rose to it, they got the idea right away at the first line. Moe Asch of the American Folkways company eventually produced the *Ding Dong Dollar* disc; it proved so successful that it was re-issued several times. It is well worthwhile to beg, borrow or steal this album from anywhere you can find it, along with its scintillating booklet.

Several more of these rebel songs should be mentioned. 'The Gleska Eskimos' title stems from Captain Lanin's gaffe in dismissing the Holy Loch demonstrators as 'Eskimos', not realising that this race had long been immortalised by the Glasgow children's street song:

> Sitting amang the Eskimos
> Playing a gemme o' dominoes,
> My Maw's a millionaire.

The tune is another American one, 'Marching through Georgia' – but it was already popular in Glasgow as 'The Brigton Billy Boys', an Orange song! So Glasgow sectarian songs were drawn into the mêlée.

The tune of 'Yankee Doodle' could hardly be missed out of all this, so 'Paper hankies' was written for it:

> (Chorus) Chase the Yankees oot the Clyde
> Away wi' Uncle Sammy,
> Chase the Yankees oot the Clyde
> An' send them hame tae mammy.

and the moving 'John Brown's Body' tune, mentioned in Chapter II, appears again as 'Ban Polaris – Hallelujah'.

The most beautiful and the most famous of all these songs was written a year before Polaris. Dedicated to the Glasgow Peace Marchers, May 1960, this is Hamish Henderson's 'Freedom Come-all-ye', written to the poet's own adaptation of the pipe tune 'The Bloody Fields of Flanders'. It is still sung frequently all over Scotland and beyond. The language is rich, yet so graphically used that the meaning is substantially clear before any glossary is consulted. It rightly took its place among the anti-Polaris songs, although – or perhaps because – its theme is broader, and the 'roch wind' is depicted as sweeping away oppression and war over the whole world. Both words and music have been widely printed and can be found in *The Scottish Folksinger,* and on Claddagh's record of Henderson's poems and songs (CC A7). Dick Gaughan wants this song to be Scotland's National Anthem.

Freedom Come-all-ye

> Roch the wind in the clear day's dawin'
> Blaws the cloods heelster-gowdie ow'r the bay,
> But there's mair nor a roch wind blawin'
> Through the great glen o' the warld the day.
> It's a thocht that will gar oor rottans
> – A' they rogues that gang gallus, fresh and gay –
> Tak' the road, and seek ither loanin's
> For their ill ploys, tae sport and play.

Nae mair will the bonnie callants
Mairch tae war when oor braggarts crously craw,
Nor wee weans frae pit-heid and clachan
Mourn the ships sailin' doon the Broomielaw.
Broken faimlies in lands we've herriet
Will curse Scotland the Brave nae mair, nae mair;
Black and white, ane til ither mairriet
Mak' the vile barracks o' their maisters bare.

O come all ye at hame wi' Freedom,
Never heed whit the hoodies croak for doom.
In your hoose a' the bairns o' Adam
Can find breid, barley-bree and painted room.
When MacLean meets wi's frien's in Springburn
A' the roses and geans will turn tae bloom,
And a black boy frae yont Nyanga
Dings the fell gallows o' the burghers doon.

Finally, one more *Ding Dong Dollar* song should be mentioned, this time in the direct line of the irrepressible Glasgow music hall tradition – with overtones of earlier American commercial popular songs – which never failed to make a hit through the next decade: 'The misguided missile and the misguided Miss'.

A curious paradox is embodied within this corpus of songs. Although the American connection was still extremely influential in the Revival, nearly all the anti-Polaris content was *ipso facto* anti-American (and with conscious irony made use of many American tunes). It is hardly necessary to add that this was not anti the American nation but anti their top brass and anti-NATO, in particular for the grossly disproportionate number of nuclear bases inflicted on a small country. Of course this enraged some Americans. But many Americans, especially those who supported the anti-nuclear arms movement, welcomed these songs and even sang them with relish. In Scotland itself, '...the anti-Polaris singers...were accepted with pride and affection by demonstrators and organisers as their own establishment singers. No-one told them what to sing, where to sing, or how to sing it. They kept to the main theme of anti-Polaris, writing and binding the many disparate organisations into one body. And to this body they gave heart, voice and laughter. They were BBC'd, STV'd, televised, NCB'd,[53] broadcast, telecast, freelanced and pirated, AFN'd,[54] Radio Moscowed, translated, interpreted and given in evidence in court.' (From disc booklet.)

With the exception of 'Freedom Come-all-ye', the songs are very seldom heard now (and the submarines have gone from the loch). One obvious reason is the 30-year-old topicality of the words. But another reason which has been put forward is that some, in common with many other songs written in the 1960s, embody male sexist attitudes which are no longer acceptable. It could be claimed that such attitudes can be traced in 'Coronation Coronach' and in 'The Misguided Missile' (if the Miss was misguided, so was the Mister, or Corporal or whatever). Insofar as this is so, these two simply followed the mainstream tradition of folksong over hundreds of years, which continued right up to the beginning of the 1970s. It took the women's movement to make people aware of these attitudes. Yet plenty of older traditional sexist-type songs are still being sung. The anti-Polaris songs served their turn, they were part of the revival at that time and they left a lasting influence on the Scottish scene. After all they were without exception couched in the Scots vernacular, more than half of the tunes were Scottish, and this strengthened the trend towards the native traditional, which was one result of the demise of skiffle. Many singers were far more interested in this than in the political or protest songs.

Two singer-songwriter individualists spring to mind here, representative of many more. Adam McNaughtan from Glasgow found the strong influence of socialist politics came as 'rather a shock…with my good Church of Scotland non-political upbringing…so being a thrawn kin' o' character, some of the early stuff I wrote was on the other side, for example, "Ye canny ban Polaris when it's raining" and other ditties. I've a bit of the rebel in me…the establishment in folk song clubs was the Left, and if anything that turned me the other way!'[55] Andy Hunter, from near Clydebank, also had similar reservations. A pupil at Allan Glen's school, and later a devoted disciple of Jeannie Robertson in Aberdeen, he found that when CND started, a dramatic choice had to be made by young people. '…I decided not to opt for it, I'd not much to do with that kind of movement…my commitment was to folk song, humanism and the regeneration of ideals… I feel it's not good for everyone to be in the same basket…' Although, speaking of the struggle to find an 'alternative music', he also said, 'Everything was against us, but everything was for us because it was against us.'[56]

Adam McNaughtan later wrote 'Blood on the Grass', about Chile, and also a song against the Argentine regime. And Andy Hunter has written several songs in the realm of local politics rather than national or international.

The annual festivals started, with the first one being in Aberdeen, in 1963. The Aberdeen story provides a good example of what happened by around the mid-1960s. People like Tom Paxton and the Corries used to come to the clubs, then when they became commercial successes – though still based on tradition – Peter Hall notes that '…there was a split, and people who came to the club to hear Paxton, went to Paxton *concerts*. Those who came to hear Jeannie Robertson or [folk] revivalists…stayed at the folk song club. This split was to some extent because of the commercial situation – the clubs could no longer afford Paxton…there were records, and he sang at concerts.'[57] As well as being one of the leading folk musicians and scholars in the North-East, Peter Hall was the first to introduce Lizzie Higgins, daughter of Jeannie Robertson, to an Aberdeen club in the late sixties, thus launching her on a distinguised career. (See Chapter IV.)

The chief Scottish folk magazine before the seventies was *Chapbook*, launched by Arthur Argo in 1964; Volume 1 was the magazine of Aberdeen Folk Club. Successive volumes, aimed at national coverage, were sponsored by the Scottish Federation of Folk Song Clubs, and continued till the end of the decade – six issues per volume, then three issues for the fifth and last volume. These are now collectors' items, containing songs with music, articles, letters and reviews. Arthur Argo as principal editor was assisted by Carl McDougall and Ian Philip, with a production team based chiefly in Aberdeen.

In addition to writing songs himself, Norman Buchan contributed between 70 and 80 traditional songs, with music, to *The Weekly Scotsman's* column on Bothy Ballads, from 1959 to 1960; many of these appeared later in *101 Scottish Songs*.

The songs sung in the first decade or so of the folk clubs were chiefly a mixture of American, Irish, Scottish and English. Occasionally one in another language, notably Scottish Gaelic, would appear, and the emphasis on Scots song increased as the 1970s approached.

The following are a few of the titles which were heard: Blowin' in the wind; Where have all the flowers gone?; Spanish boots of Spanish leather; I was born in East Virginia; The last thing on my mind; I can't help but wonder where I'm bound; This land is your land; The wild rover; The craw on the cradle (anti-war song); Fourpence a day (MacColl); The north country maid; Hawl away Joe (a shanty); Woman sweeter than man; Baby lie easy (Cyril Tawney); The jug of punch; The Irish rover; Me husband's got no courage in him (probably introduced by A L Lloyd); The Silkie of Sule Skerry; One morning fair I took the air; Plaisir d'amour; The seeds of love; The wraggle taggle gypsies; The copper kettle; Mary Hamilton; The trees do grow high; The cruel mither; The bonny hoose o' Airlie (see Chapter IV for versions of the last two); The gardener; The Highland widow's lament; Lord Gregory; Sally free and easy; To the weavers gin ye go; Rigs o' rye; and The water is wide.

Amongst songwriters not as yet mentioned were Peter Ross and actor Roddy MacMillan, both of Glasgow, Bob Bertram of Edinburgh, and Dave Goulder, who lived for some years at a youth hostel in Glen Torridon, which became a meeting place for singers as well as for climbers. Archie Fisher has been a potent influence for over thirty years, as a singer, guitarist and radio presenter as well as a songwriter. He has an understated yet compelling vocal style, with exceptionally clear diction. Danny Kyle is a brilliant MC, broadcaster, singer and guitarist.

For the words of songs supporting the Scottish National Party see Morris Blythman's article in *Chapbook* (Vol. 4:6), and Jack Brand's book *The National Movement in Scotland*. (See also Chapter VII.)

Towards the end of the 1960s the increasing popularity of instrumental music was already evident, and groups such as the Corries, and the Chieftains from Ireland, were using a wide variety of folk instruments: stringed, wind and percussion. Many young people began learning to play the pipes and traditional fiddle. Instrumental music had continued in the home and in pubs, perhaps more than in clubs or at festivals. Only within the last decade, for instance, had the enchanting whistle playing of such as Alex Green been heard at festivals; and in 1976 John Watt declared, 'There are some twelve box players in Milnathort, not one of whom has ever been in a folk club or is ever likely to be.'[58] The Fiddle and Accordion Clubs and the Reel and Strathspey Societies attracted a large membership – the latter's massed strings still produce an enormously popular sound.

By 1970 native traditional music was increasingly being heard at folk events throughout Scotland. Instrumental music, and the increasing number of groups which linked vocal and intrumental, will be the subject of a later section.

Footnotes

1. Orwell, 1968, p. 184.
2. Norman Buchan, 20 August 1977, Edinburgh.
3. Johnson, 1972, p. 6; Farmer, 1947, p. 345.
4. Elliot and Rimmer, 1973, p. 69.
5. Johnson, 1972, p. 5; pp. 7–9 provide a good summary of relevant points.

6. Robert Chambers, 'St. Cecilia's Hall', *Traditions of Edinburgh*, Edinburgh 1868. Quoted by Johnson, p. 5.
7. Tom Nairn, Brown, 1975, p. 25.
8. Kenneth Elliot, *The New Grove*, 1980, vol. 17, p. 70.
9. Craig, 1961, p. 273.
10. See Eric Anderson, 'The Kailyard Revisited', ed. Campbell 1979; also Campbell 1981.
11. Craig, 1961, p. 269.
12. Walt Whitman, 'Song of Myself', *Leaves of Grass,* 1855.
13. *The Scotsman*, 10 April 1964, letters column.
14. MacDiarmid, 1976, p. 33; reprinted from 1925.
15. Hamish Henderson, 10 December 1976, Edinburgh.
16. Francis Collinson, spring 1978, Edinburgh.
17. MacColl and Seeger, 1977 and 1986. *See* obituary on MacColl, *Folk Music Journal* vol. 6 no. 1, 1990.
18. See MacDougall, 1978, p. 90.
19. See Cowan ed., 1980, articles by Logue and Buchan.
20. Geordie McIntyre: *New Edinburgh Review*, August 1973, p. 12.
21. In Collins, 1977, the given tune, wrongly labelled, is in fact 'Maryland'.
22. Law and Berwick, 1973.
23. Donaldson, 1974, p. 22.
24. Buchan, 1962, p. 38.
25. The Stone of Destiny – officially at least – was in time returned to Westminster.
26. Without adverting to William and Mary, or to the later William.
27. This became part of the Festival Fringe.
28. Quoted by David Hamilton, *New Edinburgh Review*, August–September 1971, pp. 34–7.
29. Norman Buchan, 20 August 1977, Edinburgh. All subsequent Buchan quotes are from this interview.
30. Hamish Henderson, 6 February 1977, Edinburgh.
31. See n. 20.
32. See notes on music transcriptions, Chapter IV.
33. Morris Blythman, 11 February 1977, Edinburgh, with Josh MacRae. All subsequent Blythman quotes are from this interview.
34. Josh MacRae, 10 November 1976, Strathmiglo, Fife.
35. See the series of articles by Herschel Gower and James Porter in *Scottish Studies*: vol. 12, pp. 113–26 (1968); vol. 14, pp. 35–58 (1970); vol. 16, pp. 139–59, (1972); vol. 21, pp. 55–103 (1977). Jeannie Robertson died in 1975.
36. See Moffat, 1976, p. 20: the life-span of the People's Festival is given as two years, but in fact there were five, from 1951 to 1955. Moffat states that '…its aims to popularise the Edinburgh Festival have been realised in the seventies with the enormous local response to the Fringe from all sections of the community.'
37. See Newton, 1959, p. 244.
38. Ibid, pp. 245-6.
39. See Stearns, 1977, pp. 171–2, re the American 'spasm' band tradition.
40. Brand, 1962, p. 55.
41. Laing, 1975, p. 141.
42. Twelve years later, another concert for the same cause, in Glasgow's City Hall, celebrated Norman and Janey Buchan's Silver Wedding.
43. Moyna Flanagan, Enoch Kent, Josh MacRae and Rena Swankey.
44. Laing, 1975, p. 142.
45. See Vulliamy and Lee, 1980, pp. 5–6.
46. See Denisoff and Peterson, 1972, pp. 173–7.
47. See also MacColl, 1990, p. 288, on the 'policy' of singing songs only in a language

the singer spoke or understood.
48. See *Scottish Studies* vol. 2 (1958), pp. 213–14.
49. McVicar, 1990, p. 36.
50. *Ding Dong Dollar* disc, Folkways, FD 5444.
51. Ibid, accompanying booklet.
52. Josh MacRae, 11 February 1977, Edinburgh.
53. National Columbia Broadcasting.
54. American Forces Network.
55. Adam McNaughtan, 6 November 1976, Edinburgh.
56. Andrew (Andy) Hunter, 26 October 1976, Edinburgh.
57. Peter Hall, 9 November 1976, Aberdeen.
58. John Watt, 25 October 1976, Milnathort, Fife.

Jimmie Macgregor

Robin Hall

IV   The Story of the Revival
Songs heard in the seventies

Bright is the ring of words
When the right man rings them,
Fair the fall of songs
When the singer sings them.
Still they are carolled and said –
On wings they are carried –
After the singer is dead
And the maker buried.[1]

Robert Louis Stevenson

Dictionaries provide many different meanings of the word 'story'; the two which have seemed most apposite so far are 'facts or experiences which deserve narration', and 'past course of person's or institution's life'.[2] The latter definition covers the previous two chapters of this story.

The end of the 1960s showed an increasing number of discs – and also of television and radio performances, although these still tended to be more of the smooth, 'white heather' type than genuinely traditional in style. The steady consolidation of the trend towards Scottish material was most apparent in the festivals run by the TMSA, which have been described as the quintessence of the best in the Scottish folk scene, but it also showed in the other festivals, in the ceilidh-concerts and to a lesser degree in the folk clubs and pubs. The main 'facts and experiences' of our former definition consist now of the actual music heard; this chapter gives transcriptions of selected songs, with some commentary. Choosing songs mainly from festivals has three advantages: first, comparability – they were sung at similar gatherings which were open to all; second, familiarity on my part – as listener, recorder and adjudicator; third, availability for study – hundreds of recordings were made. Most of these songs are Scottish, either in origin or by use and adaptation, and this as we have seen was the most important emphasis in the 1970s. Disadvantages are two-fold: there are no protest songs *as such;* but a song need not be explicitly combatant to express a message of resistance as can be seen in a number of those shown here. There were some direct protest songs in the seventies but they were fewer than in the previous two decades (see Chapter III) and also, as we shall see, in the 1980s and nineties. Parallel with this, there are few *new* songs in traditional style, an important development in any revival worth its name. Both these groups will be referred to later.

Choice of Songs

In selecting the songs to be presented, I listened to over 50 tapes. These had been recorded in quantitative order, at the annual Blairgowrie/Kinross Festivals, 1970–78, at two big ceilidh concerts in Edinburgh (the *Stampede* ceilidh at the Heriot Watt University, and the Sir Walter Scott bicentenary ceilidh in

49

Edinburgh, both in 1971), at two of the annual Keith festivals which started in 1976, and at the Inverkeithing TMSA ceilidh (1970). A few were recorded in the singers' homes. These tapes contained 680 items, mostly songs but including some 74 instrumental items and ten of whistling and diddling. The final choice of the 39 below (including two versions of the same song), plus four in the Appendix, was made because certain songs were popular – four other regular festival attenders were consulted on this point – while others were interesting and significant for reasons which will emerge.

The Songs

These have been divided into groups according to themes, or verbal content. The subject matter is often wide enough for the song to be included in more than one of the categories chosen, so the final classification was made according to what seemed to be the main theme of the song. Some of these are in post-war and earlier collections, usually with skeletal tunes and with many differences in both words and tune.
The categories are:

1. Love; 2. Rejected love; 3. Comedy and music hall; 4. Feuds and war; 5. Sexual violence and seduction; 6. The pregnant woman in trouble; 7. Family pressure regarding marriage; 8. Political, social comment and work; 9. Sexual symbolism; 10. Night-visiting; 11. Elegiac; 12. Exile and emigration; 13. Wanderer's songs; 14. The supernatural; 15. Philosophical or survival.

Bothy songs or ballads are not included here as a separate category. Bothy was the name given to the outhouses in which the unmarried male labourers were quartered – particularly in the East, northwards from Kincardineshire – in farms before and after the turn of this century. Isolated as they were in country districts, these men had to rely on themselves for entertainment in the evenings after the long day's labour was over; hence the name for the songs with which they lightened these brief times of leisure, along with stories and general social intercourse. Many of these songs recount work and life on the farms, and in the feeing fairs where the men would agree to work for a spell of time with a farmer; examples of these songs are 'The Barnyards of Delgaty', 'The hairst o' Rettie', 'The hash o' Benegoak', 'Sleepy toon', 'The muckin' o' Geordie's byre', 'The weddin' o' MacGuiness and his cross-eyed pet', 'McGinty's meal and ale when the pig gaed on the spree' and 'He widna wint his gruel'. The last named is the only one transcribed on these pages (see Appendix). Interested readers should re-fer to the disc on *Bothy Ballads*, with its booklet on the songs (with their printed words) and on the background to this way of life.[3]

John Ord, however, in the preface to his collection *Bothy Songs and Ballads*, states roundly that 'Bothy song is just another name for folk song', and not a few of the songs given below, or versions of them, appear in his book.

The Songs: Assessment of Popularity

Popular

I'll lay ye doon   Sic a parcel o' rogues

The band o' shearers
Johnnie lad
Barbara Allen
I once loved a lad
Hannah, loving Hannah
The bonny hoose o' Airlie
The laird o' the Dainty doon-bye
The cruel mother
Bogie's bonny Belle
Corachree
The Magdalen Green
The dowie dens o' Yarrow

If it wasnae for the union
The Fairfield apprentice
The Berryfields o' Blair
The laird o' Udny's wa's
The college boy
Rare Willie drooned in Yarrow (two versions)
Jamie Raeburn
Tramps and hawkers
*Johnnie, my man
*He widna wint his gruel
*Willie Macintosh
*The banks o' red roses

*These four songs are in the Appendix

Moderately Popular

Huntingtower
Willie's lyke-wake
Eppie Morrie
Andrew Lammie
What can a young lassie dae wi'
    an auld man?

Sprig o' thyme
She was a rum one
The moving on song
Willie's fatal visit

Sung mainly by one person or family at this time

Betsy Bell; Here's a health to all true lovers – Belle Stewart
My bold chailin donn; When Micky comes home – Sheila MacGregor (now known as Sheila Stewart)
The belt wi' colours three – Alison McMorland
The Three Craws (with added verses); If ye only wait a wee – Adam Young

From the above 43, four are *new songs,* that is composed by contemporary authors: The berryfields o' Blair, by Belle Stewart; The moving on song, by Ewan MacColl; If it wasnae for the Union, by Matt McGinn; The Fairfield apprentice, by Archie Fisher and Bobby Campbell.

The categories are not hard and fast, for the popularity of most songs may wax or wane over a period of much less than ten years. The list gives an approximate assessment of popularity of the songs chosen and refers to a period of at least several years *during* the seventies.

'Revival' or 'Source' Singers
(Singers appearing in the Appendix are included)

It seemed worthwhile, in the present context, to attempt a classification along these lines. The late Jimmy MacBeath was clearly a source singer (he is included in the Appendix because his version of 'He widna wint his gruel', recorded in 1960, was the model for the other three given). Yet the distinction is becoming less meaningful with each decade. Out of the total, twelve are source singers: of these, seven are of traveller stock. Stanley Robertson's son Anthony, then aged eighteen, learned most of his songs from his father and grandfather, and from his great-aunt Jeannie Robertson; the travellers still have a close-knit family circle and pass on their lore orally. But after some 40 years of the revival, one can now see the time approaching when all singers in this genre will just be singers, of folk or traditional songs in the widest sense. The singers' own definitions, in replies to questions, were fairly clear-cut.

Singers were 'revival' if they had learned most of their songs from recorded or printed sources, from other revival singers or from source singers (several stressed the latter) and 'source' if the songs had been handed down in the oral tradition, or learned in childhood. But the categories are not clear-cut. Not a few revival singers have source elements in their backgrounds, while many source singers make use of the written word – both in giving copies to other singers, and in obtaining copies of words to add to their own repertoires. Maddy Taylor's answer was the most thought-provoking: *'I don't think about it at all.* These categories divide us, don't you think? Can't we just be "singers" and enjoy the music?'

Contradictions abound. One of the most curious concerns literacy; with very few exceptions all singers now consult books and use pen and paper, and I have not come across a single verbally illiterate singer in Scotland, at least amongst those involved in the revival scene. Yet although verbal literacy is now accepted, musical literacy is still comparatively rare and is often eschewed by choice in favour of repeated listening.

The singers were also asked why they liked the song in question, what they felt was its theme or 'message' (deep waters, here) and any connection between its words and their own experiences in life. The importance of the singers' own views, especially as regards the meaning of any song they choose to sing, cannot be too strongly emphasised: not enough attention and humble enquiry has been directed towards this. Few of the singers found any connection with their own experience and most gave thoughtful answers to the other two questions. Many comments by singers will be found in the notes on the songs.

Notes on the Music Transcriptions

These transcriptions are descriptive, not prescriptive,[4] and are, with a single exception in this chapter, of one verse of one singer's performance on one occasion. It must be emphasised not only that another singer's version of the song would be likely to differ in various respects, but also that the same singer might possibly sing the same song differently on another occasion. It was decided, with very few exceptions, not to include variants of the tune in other verses of the same song, although occasionally small notes, in alignment where possible with the larger notes, and distinguishable from ornament notes, show the shape of the tune in other verses. Instead, a transcription of one song, 'The belt wi' colours three', has been given in full for all six verses. Few singers vary the tune for different verses quite so freely and with such fluidity as Alison McMorland does here, but this example shows how the tune is adapted to fit different words and moods, and how such variants can and often do work out. No time signature is given for this song.

There are broadly three kinds of transcriptions of tunes. First, the skeletal type, exemplified by the majority of Bronson's *Traditional Tunes of the Child Ballads*, vols. 1–3,[5] and by most collections of folk songs. These are the bare bones which the traditional singer knows how to cover with the flesh and blood of his or her own singing style. Second, at the other extreme, are exact transcriptions which show every nuance of grace-notes, plosives, sung consonants, detailed time values, and so on. These are inordinately time-consuming to make and are also very hard to read, even for an experienced musician, so they are of value only for purposes of comparison. Examples of this kind can be found in *Scottish Studies* and in the *Journal of the Folk Song Society*.[6] Third, there is the compromise type, which we have below: most of the ornaments are given, and the main changes in time structures.

These transcriptions represent an attempt, aided by some verbal description, to give an idea of the singer's style: very necessary, especially for those readers who are unfamiliar with traditional singing.

There is no single 'correct' version of a song – as was said of the legendary Mrs Harris, 'there's no sich a person.' But there may be a single model. There are to begin with versions which are more traditional, usually because they are older and have stood the test of time, have satisfied countless people through the ages, while other versions have been thrown on the scrap heap of experience. Then there are versions which one likes better, for personal reasons; one would choose such versions to sing oneself. Value judgments are a sine qua non of all art.

Any fears that what is given here may be copied exactly by singers and so 'mummified' are groundless: tradition is far too robust a creature to be threatened by this. Realistic transcriptions in print may even reach, and awaken interest in, some people hitherto unexposed to this music, and so provide an impetus for them to listen to the thing. This is what should and must be urged, for transcriptions are at best *faute de mieux*, bound by the limitations of a book. The interested reader should try to hear the songs, either on disc or tape or – much better – should hear them live, at ceilidhs, festivals, folk concerts, clubs or pubs.

Some imitation, whether from the printed page or from recorded or live singing, is inevitable, and there is nothing wrong with this in its place. Not only is emulation the sincerest form of flattery, but all creative artists and performers learn something by copying others until they eventually find their own style. This obtains also in art music. In the seventeenth and eighteenth centuries it was the convention for singers and instrumentalists to insert their own ornaments, since they were already familiar with these in the Baroque and Classical period styles, and this practice has been revived within the last few decades. But the drawback to so many past collections of folk music is that people who studied them did not know the style or styles in which they should be performed, *because they had never actually heard this music* performed traditionally.

The sharps or flats in key signatures are given only for those notes which occur in the melody concerned.

Transcriptions made from recordings by male singers appear an octave higher than the actual sound would be.

Uncertain intonation sometimes appears and this is indicated by a downward or upward arrow above the note, which means that the sound is slightly flatter or sharper than the note given, but is nearer to it than to the note a semitone below or above. A line drawn slantingly before or after a note indicates a slide. Other signs are confined to those in common musical usage: the stress mark, a short horizontal line above or below a note, implying slight lingering, and the stronger accent mark >, are shown. The marks ≪ and ≫ , denoting variation in dynamics, are not given: they are usually omitted except in the very detailed type of transcription. This does not mean that there is no variation in volume, for some singers make considerable use of this, others less. But such variation is subtly different from that of the art singer, and is generally smaller and less frequent. The pitch of each performance is also omitted – it seems hardly important enough – the key chosen is for simplicity in reading, and in order to avoid leger lines where possible. The old convention, of separating the stalks of quavers and semi-quavers which go with different syllables, has not been adhered to. It is easier to follow the shape and rhythm of the tune when these are left joined, and slur marks show the notes which are 'set' to a single syllable. The sign (ə) denotes an extra syllable which is produced in the singing of certain words, for example, chai-r (ə) m-box instead of chairm-box.

Scottish Idioms in Song

The 'Scots snap' is the most characteristic *rhythmic* idiom: an accented short note followed by a longer, ♪♩. or ♪♩.. This tends to fit the speech-rhythm of the word in question. In *melody*, the double tonic occurs frequently; this is a temporary shifting to the (implied or explicit) key or triad a tone below the tonic. Examples of these will appear in the songs which follow.

Grace-notes: a tendency to more and yet more lavish ornamentation has been a feature of revival singing throughout Britain, with some Irish influence.

As to the *modes*: this subject has been much debated in recent years and there is now too much shifting ground to step with any surety. But references are given for readers who may wish to follow this up.[7]

In the song headings, the name preceding the song title is that of the singer; underneath is the place, the year, the recorder's initials and the tape number. The recordings were made by Kim Chambers, Peter Cooke, Hamish Henderson, Fred Kent, Ailie Munro, Allan Palmer, James Porter, Stephanie Smith and Linda Williamson. SA tapes are from the archives of the School of Scottish Studies; AM tapes are those recorded by Allan Palmer and later gifted to the School.

(Comments by the singers in this chapter and in the Appendix were made in 1981/82, so the author's comments have also been left as at that time; any changes are in the main abbreviatory.)

Group 1: Love

Jimmy Hutchison: *I'll lay ye doon*
Kinross 1972; rec. A.M. SA 1972/183.

(v.3) Though I've nae gowd nor gear tae of-fer,Nae sil-ver rings fer yer

bon-ny hands, Oh my hairt is true and my airms are strang, love,

And for you I'll work like an ho-nest man.

1. As I roved out one summer's evenin'
    Doon by the banks o' the pleasant Don,
    And as I gaed walkin' I could hear them talkin'
    Saying 'Bollel he is a sorried man.'

    (*Chorus*)
    Oh I'll lay ye doon, love, I'll treat you dacent
    Oh I'll lay ye doon, love, I'll fill yir can,
    Oh I'll lay ye doon, love, I'll treat ye dacent
    For Bollel he is a sorried man.

2. I'm bound away, my love tae leave ye
    For tae cross the hills and the bonny sands,
    But when I return then we'll get mairried
    And tae you I'll prove an honest man.

3. Though I've nae gowd nor gear tae offer,
    Nae silver rings fer yir bonny hands,
    Oh my hairt is true and my airms are strang, love,
    And for you I'll work like an honest man.

In 1972 Jimmy Hutchison said in his introduction, '…this song's in danger of becoming the most over-sung song in the festival…' It is still immensely popular, but Hutchison's singing of it is always something special. Born in South Uist, he lived there until the age of eleven, so that Gaelic was one of his two mother tongues and he heard Gaelic song from his earliest infancy. Although he has not lived in Gaelic-speaking areas since then, and does not sing Gaelic songs, it needs no stretch of aural imagination to perceive that something of this style of singing has percolated into his own, and remains there still. It is lighter than the Scots style: less earthbound, almost floating, with very delicate, fleeting ornamentation, and with an added 'something' which one might describe as a kind of tenderness. This is only one element of his style, for he is probably more Scots than Gaelic now.

The provenance of this song is uncertain, despite enquiries at Edinburgh and Dublin libraries. From Jeannie Robertson, to Enoch Kent, to Jimmy Hutchison, to Hamish Henderson – Bollel was Bolerrol and further back Bold Errol. Henderson's suspicions that the parent song was 'Muldoon the solid man', of nineteenth-century Irish music hall, was confirmed in 1954; two travellers, when asked specifically for Muldoon, sang part of our version with the same tune but ending 'And I'll go drunk like a solid man'. The letters *l* and *r* are very hard to distinguish: until Hutchison wrote the words I always thought he sang 'solid'. There is no such word as 'sorried', but oral transmission cares nothing for such unimportant details, and 'sorried' has a certain plaintive resonance. (I shall never forget the hallful of people quietly joining in the chorus, singing so softly, so meditatively, thinking their own thoughts.)

Jimmy Hutchison has been recorded by BBC records.

Norman Stewart: *Band o' shearers*
Kinross 1973; rec. A.M. SA 1973/113.

(*Chorus*)
Bonnie lassie, will ye gang
And shear wi' me the hale day lang?
Love will cheer us as we gang
To join yon band o' shearers.

1.   Until the weather it be hot
      I'll cast ma waistcoat an' my coat;
      I'll shear wi' you amang the lot
      When we join yon band o' shearers.

2.   Until the thistle it be strang,
      Until it chaps your milk-white hand,
      It's wi' ma heuch I'll cut it off
      When we join yon band o' shearers.

3.   Aye and if the weather it be fine
      They'll say there's love twixt you and I,
      But we'll shyly pass yin anither by
      When we join yon band o' shearers.

4.   And when the shearin' it's a' duin
     We'll hae some rantin' roarin' fun,
     We'll hae the rantin' roarin' fun
     An' forget the toils o' the shearin'.

Norman Stewart is of Lewis descent, on his father's side, and he can speak Gaelic although not fluently. Part of his childhood was spent in Tain and he was strongly influenced by Gaelic ornamental psalm singing in the Free Church there; one of the precentors was from Skye. The Gaelic style of singing is again unmistakable.

A version of these words, with no tune, is in Ord's *Bothy Ballads*; the intro-duction describes it as a harvest song which 'is one of the oldest and best of its kind' and 'was known in every county of Scotland'. It was heard frequently dur-ing the 1970s.

Tricia Johnstone: *Huntingtower* **(Appendix to Child 232, as** *The Duke of Atholl*)
Kinross 1975; rec. A.P. AM2.

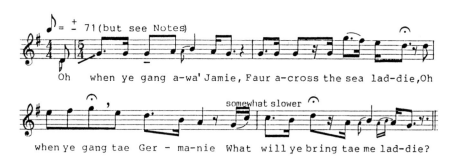

1.   Oh when ye gang awa Jamie,
     Faur across the sea laddie,
     Oh when ye gang tae Germanie
     What will ye bring tae me laddie?

2.   I'll bring ye a braw new goon Jeannie,
     I'll bring ye a braw new goon lassie,
     And it shall be o' silk an gowd
     Wi' Valencienne(s) lace a' roon' lassie.

3.   Oh that's nae gift ava Jamie,
     That wadnae dae at a' laddie,
     There's no a goon in a' the toon
     I'd wear when you're awa' laddie.

4.   When I come back again Jeannie,
     When I come back again lassie,
     I'll bring wi' me a gallant gay
     Tae be yir ain guidman lassie.

5.   Be ma guidman yersel Jamie,
     Be ma guidman yersel laddie,
     And tak' me wi' you tae Germanie
     Wi' you at hame tae dwell laddie.

6.   That wadnae dae at a' Jeannie,
     That wadna dae at a' lassie,
     For I've a wife and bairnies three
     An' I'm no sure ye'd 'gree lassie.

7.   Ye should 'a tellt me that in time Jamie,
     (Ye) should 'a tellt me that lang syne laddie,
     For had I kent o' your fause hairt
     Ye'd ne'er have gotten mine Jamie.

8.   Yir e'en were like a spell lassie,
     Yir e'en were like a spell lassie,
     That ilka day bewitched me sae
     I couldna help masel' lassie.

9.   Gae back tae yir wife an' hame Jamie,
     Gae back tae yir bairnies three laddie,
     And I will pray that nane may thole
     A broken hairt like me laddie.

10. Oh dry yir tearful e'e Jeannie,
     Ma story's a' a lee lassie,
     For I have neither wife nor weans
     An' I'll wed nane but thee lassie.

11. Think well for fear ye rue Jamie,
     Think well for fear ye rue laddie,
     For I have neither gowd nor land
     Tae be a match for you laddie.

12. Oh Blair an' Atholl's mine Jeannie,
     Little Dunkeld is mine lassie,
     Saint Johnston's Tower and Huntingtower
     And a' that's mine is thine lassie.

This is a powerful, gripping performance. Tricia Johnstone, from Glasgow, has a strong voice with very little vibrato. In eight out of the twelve verses here the second line repeats the words of the first line, and the singer soars up the octave leap with a dramatic deliberation which impressively heightens this emphasis.

Johnstone learned this song in childhood, from her father's singing: 'I was brought up in a background of Irish and Scots songs... I'm most interested in [these] songs as I feel they are "my" history and portray the feelings and events which relate to my background. I am grateful to the "revivalists". As I don't read music, hearing the singing, live, on tape or record brought many "poems" to life for me... I like "answer" songs. I can't be analytical about the songs as I find I respond to music and particularly songs emotionally... A theme which occurs again and again in folk song, where the girl is in love, the man tests her love then

reveals he is rich enough for both of them!' (No comment.)
In succeeding verses, the first half of bars 1–3 is often sung at twice the given speed. The song is in declamatory style and in very free time with some pauses during or more often at the end of the line. One feels this was originally four-beat, and the pauses at the end of each verse line fit the uncertain, tentative nature of much of the dialogue. The Scots snap is heard at 'laddie' and 'lassie'.

Vic Smith: *Johnnie lad*
Kinross 1973; rec. A.M. SA 1973/112

(V.2) When the sheep are in the fold and the cows are in the

byre   And a' the lads an'las-sies sit-tin'round a roa-rin' fire,

There is me a like-ly las-sie, just as like that I was
Jin-kin'you ma John-nie lad-die, jin-kin' you ma John-nie

mad,   Through the nooks an' bar - ley stooks jin - kin'
lad,   Through the nooks an' bar - ley stooks jin - kin'

you,   John - nie lad.
you,   John - nie   lad.

1.   Oh there is a handsome laddie, he lives down on yonder lea
      And he's lookin' and he jukin' and he's aye watchin' me;
      Oh he's teasin' me an squeezin' me but his meanin's not sae bad,
      If it's ever going to be tell me now Johnnie lad.

            Tell me now me Johnnie laddie, tell me now me Johnnie lad,
            If it's ever going to be tell me now Johnnie lad.

2.   When the sheep are in the fold and the cows are in the byre
      And a' the lads an' lassies sittin' round a roarin' fire,
      There is me a likely lassie, just as like that I was mad,
      Through the nooks an' barley stooks jinkin' you, Johnnie lad.

            Jinkin' you ma Johnnie laddie, jinkin' you ma Johnnie lad,
            Through the nooks an' barley stooks jinkin' you, Johnnie lad.

3.   Oh Johnnie is blythe an' bonny, he's the pride o' a' yon lea,
      And I love him best of ony though he's always teasin' me,
      Oh he's teasin' me an' squeezin' me an ticklin' me like mad,
      None comes near me that can cheer me like my own Johnnie lad.

            Oh it's you ma Johnnie laddie, oh it's you ma Johnnie lad,
            None comes near me that can cheer me like my own Johnnie lad.

4.   Oh Johnnie is not a gentleman nor yet is he a lord
      But I would follow Johnnie lad although he were a card,
      Oh Johnnie he is a bonny lad, he was once a lad o' mine
      And I've never had a better lad though I've had twenty-nine.

            Oh it's you ma Johnnie laddie and wi' you ma Johnnie lad,
            I wad dance the buckles off ma shoes wi' you (ma) Johnnie lad.
            Oh it's you ma Johnnie laddie and wi' you ma Johnnie lad,
            I wad dance the buckles off ma shoes wi' you (ma) Johnnie lad.

This charming song, with its jig-like tune, is sung in a suitably lively, dance-like manner. Vic Smith comes from Edinburgh but has lived mostly in Sussex. He learned this from a student who in turn had discovered it in Aberdeen, in the library of Marischal College at the University.

A similar version appears in MacColl's *Personal Choice,* but the mid-cadence above, in effect on the double tonic (its dominant note) adds more drama and interest. A similar version to Smith's words, with no tune, may be found in Ford.

Smith's first interest in folk song was stirred by his grandmother, from Aberdeenshire, who 'sang a few songs and diddled'; but he has been totally involved in the Revival for many years. 'I knew as soon as I heard a couple of lines sung that I wanted to learn this song,' he says. 'The words seem to complement the tune perfectly. I love saying to people that I'm going to sing "Johnnie lad" and seeing their faces fall as they expect the totally banal, popular version, and then seeing their interest rise as they realise they've in fact got an interesting song to listen to! The theme is "uncertainty in love", which is surely universal.'

Vic Smith has been recorded by Eron.

Sheila MacGregor: *My bold chailin donn*
Kinross 1972; rec. P.C. SA 1972/188

(V. 2) Oh ma - ny's the pro-mise he gives me When he comes e- ve - ry

Sun - day to me,   And what can I do but be-lieve him When he

whis-pers,"A chuis-le mo-chridh"? For his heart is so truth-ful and

ten-der And his bright rol-ling eyes of dark brown, And I am

sure e-ven a la-dy of splen-dour Would be charmed by my bold chai-lin

donn.

1. Oh my true love he dwells in the mountain
    Like a war eagle fearless and free,
    By the banks of a low-tuning fountain
    That wanders through Wydan Lee;
    For his heart and his soul have more honour
    Than a king with his palace an' crown.
    Like the blood of the race of O'Connor
    Fills the veins of my bold chailin donn.

2. Oh many's the promise he gives me
    When he comes every Sunday to me,
    And what can I do but believe him
    When he whispers, 'A chuisle mo chridh'?
    For his heart is so truthful and tender
    And his bright rolling eyes of dark brown,
    And I am sure even a lady of splendour
    Would be charmed by my bold chailin donn.

3. My father has riches in plenty
    And suitors for me in his eye,
    But oh come the time when I'm twenty
    If I don't wish them all the good-bye!
    For I sigh for a night in the mountains
    Far away from the dust of the town,
    By the banks of the low-tuning fountains
    To the arms of my bold chailin donn.

Along with other members of the great singing family – the traveller Stewarts of Blairgowrie – Sheila MacGregor (daughter of Belle Stewart) has a superlatively flowing style with no breaks between the different gradations of her vocal range, with some sliding, fine phrasing and clear enunciation – a kind of traditional bel canto art. She has been actively involved in traditional singing since

1954. The Stewarts got this Irish song from a friend who lives near them, Flora Beaton, a native Gaelic speaker from Lewis. Yet the Gaelic words it contains are of Irish and not Scottish Gaelic origin. 'Bold chailin donn' (pronounced 'chollion down') was probably originally the Irish 'buachaillin donn', which means brownhaired laddie and thus fits the context, whereas 'chailin donn', means brownhaired maiden. 'A chuisle mochridh' (pronounced 'a chooshla mochree') means vein of my heart, a common poetic image for 'beloved'. Sheila MacGregor has been recorded by Tangent and by Topic.

See Appendix for 'Johnnie my man', another song in this group.

Group 2: Rejected Love

Jean Redpath: *Barbara Allen* (Child 84)
Scott Ceilidh, Edinburgh 1971; rec. F.K. SA 1971/192.

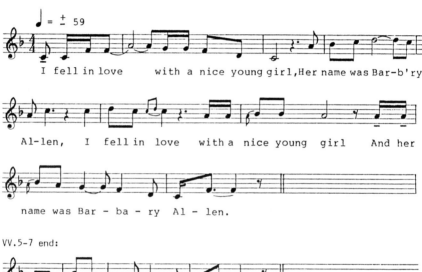

1.   I fell in love with a nice young girl,
      Her name was Barbary Allen;
      I fell in love with a nice young girl
      And her name was Barbary Allen.

2.   Till I fell sick and very ill,
      I sent for Barbary Allen;
      Till I fell sick and very ill,
      An' I sent for Barbary Allen.

3.   She pu'ed the curtains roon' my bed
      And said, 'Young man ye're dyin';'
      She pu'ed the curtains roon' my bed
      And said, 'Young man you are dyin'.'

4. 'A kiss o' you wad dae me guid,
    A kiss o' you wad cure me.'
    'But a kiss o' me ye ne'er shall hae
    Though your poor hairt were a-breakin'.'

5. 'It's look ye up at by bed-heid
    And see what you'll find hangin':
    A silver watch an' a guinea-gold chain
    That hangs there for Barbary Allen,
    That hangs there for Barbary Allen.'

6. She hidnae gaen a mile or twa
    When she heard the death bells ringin',
    And every word they seemed to say,
    'Cruel-hairted Barbary Allen,
    Cruel-hairted Barbary Allen.'

7. 'O mither dear do mak' my bed
    And mak' it saft an' narrow,
    For my true love has died for me
    And I'll die for him tomorrow,
    And I'll die for him tomorrow.'

Although Child gives only three versions of the words of this very well-known ballad, Bronson gives no less than 200 tunes (although not this one) as well as numerous sets of words.

Jean Redpath got this version from a tape of Jane Turriff's singing, recorded by Arthur Argo; Turriff herself learned it in childhood, from her mother and grandmother. It has a second 'legacy' verse which comes after verse 5 and is usually included by both Redpath and Turriff:

> It's look ye down at my bed-side
> And see what you'll find sittin':
> A basin full of my heart's tears
> That sits there for Barbary Allen.

Redpath had a kind of gut reaction to this song: 'It's possibly a step down from the real heavyweight ballads, the epic-tragic, stark spine-chillers. For every kind of hurt, and not only a hurt in your love-life, can be channelled into songs like this...'

It is interesting to note the increasing power and artistry of this brilliant singer over the years – in her 1977 televised series *Ballad Folk* (in which she introduced other singers), in her discs, in her frequent live performances in Britain and the US, and in her recent work at Summer Schools as tutor and demonstrator in traditional song. Her true, clear voice, which has had no 'training' apart from a few lessons on breathing, is a kind which is acceptable to music-lovers of all kinds, and her style, which adapts to a wide and varied repertoire, is always unmistakably traditional.

Among the many discs of Redpath's singing, an important American series should be mentioned: *The Songs of Robert Burns*. The original tunes are researched and arranged with instrumental and vocal accompaniment, by Serge Hovey (Philo 1037, 1048, 1071, 1072; further discs planned).

Caroline Carberry: *I once loved a lad*
Blairgowrie 1970; rec. P.C. SA 1970/181

(V.2)   I saw my love tae the kirk go, Wi' bride an' bride mai-den they
made a fine show; And   I fol-lowed on wi' a hairt full o' woe, But
noo he is wad tae a - no- ther.

1.   I once loved a lad, and I loved him sae weel
     I hated all others that spoke o' him ill,
     But noo he's rewarded me weel for my time
     For he's gaun tae be wad tae another.

2.   I saw my love tae the kirk go,
     Wi' bride an' bride-maiden they made a fine show;
     And I followed on wi' a hairt full o' woe,
     But noo he is wad tae another.

3.   I saw my love as he set doon tae dine,
     I stood at his elbow an' I poured oot the wine;
     An' I drank tae the laddie that should ha' been mine,
     For he's gaun tae be wad tae another.

4.   The men o' yon forest, they askit o' me,
     'How many strawberries grow in the saut sea?'
     I answered him back wi' a tear in my e'e,
     'How many ships sail in the forest?'

5.   Oh dig me a grave, an' dig it sae deep,
     An' cover it ower wi' flooers sae sweet
     That I may gaun in for tae tak' a lang sleep,
     An' maybe in time I'll forget him.

6.   They dug me a grave, an' they dug it sae deep,
     An' covered it ower wi' flooers sae sweet;
     An' I'll lay doon for tae tak' a lang sleep
     An' I'm sure that in time I'll forget him.

This is sung in true elegiac vein, and in a strong voice used at times with a fittingly harsh edge to it. Caroline Carberry achieves no easy feat in employing a fluidity of time in her singing without losing the time structure, especially at the slow tempo she has chosen. This song, now less often heard, can express a woman's or a man's feelings – 'lad' becomes 'lass', 'he' is changed to 'she', (compare with the version in Seeger and MacColl's influential collection *The Singing Island*, p. 31).

The flat seventh in bars four and seven of the tune, followed by descending notes, seems to have a darkening effect. (See also comment on blue notes, Chapter II.)

Riddles are an important element in popular story and song: correct answers are rewarded with a prize, but unsuccessful guesses with a penalty. The questions in verse four above bear some kinship to riddles, but no answers are offered – it is too late for the prize, and the penalty has already been exacted.

Allan Morris: *Willie's lyke-wake (Amang the blue flooers and the yellow)*
(Child 25)
Kinross 1973: rec. A.M. SA 1973/111

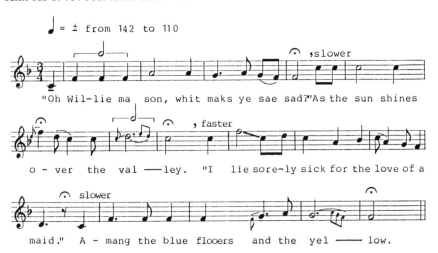

1.   'Oh Willie ma son, whit maks ye sae sad?'
     As the sun shines over the valley.
     'I lie sorely sick for the love of a maid.'
     Amang the blue flooers and the yellow.

(The internal refrain is added in the same way to each verse)

2.   'Oh is she an heiress or lady fine,
     That she winna tak' nae pity on thee?'

3.   'Though a' yir kin were aboot yon bower,
     Ye shall no be a maiden one single hour.

4.   For a maid ye cam' here wi'oot a convoy,
      But ye shall return wi' a horse and a boy.

5.   Ye cam' here a maiden sae meek and sae mild,
      But ye shall gae hame a wedded wife wi' a child.'

Allan Morris introduced this song in a not-too-serious vein: '...the story is roughly that a fellow's so much in love that he's lyin' on his death-bed...*gaspin'*...and his mother, who's got great pity for him, naturally, goes out and...*seizes* the young lady...brings her back...and nine months later she's able to go back home...wi' a baby.' This explanation was necessary, since his version of the words is incomplete; it is Bronson's number two, with substantially the same tune converted here into triple time. Morris has since adopted one of the fuller versions, which tells the story of a trick to induce the girl to come alone to Willie's house: spurred on by their mother, his brothers bribe the bellman to play his 'dead lyke-wake'. Stricken with pity the girl, thinking he is dead, goes alone to his house; she is conducted to the 'corpse' who proves he is very much alive when they're left together and who by varying methods persuades her to marry him.

'I regard the song as a lesson in singlemindedness,' says Morris, 'i.e. you can always get what you want if you try hard enough, albeit using devious and dubious methods.'

Alison McMorland

Josh MacRae   Tom Anderson   Lizzie Higgins

Aly Bain   Jane Turriff   Willie Scott

Angus Grant   Annie Bell   Matt McGinn

Belle Stewart & Sheila Stewart (MacGregor)

Alison McMorland: *The belt wi' colours three*
Kinross 1975; rec. A.P. AM26.

(V.1) The fir-sten thing ma lad-die gied tae me, It was a cap weel lined wi' lead, And the

(V.2) The nex-ten thing oh ma lad-die gied tae me, It was a man-tle wi' sor-row lined. I will

(V.3) The thir-den thing oh ma lad-die gied tae me, It was a belt wi' co-lours three. The first was

(V.4) Now I maun climb as high a tree yet, And her-ry a far far rich-er nest; And come

(V.5) But why should ye now climb a tree, may? Or pu' the cher-ries ere they be ripe? For if the

(V.6) Then up she rose and gaed on slow-ly, And state-ly step-pèd owre yon lea; And by the

Davie Stewart of Dundee: his tune of *The Dowie Dens of Yarrow*

lan-ger that I wore it The hea-vi-er grew on ma head, ma head, The hea-vi-er grew on ma head.

wear that black man-tle Till one to bor-row I find, I find, Till one to bor-row I find.

shame, the next sor-row And last of all sad mi-se-ry_____, And last of all sad mi-se-ry.

down with-out fal-ling, And mair-ry the lad that I lo'e best, And mar-ry the lad that I lo'e best.

goird-ner yince does see you He'll throw you owre yon gar-den dyke, He'll throw you owre yon gar-den dyke.

sa-men, it is weel ken-nin', That mour-ners crave nae com-pa-ny, That mour-ners crave nae com-pa-ny.

1. The firsten thing ma laddie gied tae me,
    It was a cap weel lined wi' lead,
    And the langer that I wore it
    The heavier grew on ma head, ma head,
    The heavier grew on ma head.

2. The nexten thing oh ma laddie gied tae me,
    It was a mantle wi' sorrow lined.
    I will wear that black mantle
    Till one to borrow I find, I find,
    Till one to borrow I find.

3. The thirden thing oh ma laddie gied tae me,
    It was a belt wi' colours three.
    The first was shame, the next sorrow
    And last of all sad misery,
    And last of all sad misery.

4.   Now I maun climb as high a tree yet,
      And herry a far far richer nest;
      And come down without falling,
      And mairry the lad that I lo'e best,
      And marry the lad that I lo'e best.

5.   But why should ye now climb a tree, may?
      Or pu' the cherries ere they be ripe?
      For if the gairdner yince does see you
      He'll throw you owre yon garden dyke,
      He'll throw you owre yon garden dyke.

6.   Then up she rose and gaed on slowly,
      And stately steppèd owre yon lea;
      And by the samen, it is weel kennin',
      That mourners crave nae company,
      That mourners crave nae company.

Alison McMorland introduced this beautiful song to the folk world, and so far seems to be the only person who sings it; it is the title of one of her discs.[8] She adapted it from Christie's version in *Traditional Ballad Airs from the North of Scotland* and has followed his tune in the main. She said she was strongly influenced throughout her shaping of the song by 'the sweeping feel' of old Davie Stewart's famous rendering of 'The Dowie Dens of Yarrow', in which he accompanies himself on melodeon; his tune for this, which closely resembles MacMorland's here, is given underneath. Stewart's performance of 'The Dowie Dens' is truly uninhibited, with an element of wild abandonment. MacMorland says it's the one performance of a Scots song 'which I can't hear without tears streaming down my face.' Her style has also been influenced by Lucy Stewart of Fetterangus, whose direct, minimal style of singing greatly inspired her.

MacMorland's performance has the sweeping feel of Stewart's plus her own very rich, spontaneous variation of the tune, but she eschews his wild abandonment (after all, 'The Dowie Dens' is about the death of a best-beloved). She sings with a passionate restraint which matches the poetry and the dignity of the words.

Irene Riggs: *Hannah, loving Hannah*
Kinross 1977; rec. A.P. AM10.

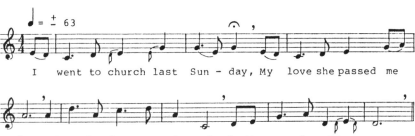

I went to church last Sun - day, My love she passed me by. I knew her heart was chan-ging By the ro-ving of her eye.

1.   I went to church last Sunday,
      My love she passed me by,
      I knew her heart was changing
      By the roving of her eye.

          By the roving of her eye,
          By the roving of her eye,
          I knew her heart was changing
          By the roving of her eye.

2.   Oh Hannah, loving Hannah,
      Come give to me your hand.
      You said that if you married
      That I would be the man.

          That I would be the man,
          That I would be the man,
          You said that if you married
          That I would be the man.

3.   My love she's pale and handsome,
      Her hands they're neat and small,
      And she is quite good-looking
      And that's the best of all.

          And that's the best of all,
          And that's the best of all,
          And she is quite good-looking
          And that's the best of all.

4.   I'll go down to the water
      When everyone's asleep,
      And I'll think on my loving Hannah
      And then sit down and weep.

          And then sit down and and weep,
          And then sit down and weep,
          I'll think on my loving Hannah
          And then sit down and weep.

5.   (As verse one)

Irene Riggs comes from Kirkcaldy, and works in Fife. She picked up this song about eight years ago, 'somewhere'; the source is forgotten, as so often in oral tradition. It is very popular in both clubs and festivals, in fact a man who frequents these described it as 'one of the anthems of folk'.

Sung here with simple artistry and in a strong, clear voice, the tune is of form AA'BC – a form rich in dramatic possibilities. Although a man's song it is sung here with total conviction by a woman – the reverse occurs in 'Johnnie lad' above.

The same tune is used for the second half of each verse, which is a kind of re-frain.

Riggs says: 'This is about a love affair gone wrong. Simply that. A rather sad

man bemoaning his lost love... I wonder if he really does something more serious than just "go down to the river and weep"!'

Group 3: Comedy and Music Hall

Sheila MacGregor: *When Micky comes home I get battered*
Scott Ceilidh, Edinburgh 1971; rec. F.K. SA 1971/191.

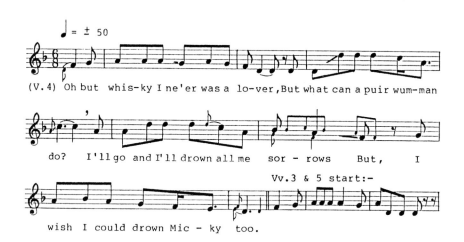

(V.4) Oh but whis-ky I ne'er was a lo-ver, But what can a puir wum-man

do?   I'll go and I'll drown all me   sor - rows   But,   I

Vv.3 & 5 start:-

wish I could drown Mic - ky   too.

1.   Oh friends I have a sad story,
     A very sad story tae tell:
     I married a man for his money
     But he's worse than the devil himsel'.

2.   For when Micky comes home I get battered,
     He batters me all black and blue,
     And if I say a word I get scattered
     From the kitchen right ben to the room.

3.   So I'll go an I'll get blue bleezin' blind drunk,
     Just to give Micky a warnin',
     And just for spite I will stay out all night
     And come rollin' home drunk in the mornin'.

4.   Oh but whisky I ne'er was a lover,
     But what can a puir wumman do?
     I'll go and I'll drown all me sorrows
     But, I wish I could drown Micky too.

5.   So I'll go an I'll get blue bleezin' blind drunk,
     Just to give Micky a warnin',
     And just for spite I will stay out all night
     And come rollin' home drunk in the mornin'.

Sheila MacGregor learned this song from her mother, Belle Stewart, who some 30 years ago heard an old ploughman sing it while tattie-lifting near Blairgowrie. His version started with verse two above, so Belle made up the first verse herself and inserted it, partly as an opening to the song and partly to provide a reason, a provocation, for the man battering his wife, namely she had married him for his money.

But in the repertoire of Alistair MacDonald, the television folk star, the song is simply about a battered wife, and it starts with the old ploughman's opening verse (verse two above). Even today the age-old practice of wife beating persists, and 'The recent laws helping battered women…do not apply here, [Scotland] limited though they are for England and Wales.'[9] I once heard a policeman say, when confronted with an injured wife (a total stranger, she had flung herself into my car to escape from her husband): 'Of course we don't know what she did to annoy him.' If comparable injuries had been inflicted in a fight between two men, the verdict would have been 'grievous bodily harm' with no excuse of provocation. But sometimes the only way people can react to ugly facts is to joke about them, and 'When Micky comes home' is obviously in this genre. Sheila MacGregor gives it the full comic treatment and it is always received with gales of laughter.

Jean Redpath comments that this is the only Scots song she knows of in which a woman is shown to be drinking: '…and this fact certainly doesn't reflect the truth!'

Belle Stewart (joined by Sheila MacGregor in chorus): *Oh ma name is Betsy Bell*
Scott Ceilidh, Edinburgh 1971; rec. F.K. SA 1971/195.

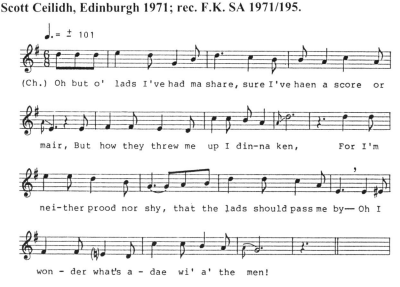

1. Oh ma name is Betsy Bell, in the Overgate I dwell,
    Nae doot ye'll wonder what I'm daein' here,
    But if ye wait a wee, sure ma tale I'll tell tae thee,
    It's a tale nae doot ye'll think is very queer.

2.   Oh for I'm lookin' for a lad an' he may be guid or bad,
      I'm gaun tae tak' the first yin that I see;
      He may be young or auld, or greyheided, freends, or bald,
      It's onything that wears the breeks for me.

      (Chorus)
      Oh but o' lads I've had ma share, sure I've haen a score or mair
      But how they threw me up I dinna ken,
      For I'm neither prood nor shy, that the lads should pass me by –
      Oh I wonder what's a-dae wi' a' the men!

3.   Noo as I gaed oot last night, sure I met wi' Sandy Wricht,
      An' he hauled me in as I was passin' by;
      He asked me if I'd wed, so this is what I said,
      'Man, if you are quite agreeable, so am I'.

4.   So I was sae prood o' the chance, sure wi' joy it made me dance,
      The mairrage it was tae be right there an' then,
      But when I got ma marriage frock, ach he said it wis a' a joke,
      So I wonder what's a-dae wi' a' the men!

      (Chorus)

5.   Noo as I gaed oot yestreen, I could scarce believe ma e'en,
      For I met auld Janet Cook wi' a lad,
      And if it's true what a' folks say she'll be wed a month the day –
      Man, the thocht's enough to drive a body mad.

6.   For I ken aul' Janet Cook and she drinks just like a deuk,
      Her age it runs aboot three score an' ten,
      And as for husbands she's had three, [slower] and there's no a chance for me.
      [usual speed] Oh I wonder what's a-dae wi' a the men!

      (Chorus)

7.   [more slowly]
      But if there's ony laddie here that wad like a little dear,
      – A widower, or a bachelor, though he be –
      If on mairrage he is bent then I'll gie him my consent
      [coyly] It's no every day ye'll get a chance like me.

8.   For I can weave an' I can work, I can wash an' mend a sark,
      I'm as thrifty as ony lass I ken,
      But on the nail I'll hing, and I'll aye get leave tae sing,
      I wonder what's a-dae wi' a the men!

Belle Stewart picked these words up as a penny broadsheet in *The Poet's Box*, a little shop in the Overgate, Dundee, when she was about twelve years old. This was during the First World War, which destroyed almost a whole generation of young men and left some two million women on the shelf. To sing it, she just picked a tune she knew which suited and fitted the words, both of verse and of chorus.

Verses seven and eight become one composite verse; the first half of the tune is sung three times, so that the second half returns only for lines three and four of verse eight. This is a common device which serves to build up tension just before the end of a song.

'Betsy Bell' is a genuine piece of Scottish music hall, and Belle Stewart's personality is one of the chief clues to its popularity. She is an extremely attractive person, she has a grown-up family and numerous grandchildren, and she puts the song over with a flirtatious, gently serio-comic kind of irony. With a different singer it could well turn into a slice of black humour.

Adam Young: *The three craws*
Kinross 1977; rec. A.P. AM10.

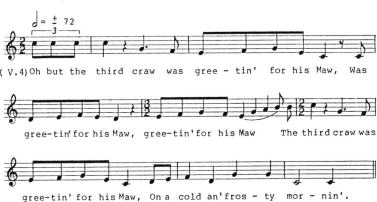

1.   Oh an' three craws sat upon a wa', Sat upon a wa', sat upon a wa', Three craws sat upon a wa', On a cold and frosty mornin'.

2.   Oh the first craw he couldna flee at a', He couldna flee at a', he couldna flee at a', The first craw he couldna flee at a', On a cold and frosty mornin'.

3.   And the second craw, he fell an' broke his jaw, (etc.)

4.   Oh but the third craw was greetin' for his Maw.

5.   Oh but the fourth craw, he wisna there at a'.

6.   Oh but the fifth craw flew awa' to Clatterha'.

7.   Oh an' the sixth craw got a job in Hornieha'.

          (pause)

8.   Oh an' the seventh craw got drunk at Justinha'

          (pause)

9.   Oh an' the eighth craw, they ca'ed him Heid-the-ba'.

          (longer pause)

10.   Oh an' the ninth craw got stuck at tap i' (o') Law.

          (still longer pause)

11.   Oh but the tenth craw – (pause) – got fed up an' walked awa'.

The first five verses are traditional. They were sung by the late Duncan MacRae, a brilliant and versatile actor with a fine flair for comedy, and were recorded by Robin Hall and Jimmy Macgregor in Volume II of *Glasgow Street Songs* (Collector JES 5). The remaining verses are 'just a make-up of my own,' says Adam Young, who lives in Forfar.

The song evoked so much laughter at this lunchtime ceilidh, that some of the words were drowned and I had to write to Adam Young. He kindly supplied notes as well as words. His allusions to local places, his gradually lengthening pauses and his straight-faced style of delivery, all combine to form a richly comic brew.

Many street songs and nursery rhymes have ancient pedigrees and sinister interpretations. In some parts of Scotland crows are still regarded with fear, as omens of death, but no such (conscious) thought has occurred to Young, who says, 'I just seem to like the song as I always fancied Duncan's songs.'

Adam Young's notes: Clatterhall was an old smiddy (smithy) between Forfar and Brechin; Horniehall is a farm up the glen, about ten miles north of Forfar; Justinhaugh is a hotel five miles north of Forfar; the Law is a hill near Dundee.

See Appendix for 'He widna wint his gruel', also in this group.

Group 4: Feuds and War

Jean Bechofer: *The bonny hoose o' Airlie* (Child 199) Kinross 1977; rec. A.P. AM9.

1.   It fell on a day, on a bonny simmer's day
     When the corn was ripe and yellow,
     That there fell oot a great dispute
     Between Argyll and Airlie.

2.   Lady Margaret looked oot o'er her high castle wa'
     And oh but she sighed sairly,
     When she saw Argyll and a' his men
     Come tae plunder the bonny hoose o' Airlie.

3.   'Come doon, come doon, Lady Margaret,' he said,
      'Come doon and kiss me fairly,
      For gin the mornin's bricht daylicht
      I winna leave a stan'in stane in Airlie.'

4.   'I winna come doon, ye fause Argyll,
      And I winna kiss thee fairly.
      I wadna kiss the fause Argyll
      Though ye didna leave a stan'in' stane in Airlie.

5.   For if my lord was noo at hame,
      As he's awa' wi' Chairlie,
      There's no a Campbell oot o' Argyll
      Dare to trod the bonny green o' Airlie.

6.   For I hae borne him seven bonny sons
      And the eighth has never seen his daddy,
      But had I borne as mony owre again
      They wad a' be men for Chairlie.'

7.   Argyll in a rage, he kin'led sic a blaze
      That it rose tae the lift red and rarely,
      And puir Lady Margaret and a' her weans
      Were smothered in the black reek o' Airlie.

8.   'Draw yer dirks, draw yer dirks,' cried the brave Lochiel;
      'Unsheath yir swords,' cried Chairlie,
      'We'll kin'le sic a lowe roond yon fause Argyll
      And we'll licht it wi' a spairk oot o' Airlie.'

Jean Bechofer, who considers herself a revival singer, was born and brought up in Shetland. She has lived in England and in different parts of Scotland, and now lives in Edinburgh. She got this song from a version in *Tocher* no. 21, 1976, which was recorded from Belle Stewart in 1956 (see Bronson no. 14). She sings here with great intensity and deliberation, and her markedly dotted rhythms are reminiscent of a slow strathspey.

This story, horrific as it is, leaves out further details of savagery which are found in some versions. Since this recording was made, Bechofer has added a verse, obtained from Belle Stewart, concerning the ravishing of Lady Margaret by Argyll – 'which she claimed she didn't sing to the School of Scottish Studies collector because it wouldn't be proper, members of the "family" still being around'. The sacking of Airlie, 1640, is brought forward to the time of Prince Charles Edward: this confusion as to dates is typical of accounts which were, at least to begin with, transmitted orally.[10]

Bechofer likes this song because 'it tells a story involving patriotism, lust, fidelity and murder, without much embellishment but very vividly... The tune...is a pipe tune and is an early version of "Loch Lomond". The regular metre of the tune suits the stark nature of this ballad... The theme is fidelity.'

See Appendix for *Willie Macintosh*, also in this group.

Group 5: Sexual Violence and Seduction

Dolina MacLennan: *The laird o' the Dainty doon-bye*
Heriot Watt University Students' Union, Edinburgh 1971; rec. A.M. SA
1971/14.

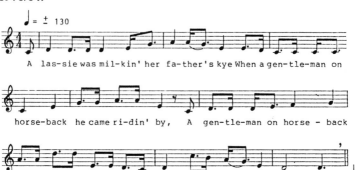

1.   A lassie was milkin' her father's kye
     When a gentleman on horseback he came ridin' by,
     A gentleman on horseback he came ridin' by,
     He was the laird o' the Dainty doon-bye.

2.   'Lassie oh lassie oh what wad ye gie
     If I were tae lie ae nicht with ye?'
     'Tae lie ae nicht that'll never never be
     Suppose ye're laird o' the Dainty doon-bye.'

3.   He took her by the middle sae sma'
     And he drew her down where the grass grew long,
     'Twas a long long time till he raised her up again
     Saying 'Ye're lady o' the Dainty doon-bye.'

4.   It fell upon a day an' a bonny summer's day,
     Tae face the lassie's father, some money he'd to pay,
     Tae face the lassie's father, some money he'd to pay
     Tae the laird o' the Dainty doon-bye.

5.   'Oh good morning and how dae ye do,
     How's yir dochter Janeky noo,
     How's yir dochter Janeky noo
     Since I laid her in the Dainty doon-bye?'

6.   'Oh my wee Janeky's no very weel,
     My wee Janeky cowks at her kail,
     My wee Janeky's lookin' unco pale
     Since ye laid her in the Dainty doon-bye.'

7.   He took her by the lily-white hand
     He showed her his rooms, they were twenty-one,
     He placed the key into her hand
     Sayin', 'Ye're lady o' the Dainty doon-bye.'

8.   'Oh,' says the auld man, 'What will we dae?'
     'Oh,' says the auld wife, 'We'll dance till we dee,'
     'Oh,' says the auld wife, 'I think we'll dae that tae
     Since she's lady o' the Dainty doon-bye.'

[Note: the usual version of lines two and three, verse eight, makes more sense:

     'Oh,' says the auld wife, 'I'll dance till I dee.'
     'Oh,' says the auld man, 'I think I'll dae that tae…']

Janeky is a diminutive of Janet.

Dolina MacLennan is a native Gaelic speaker from Lewis who has played an active and creative part in the Revival. She is chiefly known for her Gaelic songs but she also sings the Scots; for example, this song which she learned from a Ewan MacColl LP in the early 1960s.

This recording was made at a ceilidh held in aid of funds for an Edinburgh 'people's newspaper' entitled *Stampede*. After a film which showed bad living conditions in Leith, a district of Edinburgh, Dolina MacLennan introduced the song as follows: 'This next song has a – moral of a kind to it – it should suit this occasion, The Tenants' Association, because it proves that even very very far back the tenants had to – sort of – kneel down to the laird. In this case the parents of a young girl who was seduced by the laird – were delighted – that their daughter had been seduced by the laird!' The singer gave an infectious chuckle at the end of verse seven. MacLennan sums up the theme of the song: 'The audacity of the aristocracy and the acceptance of the peasant,' and adds, 'I'm aware that this attitude still exists.'

This song appears to be very popular among both men and women; it is at least 200 years old. It's worth comparing this version with the one in Herd.[12]

The story in the version given here is told in a kind of minimal short-hand. The sting is in the tail – 'the parents…were delighted' – but were they pleased for their daughter's sake or for their own? Possibly for both. If for themselves only, they have in effect sold her; in either case they may even have in some way engineered the situation. On the other hand they could simply be making the best of a fait accompli, in which case the father's reply (verse 6) is a bold challenge, the suggestion being 'You've got her into this, now get her out of it'. (Imagine Mozart's Figaro, some twenty years after his marriage, scheming for his daughter with a son of Count Almaviva…a son who has not inherited his father's humane views regarding the *droit du seigneur* syndrome.) The daughter's wishes are not considered at any time, and in view of her spirited refusal (verse 2) this is initially a story about rape or near-rape. The laird makes a tentative declaration; he then delays his next visit, ostensibly till rent-collection day, but possibly also until enough time has elapsed to establish whether or not she is pregnant. Insofar as this hypothesis may be true, the story follows a pattern which was found until recently in parts of Scotland. For instance in Aberdeenshire, within living memory, pregnancy before marriage was considered advisable in some circles as a safeguard against possible infertility in either husband or wife. Two centuries ago arranged marriages were more common, while expectation of romantic love was comparatively rare. Janet's parents knew the struggle for existence of tenant farmers and farm workers, and might quite sincerely decide that a shot-gun marriage to the laird would by no means be a fate worse than death.

This song is obviously seen as embodying a hard and humorous realism. It is usually sung at a lively tempo, as here.

Dolina MacLennan has been recorded by Topic and by Decca.

Walter Allan: *Eppie Morrie* **(Child 223)**
Blairgowrie 1970; rec. P.C. SA 1970/180.

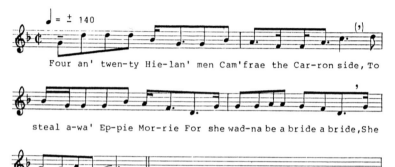

Four an' twen-ty Hie-lan' men Cam'frae the Car-ron side, To

steal a-wa' Ep-pie Mor-rie For she wad-na be a bride a bride, She

wad-na be a bride.

1.   Four an twenty Hielan' men
       Cam' frae the Carron side,
       To steal awa' Eppie Morrie
       For she wadna be a bride a bride,
       She wadna be a bride.

2.   It's oot an cam' her mither then,
       It was a moonlicht nicht;
       She couldnae see her dochter
       For the waters shone sae bricht sae bricht.
       The waters shone sae bricht.

3.   'Haud awa' frae me, mither,
       Haud awa' frae me!
       There's no a man in a' Strathdon
       Shall mairriet be wi' me wi' me,
       Shall mairriet be wi' me.'

4.   They've taken Eppie Morrie then
       And a horse they've bound her on;
       And they hae rid to the minister's hoose
       As fast as horse could gang could gang,
       As fast as horse could gang.

5.   And Willie's ta'en his pistol oot
       And held it tae the minister's breist;
       'Oh marry me marry me minister,
       Or else I'll be yir priest yir priest
       Or else I'll be yir priest.'

6. 'Hand awa' frae me Willie,
    Hand awa' frae me!
    I daurna vow tae marry you
    Except she's willin' as thee as thee,
    Except she's willin' as thee.'

7. 'Hand awa' frae me guid sir,
    Hand awa' frae me!
    There's no a man in a Strathdon
    Shall wedded be by me by me,
    Shall wedded be by me.'

8. They've taken Eppie Morrie then
    Sin' better couldnae be,
    And they hae rid owre Carron side
    As fast as horse could flee could flee,
    As fast as horse could flee.

9. Then mass was sung and bells were rung
    And they're awa' tae bed,
    And Willie and Eppie Morrie then
    In ane bed they were laid were laid,
    In ane bed they were laid.

10. He's ta'en the sark frae off his back
    And kicked awa' his shoon.
    He's thrawn awa' the chaumer key
    And naked he lay doon lay doon,
    And naked he lay doon.

11. He kissed her on the lily breist
    And held her shouthers twa
    But aye she grat and aye she spat
    And turnèd tae the wa' the wa',
    And turnèd tae the wa'.

12. 'Haud awa' frae me, Willie,
    Haud awa' frae me!
    Before I lose ma maidenheid
    I'll try ma strength wi' thee wi' thee,
    I'll try ma strength wi' thee.'

13. A' through the nicht they warstled then
    Until the licht o' day,
    And Willie grat and Willie swat
    But he couldnae streitch her spey her spey,
    He couldnae streitch her spey.

14. Then early in the mornin'
    Before the licht o' day,
    In cam' the maid o' Scallater
    Wi' a goon and shirt alane alane,
    Wi' a goon and shirt alane.

15. 'Get up get up young woman
     And drink the wine wi' me!'
     'You micht hae ca'ed me maiden
     For I'm sure as hale as thee as thee,
     For I'm sure as hale as thee.'

16. 'Weary fa' you Willie then
     That ye couldnae prove a man;
     You micht hae ta'en her maidenheid,
     She wad hae hired your hand your hand,
     She wad hae hired your hand.'

17. Then in it's cam' young Breidalbane,
     A pistol on each side.
     'Oh come awa' Eppie Morrie
     And I'll mak' you ma bride ma bride,
     And I'll mak' you ma bride.'

18. 'Go get to me a horse Willie,
     Get it like a man!
     And send me back to ma mither
     A maiden as I cam' I cam'
     A maiden as I cam'.'

19. The sun shines owre the westlin' hills
     By the lamplicht o' the moon;
     'Oh saddle your horse young John Forsyth
     And whistle and I'll come soon come soon,
     And whistle and I'll come soon.'

This ballad was made popular by Ewan MacColl. The words from Maidment's *North Countrie Garland* form the only version in Child – and (conflated as here) in Bronson who gives MacColl's tune alone, 'learned from his father', with the disc number. In 1824 Maidment wrote: 'This ballad is probably much more than a century old, though the circumstances which have given rise to it were unfortunately too common to preclude the possibility of its being of a later date.'

Norman Buchan has described the time he first heard MacColl sing it, at the late night ceilidh in St Columba's Church after the first Edinburgh People's Festival Ceilidh; he said MacColl leaned against a pillar – 'I could almost take you to the particular pillar' – 'and belted out "Eppie Morrie", and it came like a charging gallop.'[13]

Walter Allan's version, very nearly the same as MacColl's,[14] is also taken at 'charging gallop' speed. It's a superb performance. He never falters, his diction is clear and he is as if possessed by the rhythmic drive of the music and story. Allan says that he identified with Willie to some extent; he continues, 'I like the story content of the song and the way it is made to fit the tune. The tune is also powerful and I think echoes the speed with which Wullie tries to gain his maid, then the hard struggle, and ultimate frustration. I think it is purely a story, perhaps based on true historical personalities although I don't find that quite important. Since Eppie Morrie at the end reveals her love for John Forsyth and not Wullie, perhaps there's also a moral in it!'

See Appendix for 'The banks o' red roses', also in this group.

Group 6: The Pregnant Woman in Trouble

Gordeanna MacCulloch: *The cruel mother* (Child 20)
Kinross 1971, rec. P.C. SA 1971/243.

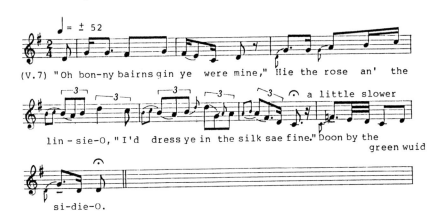

1. There was a lady in the North,
   Hie the rose and the linsie-O,
   And she's fa'en in love wi' her faither's clerk,
   Doon by the green wuid sidie-O.

[The internal refrain is added in the same way to each verse]

2. She's leaned her back against a tree,
   And there the saut tears blint her e'e.

3. She's leaned her back against a thorn,
   And there twa bonny boys has she borne.

4. She's ta'en oot her little pen-knife,
   And she's twined thae twa bonny boys o' their lives.

5. She's buried them 'neath a marble stane,
   Thinking to gyang a maiden hame.

6. She's looked owre her faither's wa',
   And she spied thae twa bonny boys playin' at the ba'.

7. 'Oh bonny bairns gin ye were mine,
   I'd dress ye in the silk sae fine.'

8. 'Oh cruel mither, when we were thine,
   We didna see aucht o' the silk sae fine.'

9. 'Oh bonny bairns come tell tae me,
   What kind o' a death I'll hae tae dee.'

10.   'Seeven years a fish in the flood,
       And seeven lang years a bird in the wood.

11.   Seeven years a tongue tae the warnin' bell,
       And seeven lang years in the cave o' hell.

12.   'Welcome, welcome, fish in the flood,
       Welcome, welcome, bird in the wood.

13.   Welcome, tongue tae the warnin' bell,
       But God keep me frae the flames o' hell.'

('Hie' is pronounced 'high')

Vic Smith's tune
Kinross 1973; rec. A.M. SA 1973/112

A former pupil of Norman Buchan's at Rutherglen Academy, Gordeanna MacCulloch is a member of The Clutha, a Glasgow group, one of whose thumb prints of style is solo or unison singing, with harmonic content coming only from the instruments.

MacCulloch has become one of the finest of Scottish singers today. She uses her strong voice here with a fluid drive which conveys the dramatic compulsiveness of the story. She got the words from Norman Buchan at her school folk club; they are very similar to the *Last Leaves* version, with four verses omitted. Greig and Keith state, 'The numerous versions of this ballad are almost all Scottish.' The implied tritone ending to the third line of the verse-tune (F sharp to C) leads with poignant effect to the inflected, now flattened seventh at the word 'Doon'.

The tune is that used by Ewan MacColl for his version of this ballad: he learned and possibly adapted it from the singing of his aunt, Maggie Henry Logan.

In verse seven, transcribed above, the mother's words including the first re-frain 'Hie the rose and the linsie-o' are sung as a cry of limitless yearning and regret; in contrast, the end-refrain 'Doon by the green wuid sidie-O' is hushed, impersonal, age-weary... MacCulloch describes this second refrain as 'eerie...it seems to take you back to the scene of the crime.' She has always liked the big ballads: 'This one appeals to me mainly because of the words I think, because it is a situation which any young female can get into today although not all take such drastic measures as a solution. I think also the female getting her "just deserts" appeals to me. I'm not sure that there is a message in ballads as I believe they were used as a method of carrying news from one community to the next. If there is any message it must be a warning to young females to beware of the same fate.' Gordeanna MacCulloch has been recorded by Argo, by Topic and by Claddagh.

All the fuller versions in Child end with the Hell motif, and several include the 'Welcome, welcome': the mother does not merely accept expiation, she *wants* it (cf. the murderer in Dostoyevsky's *Crime and Punishment*) – provided it ends at last.

Vic Smith's version, the tune of which is added above as a contrast, has rather appropriate words for the first of the two internal refrain lines: 'All alone and alonie-O'.

Owen Costello: *Bogie's bonny Belle*
Kinross 1973; rec. A.M. SA 1973/111

(V.5) Doon be the banks o'Cair-nie There we en-ded mo-ny's a day, And when

Bo-gie wis-na wat-chin' It was there we'd sport an' play.

1. Ae Whitsunday in Huntly toon
    'Twas there I did agree
    Wi' Bogie o' Cairnie
    For six months tae fee.

2. For tae drive his twa best horses,
    'Twas a job that I could do,
    Oh tae drive his twa best horses
    At ma harrow an' ma ploo.

3. Noo Bogie had a dochter
    Her name was Isabel,
    And oh but she was bonny
    And she knew I lo'ed her weel.

4. When she gaed oot walkin'
    She chose me for her guide
    Tae watch the trooties lowpin'
    By Bogie's waterside.

5.   Doon be the banks o' Cairnie
There we ended mony's a day,
And when Bogie wisna watchin'
It was there we'd sport an' play.

6.   Doon be the banks o' Cairnie
Where we watched the fishes glide,
It was there I had my will o' her
By Bogie's burnside.

7.   And the first three months being scarcely owre
This lassie lost her bloom,
And the reid fell fae her rosy cheeks
And her eyes began tae swoon.

8.   And when six months were nearly owre
Her waist began tae swell,
And when her mother speired at her
Oh the truth she had tae tell.

9.   And when nine lang months were past an' gane
She brocht forth tae me a son,
And I was quickly sent for
Tae see what could be done.

10.   I said that I wad mairry her
But oh no that wouldna dae;
'For ye're nae match for ma bonny Belle
And she's nae match for ye.'

11.   An' noo she's mairried til a tinkler chiel
Wha bides in Huntly toon,
He mends pots an pans an' ladles,
An' he scoors the country roon'.

12.   And maybe she's gotten a better match,
Auld Bogie canna tell,
But it's me that stole the maidenheid
Fae his bonny Isabel.

The popularity of this bothy song may be due partly to the weel-gaun, up and down swing of its tune, but the words form at least an equal attraction. Owen Costello of Cumbernauld, originally from Glasgow, conflated his version from many others he had heard, as well as from records and books. He says, 'I like this song because it's political in the widest sense: it's untypical of bothy songs, most of which express grumbles against individual employers but that's about all. The song is a very bitter comment on the conditions and attitudes of farm life. Although the complaint here is underscored, this brings out the bitterness all the more.'

Boasts about maidenhead stealing can be supremely boring, but in this particular situation the last verse is a biting comeback, a piece of one-upmanship and nose-thumbing. 'I had my will o' her' (verse six) is a well-worn cliché in Scots folk song; its implications are various.

It is interesting that the 'tinkler chiel', or tinker, whom Belle married seems to have been more of a social catch than a farm worker would be: the song may thus have a fairly ancient ancestry, for it is a long time since the travelling tinsmiths lost their former status as skilled craftsmen. But in verse eleven the speaker suggests that the life of a tinker's wife is hard: 'he scoors the country roon'' probably refers to moving camp – another piece of one-upmanship with which the rejected suitor comforts his bruised ego.

Cy Laurie: *Corachree*
Kinross 1971; rec. J.P. SA 1971/242.

(V.2)Noo half-wey up the a-ve-nue they baith set doon tae rest. He

put his airms a-roon' her sayin','"Ma dear, I love ye best, A

mai-den ye hae sit-ten doon, a maid ye're aye tae me But a

maid-en ye'll ne'er walk a-gain the grass o' Co-ra-chree".

1.   It was on a summer's evenin' I gaed oot tae tak' the air
When comin' in be Tarlin toon I spied a lonely pair.
The youth was tall and handsome and the maid fair tae see
An' I kent their destination wasnae faur frae Corachree.

2.   Noo halfwey up the avenue they baith set doon tae rest.
He put his airms aroon' her sayin', 'Ma dear, I love ye best,
A maiden ye hae sitten doon, a maid ye're aye tae me
But a maiden ye'll ne'er walk again the grass o' Corachree.'

3.   'O Sandy lad ye'll ne'er deny this deed ye hae dene
My apron-strings are broken, Lord ma hairt flees wi' the win',
Ma maidenheid has ta'en a fricht, it's fairly flown awa'
An' the session clerk'll get tae ken this deed ye hae dene.'

4.   'Cheer up ma bonny lassie ye neednae care a fig,
There's mony's a bonny lassie gaes daily on the rig.
There's mony a bonny lassie aye an' juist as guid as thee
But a maiden ye'll ne'er walk again the grass o' Corachree.'

5. Well he comes doon in the evenin' as often as he can,
    He comes doon in the evenin' juist tae see his lonely Anne.
    They tak' their lane o' auld lang syne faur naebody can see
    But ye'll easy fin' oot a' their beds aroon' be Corachree.

'My apron-strings are broken' is one of the recognised traditional ways of an-
nouncing pregnancy and it is received here with apparent insouciance (verse
four, line one).

Although Cy Laurie's time is free he achieves a firm base of time-structure,
unlike some interpretations where the tune seems to wander rather aimlessly; he
sings with a warm melancholy.

This song, although perhaps less popular than a few years ago, is still heard
quite frequently, especially at competitions and in pubs; it is usually sung by
men. Its origin has not been traced or any printed version found, but the fear of
the session clerk takes us back at least 160 years or so.

Janet Weatherstone: *The Magdalen Green*
Kinross 1977; rec. A.P. AM9.

(V.2) Wi' a roguish smile upon her face she answered me and
said, "Young man I would a-walk wi' you, but you know I am a-
fraid, For the paths they are so slippery, the nicht be cauld an'
keen, And it would not do for me tae fa' doon by the Mag-d'len Green".

1. 'Noo here am I a sailor lad just newly hame frae sea,
    My ship it lies at anchor in the harbour o' Dundee,
    And your face it is the fairest that I hae ever seen,
    Oh fair maid wad ye walk wi' me doon by the Magdalen* Green?'

2. Wi' a roguish smile upon her face she answered me and said,
    'Young man I would a-walk wi' you, but you know I am afraid,
    For the paths they are so slippery, the nicht be cauld an' keen,
    And it would not do for me tae fa' doon by the Magdalen Green.'

3. Wi' kind words and promises alang wi' me she went,
    We wandered here, we wandered there, mid love and pleasure brent,
    Day after day we met and roved amid yon pleasant scene,
    And I fear that maid fell more than once doon by the Magdalen Green.

4. Well soon the time for partin' came, my ship had hoisted sail,
    Nae langer could I see yon lass tae tell a pleasant tale,
    So I bid fareweel tae her thon day, whaur I hae happy been,
    And she was left to weep alone doon by the Magdalen Green.

5. One night as I lay in my bed when my weary watch was done
    I dreamt I was the father o' a darlin' little son';
    Aye and in the dream his mither tae richt plainly could I see
    And she was weeping bitterly doon by the Magdalen Green.

6. So when my ship puts in again in the harbour o' Dundee
    I'll search that town all up and down until my girl I see,
    And I'll ask her tae forgi'e me for the rascal I hae been,
    And I will make it up tae her doon by the Magdalen Green.

7. So come a' ye jolly sailor lads, a warnin' tak be me,
    Never slight that poor lass for a' her poverty;
    For tae lichtlie love and sail away, 'tis neither strecht nor clean,
    Aye 'n' never dae as I once did doon by the Magdalen Green.

* Pronounced 'Maudlen'

The Weatherstones of Barnton, Edinburgh, have recently come to the fore as another singing family, with their mother the immediate source of many songs which Jock and Janet sing. Jock is well known for his racy and authentic renderings of such rollicking Aberdeenshire tongue-twisters as 'McGinty's meal and ale when the pig gaed on the spree', and 'MacFarlane o' the Sprotts o' Birniboosie (both in Greig's *Folk-Song of the North East*), as well as for his more serious songs.

Janet Weatherstone got her version of 'The Magdalen Green' from her mother: it was her favourite, and is now Janet's. The words are almost the same as those obtained from *The Poet's Box*.

With her powerful voice, which has great sustaining powers, her clear enunciation, and hardly any vibrato or ornamentation, this singer's straightforward version is sung to a very steady beat; but there's much tight-lipped feeling too.

Group 7: Family Pressure Regarding Marriage

Jane Turriff: *Andrew Lammie* (Child 233)
Fetterangus 1974; rec. H.H. and P.C. SA 1974/150.

At Mill o' Tif-ty lived a man In the neigh-bour-hood o'

Fy-vie, And he had a love-ly daugh-ter fair, Her name was bon-ny

An - nie.

1.   At Mill o' Tifty lived a man
     In the neighbourhood o' Fyvie,
     And he had a lovely daughter fair,
     Her name was bonny Annie.

2.   Lord Fyvie had a trumpeter
     An' his name was Andra Lammie,
     And he had the art to gain the heart
     O' bonny Tifty's Annie.

3.   Her mother called her to the door,
     'Come here tae me, my Annie.
     Did e'er you see a prettier man
     Than the trumpeter o' Fyvie?'

4.   Oh nothing she said but sighin' sore,
     Alas for bonny Annie!
     But she durst not own that her heart was won
     By the trumpeter o' Fyvie.

5.   Oh the first time me an' my love did meet
     It was in the woods o' Fyvie,
     And he ca'ed me 'Mistress' – I said, 'No,
     I am Tifty's bonny Annie.'

6.   With apples sweet he did me treat,
     And kisses soft an' many,
     And he had the art to gain the heart
     Of bonny Tifty's Annie.

7.   Oh loves comes in at my bedside,
     And love lies down beyond me:
     And love so oppressed my tender breast,
     Oh but love will waste by body.

8.   'Oh lovey I must go to Edinburgh toon
     And for a whilie I must leave ye'.
     'Oh but I'll be dead or you come back,
     Oh bonny Andra Lammie.'

9.   'I will buy you a bridal goon,
     And dearie it will be bonny'.
     'Oh but I'll be dead or you come back,
     Oh ma bonny Andra Lammie.'

10.   'I will buy tae you a bridal shoon
       And oh but they will be bonny.'
       'Oh but I'll be dead or you come back,
       Oh ma bonny Andra Lammie.'

11.   Oh love comes in at my bedside,
       And love lies down beyond me:
       And love so oppressed my tender breast,
       Oh but love will waste my body.

12.   Oh but lay me doon to rest a while
       And turn my face to Fyvie,
       That I may see before I dee
       Oh ma bonny Andra Lammie.

13.   Oh it's up and doon in Tifty's glen,
       Whaur the burn lies clear and bonny;
       Whaur oft-times I have run tae thee,
       Oh my bonny Andra Lammie.

14.   Oh love it dwines and love it twines,
       And love decays ma body:
       And love so oppressed my tender breast,
       Oh but love will waste my body.

15.   Oh Andra hame fae Edinburgh toon
       Wi' muckle grief and sorrow,
       And he sounded his horn right loud and clear
       In the low lands o' Fyvie.

16.   Oh Fyvie's lands are broad an' wide
       And Fyvie's lands are bonny,
       Whaur oft-times I have gone tae meet
       My bonny Tifty's Annie.

This is a lengthy ballad. Jane Turriff, formerly of Fetterangus but now living in Mintlaw, has 52 verses, but for reasons of time she usually cuts it to about a third of this length. *She assumes that her audience knows the story.* The verses cut include those describing the physical brutality; 'I don't like to sing that verses,' says Turriff. Her tune is closest to Davie Stewart's for 'The dowie dens', given above under 'The belt wi' colours three'. Stewart was Jane Turriff's uncle and a constant visitor to her home. (Detailed notes on the music of 'Andrew Lammie', with Turriff's harmonium accompaniment compared with Davie Stewart's melodeon accompaniment to 'The dowie dens', may be found in *The Muckle Sangs* booklet.[15]) Turriff is of the travelling people. Crippled since her childhood, she was nearly always in the house and so learned many songs, including this one, from her mother's, her grannie's and her uncles's singing. Of folk song generally she says '…it's *real*, and something that gets ye going.'[16]

The rest of the ballad story: Annie's family strongly disapprove of the trumpeter as a suitor – musicians are of low status – and her father accuses him of having bewitched her by 'wicked art'. While Andra is in Edinburgh, Annie's family turn on her: her father, her mother, and – most violent of all – her brother.

At first Annie shows some spirit:

> But if ye strike me I'll cry out,
> And gentlemen will hear me;
> Lord Fyvie will be riding by,
> And he'll come in and see me.

The laird does hear her cries, and comes in to intercede for her, but to no avail. When he leaves, the violence is in fact intensified, probably because Annie has dared to invoke help (this pattern may be found even today, if a battered woman reports her ill-treatment). Eventually the brother breaks her back, and Annie dies. Andra says later, 'My love has died for me today, I'll die for her to-morrow.'

This dreadful story is based on historical fact. In his notes on this ballad in *The Muckle Sangs* Hamish Henderson relates how Arthur Argo led the two recorders to the actual ruined mill, in Aberdeenshire, and saw 'Annie's flat grave-stone in Fyvie kirkyard – dated 1673, and surmounted by a nineteenth-century monumental stone on which are carved the leaves of two intertwining trees'; also to Fyvie Castle nearby, with the stone figure of the trumpeter on one of the turrets.

Child remarks, '…the gentleness and fidelity of Annie under the brutal behaviour of her family are genuinely pathetic, and justify the remarkable popularity which the ballad has enjoyed in the North of Scotland.' One's first reaction might be that 'pathetic' is the word in more senses than one: the slang meaning appears applicable to Annie's passivity. But on second thoughts, what more could she have done? She tries three times to warn Andra of the fate in store for her during his absence, but he ignores this warning.

Professor Trevelyan in his *History of England* writes: 'Wife-beating was a recognised right of man, and was practised without shame by high as well as low… Similarly, the daughter who refused to marry the gentleman of her parents' choice was liable to be locked up, beaten and flung about the room, without any shock being inflicted on public opinion. Marriage was not an affair of personal affection, but of family avarice…'[17] The historian is speaking here of the year 1500, but these practices continued for many long years and died hard. (And violent treatment of women by members of the family still continues, in Scotland and elsewhere.[18]) The 'remarkable popularity' of the ballad may have had something to do with an atavistic clinging to outworn mores. Women were supposed to be gentle and passive – 'under the bludgeonings of chance' their heads should be bloody *and bowed*. Also this continuing popularity could possibly imply a touch of the sadism-masochism vicious circle; many people enjoy the depiction of violence.

Yet violence cannot be ignored, and it is of course an ingredient in many of the finest ballads. 'Andrew Lammie' has an epic quality, with some powerfully evocative language. Above all it is a true love-story; a story which ends on a note of apocalyptic doom, with a hint of the Pauline 'last trump':

> And he sounded his horn both loud and clear
> In the low lands o' Fyvie.

Jane Turriff's complete version ends on this repeated note:

He hied him to the head of the house,
To the house-top o' Fyvie;
He blew his trumpet loud and shrill,
'Twas heard at Mill o' Tifty.

Heather Heywood: *What can a young lassie dae wi' an auld man?*
Kinross 1975; rec. A.P. AM2.

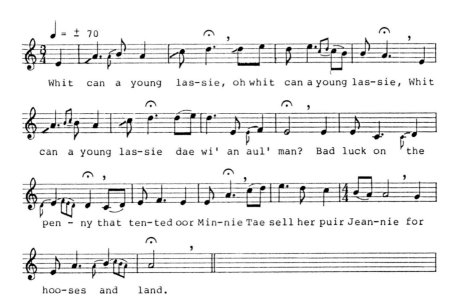

Whit can a young las-sie, oh whit can a young las-sie, Whit
can a young las-sie dae wi' an aul' man? Bad luck on the
pen - ny that ten-ted oor Min-nie Tae sell her puir Jean-nie for
hoo-ses and land.

1.   Whit can a young lassie, oh whit can a young lassie,
     Whit can a young lassie dae wi' an aul' man?
     Bad luck on the penny that tented oor Minnie
     Tae sell her puir Jeannie for hooses and land.

2.   He hums and he hankers, he frets and he cankers,
     I never cuid please him, dae a' that I can.
     For he's peevish and jealous o' a' the young fellas
     Oh weary's me life wi' me crazy aul' man.

3.   Ma auld Auntie Kitty, on me she taks pity,
     I'll dae ma endeavour tae follow her plan;
     For I'll cross him, I'll crack him, until I hairt-brak him
     And wi' his aul' brass I will buy a new pan.

4.   For he's aye-ways complainin' frae mornin' till evenin',
     He hoasts and he hirples the weary day lang,
     He's dowie an' dosin' and his blood is gey frozen,
     Oh I rue on the day I met wi' ma aul' man.

5.   Whit can a young lassie, oh whit can a young lassie,
      Whit can a young lassie dae wi' an aul' man?
      Bad luck on the penny that tented oor Minnie
      Tae sell her puir Jeannie for hooses and land.

The villain of this piece is the mother. The pauses shown in the transcription are not as frequent in subsequent verses. This opening, and concluding, verse conveys a dull, dragging hopelessness, an incapacity for looking forward, with frequent stops as if for bitter reflection. Yet 'for a' that' a youthful vitality surges through especially in the other verses, in Heather Heywood's clear, resonant voice and her thoughtful shaping of the melody.

The words are substantially those of Burns (see Kinsley,[19] though the order of verses is changed); but, as with Allan Morris' 'Parcel o' rogues' below, these words are even more Scots than are Burns's, thus showing signs of oral tradition at work.

Heywood's changing of the original, lilting jig tune to this slower, more pensive tempo is entirely convincing and far more suitable. She learned this song from the singing of Janice Clark, and also that of Jane Turriff.

'The theme is the old saying "It's better to marry for love and not for money",' says Heather. 'It's obvious that all the man's money can't make up for the fact that he's far too old for the girl… This song is usually a favourite of our local Folk Club' (in Kilmarnock). Heather has been recorded by Springthyme and by Ayrshire Folk Club.

Jane Turriff: *The dowie dens of Yarrow* **(Child 214)**
Kinross 1977: rec. A.P. AM9.

1.   As he's gaen tae his lady gang
      As he had done before-O,
      Sayin', 'Madam I maun keep a tryst
      On the dowie dens o' Yarrow.'

2.   'Oh bide at hame, my lord,' she said,
      'Oh bide at hame, my marrow,
      For my three brothers will slay thee
      On the dowie dens o' Yarrow.'

3. Oh she kissed his cheeks and she kissed his hair,
    As she had done before-O,
    Gied him a brand down by his side
    And he's awa' tae Yarrow.

4. So he's gaed up yon Tenniesbank,
    And I wyte he gaed wi' sorrow,
    For there he met nine armed men
    On the dowie dens o' Yarrow.

5. 'Oh come ye here tae hawk or hound,
    Or drink the wine sae clear-O,
    Or come ye here tae pairt yir land
    On the dowie dens o' Yarrow?'

6. 'I come not here tae hawk or hound,
    Nor drink the wine sae clear-O,
    Nor come I here to pairt my land
    But I'll fight wi' you in Yarrow.'

7. So four he's hurt, and five he's slain
    On the bloody dens o' Yarrow,
    Till a cowardly man came him behind
    And he's pierced his body through-O.

8. 'Gae hame, gae hame, ma brither John,
    Whit's a' the dule an' sorrow?
    Gae hame an' tell my lady dear
    That I sleep sound in Yarrow.'

9. So he's gaed up yon high, high hill
    As he had done before-O,
    And there he spied his sister dear
    She was comin' fast tae Yarrow.

10. 'Oh I dreamed a dreary dream yestreen,
    God keep us a' fae sorrow;
    I dreamed I pulled the birks sae green
    On yon dowie dens o' Yarrow.

11. 'Oh sister I will read yir dream
    And oh it has come sorrow,
    For yir true love he is dead and gone –
    He's killed, he's killed in Yarrow.'

Jane Turriff says, 'When I sing my old songs my mind and memories go far back, and I always think I hear my mother singing.' Her clear voice with its soaring high notes has an arresting edge to it. It is difficult to describe the impact her singing makes, in particular her production of the first syllable of 'Yarrow', which ends each verse, except verse seven, and gives one of the most unforgettable and hard to analyse sounds heard in Scottish traditional song. There is a kind of break in her voice here – one might almost say heart break, so poignant is its effect. The words 'tell' and 'my' (verse 8) are also given something of this treatment, without any further ornamentation.

There is a strong suggestion here that the *coup de grâce* (verse 7) was delivered by a brother of the lady – this is supported by many versions in Bronson but by fewer in Child. And 'my brother John' (verse 8) sometimes appears as 'my good-brother', meaning brother-in-law. Turriff's final line is the best of all in any version.

Tenniesbank is on the Tinnis Burn, near Newcastleton.

Group 8: Political, Social Comment and Work

Allan Morris: *Sic a parcel o' rogues in a nation*
Kinross 1973; rec. P.C. SA 1973/109.

1.   Fareweel tae a' oor Scottish fame,
      Fareweel oor ancient glory;
      Fareweel even tae the Scottish name
      Sae famed in martial story.
      Noo Sark rins owre the Solway sands
      And Tweed rins tae the ocean,
      Tae mark whaur England's province stands;
      Sic a parcel o' rogues in a nation!

2. What force or guile could not subdue
    Through many warlike ages,
    Is wrought now by a coward few
    For hireling traitors' wages.
    The English steel we could disdain,
    Secure in valour's station,
    But English gold has been oor bane;
    Sic a parcel o' rogues in a nation!

3. Oh would, or I had seen the day
    That treason thus could sell us,
    My auld grey heid had lain in clay
    Wi' Bruce an' loyal Wallace!
    But pith an' power till my last hour,
    I'll mak' this declaration:
    We're bought and sold for English gold.
    Sic a parcel o' rogues in a nation!

This version follows Burns' including the tune, almost exactly, although the words are even more Scots ('oor' for 'our', 'sic' for 'such', etc.). Thomas Crawford suggests that the original may have been one of the Jacobite songs which Burns altered or touched up, although as always 'it is extremely difficult...to say where tradition leaves off, and Burns...begins.'[20] Allan Morris introduces the song by making in effect this last point, and adds, 'I regard it as the first "folk song" I ever learned. It's a protest against the Anglo-Scottish union of 1707...and still remains to my mind one of the finest national songs we have.' (See Francis Collinson on the distinction between national and traditional songs.[21])

The noble, wide-ranging tune, with its constant shifts from minor to major and back again, fits the corresponding changes of mood in the words which express alternating feelings of melancholy and of pride. Burns had an uncanny gift for matching words and music.

Morris first heard this sung in the mid or late sixties, probably by the Corries or the Dubliners. A member of the SNP since 1959, when he was seventeen, he comments: 'The theme is the betrayal of Scottish nationhood in 1707...such betrayal still proceeding today, with tacit agreement of some sections of the Scottish populace.'

Hamish Imlach: *If it wasnae for the Union*
Heriot Watt University Students' Union, Edinburgh 1971; rec. A.M.
SA 1971/15.

(Ch.)   Too-ra loo-ra loo-ra loo, I'll tell ye some-thin' aw-fa true Ye

would-nae hae yer tel-ly the noo If it was-nae for the U-nion.

Note: each verse ends:—

(*Chorus*)
Toora loora loora loo,
I'll tell ye somethin' awfa true
Ye wouldnae hae yir telly the noo
If it wasnae for the Union.

1.   Noo I had a boss in Aiberdeen,
    The nicest fella that ever was seen,
    But he must 'a' thought me hell of a green
    Before I joined the Union.

2.   And I had a boss named Allardyce,
    He was really hell of a nice,
    Except for the way he loaded the dice
    Before I joined the Union.

3.   A pal o' mine has bought a car,
    A second-haunded Jaguar –
    He wouldn't 'a' travelled half as far
    If it wasn't for his Union.

4.   The bosses they were daein' fine,
    Wee weans workin' doon the mine –
    They'd have them on the assembly line
    If it wasn't for the Union.

5.   So men and women, all agree
    It's time to rise up off yir knee
    And raise the banner of unity –
    Forward with the Union!

This is one of the many songs written by Matt McGinn of Glasgow. For some he composed his own tunes (for example 'A Miner's Lullaby'); others, as here, he wrote to existing tunes. The following is part of Hamish Imlach's introduction to it, spoken, while he strummed his guitar as background: '…Matt's song…I've sung it every night for eighteen months…it's a song written in the days when Trade Union leaders were…sort of…working for the people who paid them, not messing about getting on television… – When the TUC motto was still "Non illegitimi carborundum" …"Don't let the bastards grind you down"…' – with other topical and humorous cracks. After the first chorus he says (still with guitar strumming), 'It's my favourite song of Matt's. For any tourists here, that's "Toora loora loora loo, you wouldn't have your television sets at present, if it wasn't for the Trade Unions".'

The tune is almost the same as Jeannie Robertson's for 'Killicrankie' in her disc *Jeannie's Merry Muse*[22], but McGinn has greatly improved on this by making the verse end on a dominant cadence.

Hamish Imlach, a popular soloist, was born in Calcutta of Scottish parents; after eight years in India and five years in Australia, he came to Glasgow, and was at Hyndland School with Archie Fisher. He remembers Norman Buchan visiting the school with his Reivers group. An honorary member of the Indian Students' Club in Motherwell since 1961, Imlach studied engineering but has been a professional singer for some twenty years. 'Matt wrote this song about 1964,' he says. 'The press were vilifying the unions…both Matt and I adapted the words from time to time…it's an Irish tune, often sung to words which end, "Come and join the British army". People get ideas from the media, and it's good if they can get them in an entertaining way… I still do anti-Polaris songs… "You canny spend a dollar when you're deid" is still topical because the subs are still in the loch.'

Imlach puts over this song with a kind of cool verve, never over-using his powerful voice. It is still popular in the more politically minded west, McGinn's old home territory. Protest songs in general appear to be on the decline at present.

Imlach has been recorded by Transatlantic and by Autogram.

Ray Fisher: *The Fairfield Apprentice* (also called *The Shipyard Apprentice*)
Kinross 1973; rec. P.C. SA 1973/109.

I was born in the sha-dow of a Fair - field crane, And the blast of a freigh-ter horn Was the ve-ry first sound that reached my ears On the mor-ning I was born. I lay and lis - tened to the ship - yard noise Co-ming out of the big un - known, And was sung to sleep by the mo-ther tongue That was to be my own.

1.   I was born in the shadow of a Fairfield crane,
      And the blast of a freighter horn
      Was the very first sound that reached my ears
      On the morning I was born.
      I lay and listened to the shipyard noise
      Coming out of the big unknown,
      And was sung to sleep by the mother tongue
      That was to be my own.

2.   And when I was barely one year old
      I heard a siren scream
      As that city watched in the blacked out night
      A wandering search light beam.
      And then one day I awoke and rose
      To my father's day of peace,
      And I knew the battle to stay alive
      Was never going to cease.

3.   For I sat and listened tae my father tell
      Of the Clyde that he once knew
      Where you either sweated for a measly wage
      Or joined in the parish queue.
      Where life grew harder day by day
      Along the riverside:
      Oh it's oft I've heard my mother say
      It was tears that made the Clyde.

4.   When I've sat in the school fae nine to four,
      And I've dreamed of the world outside
      Where the riveters and the platers watch
      Their ships slip tae the Clyde.
      And I'm serving my time behind ship-yaird gates
      And sometimes mourn my lot
      But if ever the bad old times return
      I will fight as my father fought.

5.   For I was born in the shadow of a Fairfield crane
      And the blast of a freighter horn
      Was the very first sound that reached my ears
      On the morning I was born.

Still in the west of Scotland – with two of the best-known members of the singing Fisher family of Glasgow. The words and tune of this song were written by Archie Fisher and Bobby Campbell respectively.

Ray Fisher accompanies herself here on guitar and achieves some interesting shifts of rhythm by pausing vocally on certain notes, thus lagging temporarily behind the stricter rhythm of her instrumental backing. She has a strong voice of impressive quality, with an abrasive edge to it where needed. Her spoken introduction on this recording refers to the shipbuilding industry and she says, 'Imagine I'm a seventeen-year-old apprentice...' She has had a powerful influence on the folk scene, and continues to help other less experienced singers.

This song was first heard in a series of six radio programmes called *Landmarks* (subtitle: *From the cradle to the grave*) broadcast during 1964–65.

Like the *Radio Ballads* series described in Chapter III, these were devised and presented by Charles Parker in conjunction with Ewan MacColl. 'The Fairfield apprentice' song was in the programme entitled *School.* 'It pinpointed the hardships on Clydeside in the "bad old days" – parish queues and all – people's utter dependence on the Clyde's industries.'

Ray Fisher has been recorded by Topic and by Leader.

Belle Stewart: *The berryfields o' Blair*
Kinross 1972; rec. P.C. SA 1972/188. (Farewell ceilidh)

(V.3) Noo there's traiv-'lers fae the Wes - tern Isles, fae

Ar-ran, Mull an' Skye, Fae Har-ris, Le-wis an'Kyles o'Bute they

come their luck tae try; Fae In-ver-ness and Ai-ber-deen, fae

Stor-no-way and Wick, A' flock tae Blair at the ber-ry-time the

straws an' rasps tae pick.

1.   Oh when berry-time comes roond each year, Blair's population swellin',
There's every kind o' picker there an' every kind o' dwellin'.
There's tents an' huts an' caravans, there's bothies and their bivvies,
And shelters made wi' tattie-bags an' dug-oots made wi' divvies.

2.   Noo there's corner-boys frae Glesgie, kettle-boilers fae Lochee,
An' miners fae the pits o' Fife, mill-workers fae Dundee,
An' fisher-folk fae Peterheid an' tramps fae everywhere
A' lookin' for a livin' aff the berryfields o' Blair.

3.   Noo there's traiv'lers fae the Western Isles, fae Arran, Mull an' Skye,
Fae Harris, Lewis an' Kyles o' Bute they come their luck tae try;
Fae Inverness and Aiberdeen, fae Stornoway and Wick,
A' flock tae Blair at the berry-time the straws and rasps tae pick.

4.   Noo there's some who earn a pound or twa, some cannae earn their keep,
      And some wad pick fae morn tae nicht, an' some wad raither sleep.
      But there's some wha has tae pick or stairve, and some wha dinnae care,
      And there's some wha bless, an' some wha curse, the berryfields o' Blair.

5.   Noo there's faimilies pickin' for one purse an' some wha pick alane,
      And there's men who share an share alike wi' wives that's no their ain.
      There's gladness and there's sadness tae, there's happy hairts an' sair,
      For there's comedy an' tragedy played on the fields o' Blair.

6.   But afore I put my pen awa' it's this I wad like to say,
      Ye'll traivel far before you'll meet a kinder lot than they,
      For I've mixed wi' them in field an' pub, and while I've breath to spare
      I'll bless the hand that led me tae the berryfields o' Blair.

Belle Stewart wrote these masterly words herself. As Geordie McIntyre points out in his sleeve notes for her disc,[23] 'this composition of Belle's, written in 1930 and set to "The Queer Folk o' the Shaws" or "Pair o' Nicky Tams" tune, had entered the anonymous stream of oral tradition before the authoress was known.' Her voice is somewhat lighter than that of her daughters Sheila and Cathy but is perhaps even more persuasive and flexible. In the first half of verse-lines one and four the tune shows the characteristic double tonic.

One of the chief means of livelihood of the travellers was and still is seasonal farm work, but people of many other different origins converge on the fertile fruit-growing land around Blairgowrie when the berries are ready for picking. The crop has been gathered every year since around the end of last century.

Songs, storytelling and instrumental music making often arose spontaneously after the day's work, in many a field or pub or around the camp-fires, and the scene came to be described as 'the first unofficial folk festival in Scotland'. When in 1966 the first Traditional Music and Song festival was held in this little town, it was in a sense simply a more organised version of what had already been going on for many years. (In 1971 the locale of this festival was changed to Kinross.)

Belle Stewart's compound of charm, friendliness and complete naturalness gives her instant audience appeal: she has them eating out of her hand before you can say 'The berryfields of Blair'.

Three other songs about work should be mentioned here: 'The wark o' the weavers' (AM1, Adam Young, Kinross 1975); 'Jute-mill song' (AM6, Bobby Dunbar, Kinross 1976) by Mary Brooksbank, a worker in the Dundee mills, which includes these memorable lines:

Oh dear me, the world's ill divided,
Them that works the hardest are the least provided;

and 'The Blantyre explosion' (SA 1973/111, Owen Costello, Kinross 1973) about a mining disaster. Versions of these, in the order given, are in *101 Scottish Songs, The Singing Island* and *A Collection of Scots Songs* (School of Scottish Studies).

Group 9: Sexual Symbolism

Bobby Dunbar: *Sprig o' thyme*
Kinross 1976; rec. A.P. AM 6.

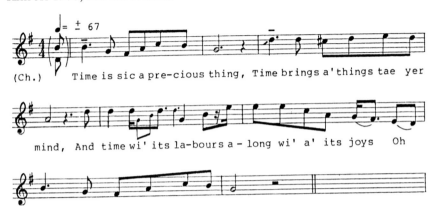

(Ch.) Time is sic a pre-cious thing, Time brings a' things tae yer

mind, And time wi' its la-bours a - long wi' a' its joys Oh

time brings a' things tae an end.

1. Aince I hed a sprig o' thyme,
   I thocht it never wad gae duin,
   But along there cam' a bonny sailor lad
   And he stole awa' ma sprig o' thyme.

   (*Chorus*)
   (For) time is sic a precious thing
   Time brings a' things tae yir mind,
   And time wi' its labours along wi' a' its joys
   Oh time brings a' things tae an end.

2. The sailor gied tae me a rose,
   He said it never wad decay,
   He gied it tae me tae mind me o' the day
   He stole awa' ma sprig o' thyme.

3. Come a' ye maidens young and fair
   That are juist noo bloomin' in yir prime,
   Oh I wad like to see ye keep yir gairdens clean
   And let nae man steal awa' yir thyme.

This is another reflective song, meditating on a matter of deep importance, whether time or thyme, and on the mysterious connection between the two. In *lingua franca* certain flowers are considered to represent human attributes: for instance thyme is virginity (though here it clearly means far more), the rose is passion, and so on. The song is related to 'The seeds of love'.[24]

Anna Knight gave another fine rendering of the song at Kinross in 1975, with several felicitous phrases. A possible conflation of these two versions is the following:

Line one of chorus: Time it is a precious thing…
Verse one as above.

Verse two, lines three and four: He gied it tae me tae mind me o' yon time,
'Twas then I heard ma mither say:
Verse three: Come a' ye maidens young and fair,
A' ye that are bloomin' in yir prime:
Now you be aware and keep yir gairdens fair
And let nae man steal awa' yir thyme.

Bobby Dunbar sings this with a lyrical simplicity. His own guitar accompaniment adds a welcome dimension, for this tune's harmonic implications seem to clamour for some concrete expression. When set down in cold print this tune does not 'look' so good: bars three-four in particular seem distressingly banal, with a kind of insipid sentimentality. Yet both the singers listened to make the song as a whole sound good, their performance causes the tune as it were to rise above itself. This shows the limitations of all transcription, descriptive or prescriptive. It also underlines the folly of judging either words or tune of a song in isolation one from the other. I have already referred to the transforming effect of music on words, and the same is true in reverse: good words can have a magical influence on the tune they are sung to.

A postal officer, Dunbar has lived in Elgin all his life apart from army service during the Second World War. He heard this from an Englishman, at a ceilidh in Torridon, and remembered that his mother used to sing it. He is a songwriter as well as singer.

Arthur Watson: *She was a rum one*
Blairgowrie 1970; rec. P.C. SA 1970/180.

1.   As I gaed oot on a fair muin nicht
On a fair muin nicht in winter,
It was there I spied a pretty fair maid,
(*Chorus*)
(An') she was a rum one, falla-diddle-i-do-ay,
But a bonny one, falla-diddle i-doh.

2. It's she's walked up an' she's walked doon
    An' I've walked close beside her,
    An' I've askit tae her ae reason why
    That she cuidna step nae wider.

3. 'Go 'way, go 'way, ye foolish young man
    An' stop yir idle talkin',
    For it ill becomes young men,' she said,
    'Tae pick up young weemen walkin'.'

4. 'But I'm a doctor tae ma trade
    An ma freends they cry me rare-O,
    An' gin ye tell me faur yir trouble lies
    I'll fix it neat an' fair-O.'

5. 'Oh ma trouble lies in atween ma thighs
    And it's there it is abidin',
    An' it kittles me baith nicht an' day
    An' it keeps me fae ma stridin'.'

6. Oh I laid her doon upon the bank
    An' I've provided the plaister;
    She's lowpt up tae her feet again
    And says, 'I think ye've cured me, maister.'

7. She's gien tae me ma winter's meat
    Likewise ma winter's firin';
    Far better than that she's gien tae me,
    It was a stable for ma stallion.

Arthur Watson of Aberdeen sings this vigorously, with an infectious lilt. In verse one, line four of the verse is missed out and so the tune goes straight from 'fair maid' to the chorus, with a quaver on low D for 'An''. Peter Hall tells me that Jeannie Robertson sang her verse one in exactly this way, so that yet again she was the revival source and many singers learned it from her. Old Davie Stewart also sang it. Arthur Watson thinks he learned it from Norman Kennedy, and adds that many people have asked him for the words – he still sings it. It could once have been a broadside, probably English (the travellers may have got it thus): the word 'rum', in the sense used here, is more an English than a Scots word. But the song has clearly become transmuted into something unmistakably Scottish.

Watson, director of the Aberdeen Artists' Printmaking Workshop, comments: 'I found the song totally irresistible, with amazing flow in both words and tune as if honed down with all irrelevant detail removed. The singer is, I think, deliberately understating the case of his conquest and, in the last triumphant verse, its permanence.'

Arthur Watson has been recorded by Topic.

Another song in this group is the much newer 'Oh Mither, Mither' by Sheila Douglas (Kinross 1976; rec. A.P. AM7). This entertaining dialogue between daughter and mother exploits the symbolism of various instruments; two deathless verses cannot possibly be omitted:

5.   Oh Mither, Mither, what can a lassie dae,
      If I'm coorted by a piper in the merry month of May?
      He has a braw chanter and his bag is never dry,
      And I'm feart I may rue it in the mornin' O.

6.   Oh lassie, lassie, when ye hear him play the ground,
      You'll learn the variations that mak' the pibroch sound.
      You'll forget aboot *ceol beag* when *ceol mor* comes around
      And never fear tae rue it in the mornin' O.

Group 10: Night-Visiting

The night-visiting custom is found in many countries, and the ambient mores are
varied. Ewan MacColl wrote, of the Scots and English tradition, 'The night-visit
was essentially a consummation of love sanctioned by the girl's parents on the
night before the wedding.'[25]

Belle Stewart: *Here's a health to all true lovers*
Blairgowrie 1970; rec. P.C. SA 1970-181.

1.   Here's a health to all true lovers
      And here's to mine wherever she may be.
      This very night I will go and see her
      Although she is many a long mile from me.

2.   Let the night be dark as the very dungeon,
      Let not a star shine from the bowl,
      Still I will be guided, oh safely guided,
      Into the arms of my own true love.

3.   He then approached her bedroom window,
      His knee he placed on a cold damp stone;
      Through the panes of glass he softly whispered,
      'My darling maid do you sleep alone?'

4.   She raised her head from her soft white pillow,
      Her hand she placed o'er her lily-white breast;
      Through the panes of glass she gently answered,
      'Who is this that disturbs my quiet night's rest?'

5.   ''Tis only I, my darlin' lover,
      Open the door love and let me in,
      For I am tired of this long night's journey
      And besides I am drenched to the very skin.'

6.   She opened the door with the greatest of pleasure,
      She opened the door and he walked in.
      They both embraced and they kissed each other
      Till the dawning of the day it came creeping in.

7.   'The cocks are crowing love I must be going,
      The cocks are crowing love I must away,
      The cocks are crowing love I must be going
      For we are but servants and I must obey.'

Both words and tune of this song are close to the version in *The Singing Island.*

This is Belle Stewart in her most seductive vein: her flexible voice glides and slides its way till one feels, if female, one would definitely open that door, and, if male, would consider the long walk and getting drenched to the skin (a good line, that) well worthwhile. The tune, with its swooping intervals, is in what would appear to be a favourite mode for the Stewarts: a minor inversion of the pentatonic scale. The form is ABCA¹.

The melody is sung so smoothly, with such roundness and such understatement of accentuation, that the transcription poses a problem in rhythm. The time is certainly triple, but the bar lines could all be placed one beat later.

Cilla Fisher, with Artie Tresize: *The laird o' Udny's wa's (This ae nicht)*
Kinross 1976; rec. A.P. AM7.

(V. 3)   When he got in he wes sae gled He pu'ed the bun-net frae

aff o' his head, He kissed her on the cheek sae red   And the

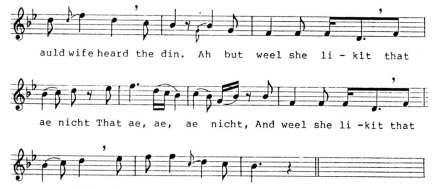

auld wife heard the din. Ah but weel she li - kit that

ae nicht That ae, ae, ae nicht, And weel she li -kit that

ae   nicht She let her lad-die in.

1.   Noo I'm the laird o' Udny's Wa's
      And I've come here withoot guid cause,
      And I've had mair than thirty fa's
      Comin oot owre the hill.
              Ah but let me in this ae nicht
              This ae, ae, ae nicht,
              Aye let me in this ae nicht
              And I'll be back nae mair.

2.   We'll oil the door when it gets weet
      And it'll neither chirp nor cheep,
      No it'll neither chirp nor cheep
      And I'll gae slippin' in.
              Ah but let me in this ae nicht,
              This ae, ae, ae nicht,
              Aye let me in this ae nicht
              And I'll be back nae mair.

3.   When he got in he wes sae gled
      He pu'ed the bunnet frae aff o' his head,
      He kissed her on the cheek sae red
      And the auld wife heard the din.
              Ah but weel she likit that ae nicht
              That ae, ae, ae nicht,
              And weel she likit that ae nicht
              She let her laddie in.

4.   For when he got in he wes sae gled
      He knockit the bottom boards oot o' the bed,
      He stole the lassie's maidenhead
      And the auld wife heard the din.
              But weel she likit that ae nicht
              That ae, ae, ae nicht,
              And weel she likit that ae nicht
              She let her laddie in.

Cilla Fisher and Artie Tresize have become increasing popular, and not only in Scotland. Cilla sings here in a relaxed, matter-of-fact way, with Artie's effective guitar backing, and everyone joins in the refrains.

A member of the famous Glasgow singing family, Cilla Fisher has been a professional singer for the last six years. She learned this song from Jimmy Hutchison around 1973 – she draws most of her material from source when possible. She writes: 'Seducation [sic] is timeless – so if it happened in a cottage or a block of flats it's the same. The theme is a story of an everyday happening (if you're lucky).'

Both words and tune of this song are almost identical with Jeannie Robertson's 'The laird o' Windy Wa's' on her EP disc, and on Prestige International no 13006. There is also a close resemblance in the words, though less in the tune, to 'As I cam' ower the Muir o' Ord' in the *Bothy Ballads* disc (*Scottish Tradition* series). The 'Muir of Ord' version has one appearance of the 'O she likit that ae nicht' theme (as in the second half of verses three and four above) but the ending is changed to 'For O she rued that ae nicht'. In the bothy version the use of the first person singular continues to the end, and the final effect is one of male boastfulness at success achieved against the woman's will. A whiff of this remains in the otherwise more equalitarian version given above.

Morag MacLeod comments on the differences between Scots and Gaelic songs in this genre:

Overt references to sexual success from the male point of view, boasting, almost, about stealing the girl's maidenhead and so on, hardly occur in Gaelic song. The majority of songs about sexual encounters are from the girl's point of view. Most of the bawdy songs in Scots probably originated in the bothy, and in such an exclusively male environment it would be natural for men to compensate for the lack of female company by talking and joking about women, boasting about their own sexual prowess and composing songs which were not meant for female ears.

Gaelic males did not suffer the same deprivations. At the same time, in many accounts of waulkings it is said that men were not allowed to be present, and among the waulking songs you get 'Young Alasdair son of MacNicol/I wish I could bear a son to you/Five or six or seven/...' The theme of women's songs relating to sexual encounters is more often regret: 'My laugh of last year/Has made my step heavier' and 'I had an apron of smooth silk/Prettily embroidered/And had I been so modest as to lie alone/I would not be heavy and pregnant under my apron.'

There are references to night-visiting from both viewpoints. There is no indication that the intimacies involved were reserved for the night before the wedding, but regular visits by the same suitor led to expectation of marriage. Disappointment in this expectation would lead to complaint, for example: 'That's how I passed the winter/Always longing for my sweetheart's love... Many a night throughout the season/Did I get up to the bench/My advice to other girls/Is to lie reasonably in their beds' (that is, not to bother with such a man!).

Songs by men about night-visits that give details, are usually humorous and self-deprecating. The element of forcing unwanted attentions on the girl does not show itself. Two friends decide to visit a girl in a shieling. When the bard approaches her she turns him down at first, but then she says, 'All right, then, put off your clothes/I'll let you lie beside me/For fear you may satirise me/And not for love of your charms.' There is an equality here that is missing, I think, in the Scots songs on this subject. This is not to say, of course, that Gaelic men did not take advantage of girls. But they did not make songs about it.

Cilla Fisher has been recorded by Topic, Autogram, Trailer/Leader, Kettle, and the BBC.

Group 11: Elegiac

Lizzie Higgins: *The college boy*
Aberdeen 1970; rec. A.M. SA 1970/20.

1.   Oh father, dear father, pray what is this ye've done?
      You have wed me to a college boy, a boy that's far too young,
      For he is only sixteen years and I am twenty-one;
      He's ma bonny, bonny boy, and he's growin'.

2.   As we were going through College wyn' some boys were playing ball
      When there I saw my own true love, the fairest of them all,
      When there I saw my own true love, the fairest of them all;
      He's ma bonny, bonny boy, and he's growin'.

3.   At the age of sixteen years he was a married man,
      An' at the age of seventeen the father of a son,
      An' at the age of twenty-one he did become a man,
      Though the green grass o'er his grave it was growin'.

4.   I will buy my love some flannel an' I'll make my love's shroud,
      With every stitch I put in it the tears will flow down.
      With every stitch I put in it the tears will flow down
      For cruel fate put an end to his growin'.

Only verse one begins half a bar earlier on high F, and descends by a step and leaps to low D as here at 'years' in bar two.

In the passage from his *History of England* quoted above (in the notes for 'Andrew Lammie') Trevelyan continues: 'Betrothal often took place when one or both of the parties was in the cradle, and marriage when they were scarcely out of the nurses' charge.'

This is Lizzie Higgins's own version, both words and tune, of 'The College Boy', sung here with all the impressive dignity and restraint at her command. She underlines the point that, after this arranged marriage took place, the girl 'fell very much in love with her young husband'. Other versions are known as 'The trees they do grow high', 'Still growing', 'Lang a-growing', 'Lady Mary Ann' and 'Young Craigston'. Interesting notes on the last named can be found in *The Singing Island*.

Lizzie Higgins uses ornamentation as an important means to expressiveness. Now a tendency towards increased ornamentation has been a feature of revival singing in recent years. The original impetus towards this probably came from Ireland, but as Peter Hall points out in his notes on her last record, *Up an' awa' wi' the Laverock*, the suggestion made by Hamish Henderson that her ornamented singing style 'almost recalls the *sean-nos* of the West of Ireland'[26] is mistaken, for, says Hall, 'her style is distinctly Scots'. He quotes Samuel Bayard's description of Irish ornamentation as 'almost impeding the onward course of the melody', and as 'wavering and unemphatic', and rightly comments, 'This could never be a description of Lizzie's style'.

She was of course strongly influenced by her famous mother Jeannie Robertson, but she was also influenced by her father Donald Higgins, a fine player of the Highland bagpipes and no mean singer himself. There has been much debate concerning Lizzie's claim that her father taught her to imitate the ornaments of pipe music. To reproduce these ornaments vocally is literally a physical impossibility, and Lizzie has certainly been influenced by the general trend towards increased decoration. Nevertheless there's an unmistakable sound of the pipes in her singing – including, in some ways as yet not fully analysed, her ornamentation. More laboratory analysis needs to be done on this. But, '...it is possible that her comparative lack of dynamic variation and her freedom from vibrato may be attributable to the strong influence of pipe music, since one of the chief characteristics of this music is its unwavering uniformity of volume'.[27]

If you have never heard Lizzie Higgins sing, you have an unforgettable and unique musical experience yet to come. Her voice combines a husky tone, a kind of gutsiness, with a bell-like quality and very true pitch. Her large repertoire varies from the big ballads, or muckle sangs, to lighter songs such as the entrancing little 'Tammy Toddles' which she sings to a strathspey-type tune.

Annie Bell: *Rare Willie drooned in Yarrow* (Child 215)
Kinross 1975; rec. A.P. AM2.

Down in yon gar-den sweet and gay Where bon-ny grows the

li-ly, I heard a mai-den sing-in' say, "My wish is wi' sweet

Wil-lie, My wish is wi' sweet Wil-lie".

1.   Down in yon garden sweet and gay
      Where bonny grows the lily,
      I heard a maiden singin' say,
      'My wish is wi' sweet Willie,
      My wish is wi' sweet Willie.

2.   For Willie's fair and Willie's rare
      And Willie's wondrous bonny,
      And Willie's hecht tae mairry me
      Gin e'er he mairries ony,
      Gin e'er he mairries ony.

3.   But Willie's gaen whom I thocht on
      And does not hear me weepin',
      O spare a tear frae true love's e'e(n)
      When other maids are sleepin',
      When other maids are sleepin'.

4.   Oh gentle wind that bloweth south
      From where my love repaireth,
      Carry a kiss from his sweet mouth
      And tell me how he fareth,
      And tell me how he fareth.

5.   And tell sweet Willie tae come doon
      And hear the mavis singin',
      Tae see the birds on ilka bush
      And leaves aroond them hingin',
      And leaves aroond them hingin'.

6.   She socht him east, she socht him west,
      She socht him braid and narrow;
      Syne in the cleavin' o' a craig
      She fund him droon'd in Yarrow,
      She fund him droon'd in Yarrow.

John Barrow: *Rare Willie drooned in Yarrow* (Child 215)
Kinross 1973; rec. A.M. SA 1973/112.

Oh Wil-lie's fair and Wil-lie's rare And Wil-lie's won-drous

bon-ny, And Wil-lie hecht tae mar-ry me Gin e'er he mar-ried

o - ny.

1. Oh Willie's fair and Willie's rare
    And Willie's wondrous bonny,
    And Willie hecht tae marry me
    Gin e'er he married ony.

2. Yestreen I made ma bed fu' braid,
    The nicht I'll mak' it narra,
    An' a' the live-long winter's night
    I lie twined of me marra.

3. O come ye by yon water-side,
    Pulled you the rose or lily?
    Oh come ye by yon meadow green
    Or ye saw ye ma sweet Willie?

4. Oh she sought him east an' she sought him west,
    She sought him braid and narra;
    Syne in the cliftin' o' a crag
    She found him drowned in Yarrow.

Annie Bell of Blairgrowrie was born and brought up in Fife, and she has also lived in the Borders and in Angus. She is well known at Kinross Festival as a champion whistler, diddler and melodeon player, has adjudicated for these classes and been a guest artiste. In recent years she has added singing to her accomplishments: she prefers 'good Scots songs with good lyrics', and finds some of the longer traditional songs 'repetitive and boring…too much dwelling on the theme of death'.

The mixture of styles in this version is most striking in verse four, which in contrast to the rest contains no Scots words or pronunciations. She found it in a book in her local library. Various collections, such as Greig's *Folk Song of the North East*, Palgrave's *Golden Treasury*, and Robert Chamber's *Scottish Ballads* include six similar verses. The beautiful tune (no. 5 in Bronson) was learned orally from other singers. Annie Bell sings flowingly in moderately free time and with some variation in dynamics, and her clear, true voice is pitched in a high register.

The words of John Barrow's version are Child A, with a few Tyneside pronunciations: he got it from *A Book of Scottish Verse* (Mackie, 1960). Its brevity
was an attraction to him at that time. Not knowing of any tune for this Border
ballad when he first found it, he made up his own – and a very good tune it is,
suitable to the elegiac words. It is sung quietly and with warmth.

Barrow was director of Edinburgh Folk Festival for its first four years. He regards this as 'a fairly straight love song ending in tragedy', but to Annie Bell it is
'a song of unrequited love where the heroine gives love which is not returned,
and because of this fact, rather than let her down or marry her, he decides to take
his life.' It is clear that a singer may put his or her own interpretation into a song,
with the aid of imagination, memory or fantasy.

Group 12: Exile and Emigration

Willie Scott: *Jamie Raeburn*
Blairgowrie 1970; rec. P.C. SA 1970/179.

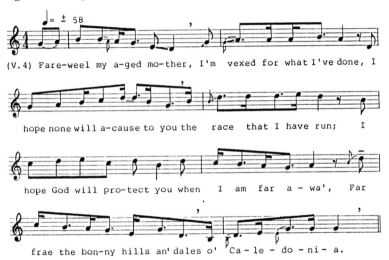

(V.4) Fare-weel my a-ged mo-ther, I'm vexed for what I've done, I
hope none will a-cause to you the race that I have run; I
hope God will pro-tect you when I am far a - wa', Far
frae the bon-ny hills an' dales o' Ca - le - do - ni - a.

1. My name is Jamie Raeburn, in Glasgow I was born.
    My place of habitation I now maun leave wi scorn,
    My place of habitation I now maun gang awa'
    Far frae the bonny hills an' dales o' Caledonia.

2. It was early one morning just by the break o' day.
    I overheard the turnkey, which unto us did say,
    'Arise ye helpless convicts, arise ye yin and a',
    This is the day that we maun stray frae Caledonia.'

3. We all arose, pit on oor clothes, oor hairts were filled wi' grief,
    And a' oor freends stood roond the coach, to grant us nae relief,
    And a' oor freends stood roond the coach to see us gang awa',
    Tae see us leave the hills an' dales o' Caledonia.

4.   Fareweel my aged mother, I'm vexed for what I've done,
     I hope none will a-cause to you the race that I have run;
     I hope God will protect you when I am far awa',
     Far frae the bonny hills an' dales o' Caledonia.

5.   Fareweel my aged faither, he is the best o' men,
     Likewise my sweetheart, young Catherine was her name.
     Nae mair I'll walk by Clyde's clear stream or by the Broomielaw,
     Fareweel my freends, ye hills an' dales, o' Caledonia.

6.   But oh perchance we'll meet again, I hope 'twill be above
     Where hallelujahs will be sung to him wha rules in love.
     Nae earthly judge shall judge us there, but him wha rules us a'.
     Fareweel my freends, ye hills an' dales, o' Caledonia.

It is not so long ago that comparatively trivial offences such as poaching
could be punished by transportation for life to a convict settlement, such as Van
Diemen's Land (see *MacCall's Personal Choice* for a song with this title).
'Jamie Raeburn', which describes the convicts' farewells in harrowing detail, is
sung here by a veteran and much-travelled singer, a retired shepherd now in his
eighties: Willie Scott of Hawick, known as the Border Shepherd. He is a source
rather than a revival singer, in that he has absorbed his large repertoire of songs
from his earliest years on, but he has been closely involved in revival events, and
at festivals he has been an invited guest or adjudicator. He uses his rather light
tenor voice with great musical charm and his enunciation is clear but unforced,
with the added bonus of a fine Border accent. Scott says, 'My mother used to
sing "Jimmy Raeburn" when I was a wee boy, and my brother Tom gave me the
words before I left school.' He has a special feeling for this 'great song', and
comments, 'A shepherd has to be responsible for his sheep, and if not is just not
wanted. Long ago sheep stealers were hanged… As far as I have been told, he
[Jamie Raeburn] stole a hen – and that was what he was transported for – and his
girlfriend said he was not near the place as they had a date that night.'
    'Jamie Raeburn' has been recorded by Willie Scott in *Border Ballads* (Topic
12T 183).

Group 13: Wanderers' Songs

Charlie Murray: *Tramps an' hawkers*
Blairgowrie 1970; rec. P.C. SA 1970/184

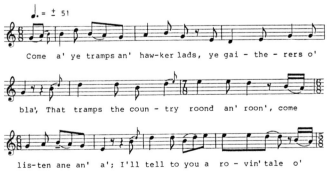

Come a' ye tramps an' haw-ker lads, ye gai - the - rers o'
bla', That tramps the coun - try roond an' roon', come
lis-ten ane an' a'; I'll tell to you a ro - vin' tale o'

sichts that I hae seen Far up in-tae the sno-wy north an'

sooth by Gret-na Green.

1. Come a' ye tramps an' hawker lads, ye gaitherers o' bla',
    That tramps the country roond an' roon', come listen ane an' a';
    I'll tell to you a rovin' tale o' sichts that I hae seen
    Far up intae the snowy north an' sooth by Gretna Green.

2. I have seen the high Ben Nevis 'way towerin' tae the muin,
    I have been by Crieff and Callander an' roond by bonnie Doon,
    An' by the Nethy's silvery sands and places ill tae ken
    Far up intae the snowy north lies Urquhart's fairy glen.

3. Noo I aften laugh untae masel' when trudgin' on the road,
    A bag o' bla' upon ma back, my face as broon's a toad,
    Wi' lumps o' cake an' tattie scones, wi' cheese an' braxy ham,
    Wi' little thocht whae far I've come an' less where I am gaun.

4. Noo I've dene ma share o' huntin' wi' the gagers on the Clyde.
    I've helped in Buckie trawlers hawl the herrin' owre the side.
    I've helped tae build the mighty bridge that spans the hazy Forth,
    An' wi' mony an Angus fairmer I hae ploo'ed the banks o' Esk.

5. Noo I'm happy in the summer time beneath the bright blue sky,
    Little kennin' in the mornin' where at nicht I'll hae tae lie,
    In barn or byre, or anywhere, dossin' oot amang the hay,
    An' if the weather suits me right I'm happy every day.

6. Noo Loch Katrine an' Loch Lomond, they've a' been seen by me,
    The Dee, the Don, the Deveron hurries tae the sea.
    Dunrobin Castle, by the way, I very near forgot,
    And aye the rickle o' cairn marks the hoose o' John o' Groats.

7. Noo I'm often doon by Gallowa' and roon' aboot Stranraer,
    My business takes me anywhere, sure I've wandered near and far;
    I've got the rovin' notion there's nothing what I loss
    In a' ma days, ma daily fare, an' what'll pey my doss.

8. But I think I'll go to Paddy's land, I'm makin' up ma min',
    For Scotland's fairly altered noo, I canna raise the win'.
    But I will trust in providence, if providence proves true,
    Then I will sing of Erin's isle when I come back to you.

This song breathes the very essence of the nomadic life – but the speaker is an itinerant worker, not a layabout: a loner describing the different jobs he has done and the places he has visited. Unlike Woody Guthrie's migrant workers, forced to travel in search of work, this man has chosen his way of life and enjoys it.

Charlie Murray of Forfar, a weel-kent figure on the East and North-East scene, has a really beautiful voice with a relaxed, vigorous springing quality. He got this song from Jimmy MacBeath at Banff feeing market, around 1934–35 when MacBeath was in his heyday as an itinerant singer. The fourth verse is less well-known, and Murray says he 'concocted' the last line himself. He has been recorded by Tangent, Springthyme, and BBC records.

Charlie Murray has always worked as a cattleman, in Banff, Ross-shire (Black Isle) and now Forfar district. He learned a few songs from his parents, and others from street singers and from old 78 records. Of 'Tramps and Hawkers', he says, 'In Jimmy MacBeath's case I think he let the establishment know that despite hardships and harassment by police to street singers, he made a living by what he liked doing. Farm work in the thirties was rough, for little reward, and I think if I had not had family responsibilities in early life, I would have liked to have done the same as Jimmy.'

Ray Fisher: *The moving on song*
Heriot-Watt University Students' Union, Edinburgh 1971; rec. A.M. SA 1971/13.

(V. 3) Born on a com-mon near a buil-ding site Where the ground is rut-ted wi' trac-tors' wheels. The lo-cal peo-ple said to me, "You lower the price of our pro-per-ty. (Ch.) You bet-ter get born in some place else, Oh move a-long, get a-long, move a-long, get a-long, Go! Move! Shift!".

1. Born in the middle o' the afternoon
    In a horse-drawn wagon on the old A5;
    The big twelve-wheeler shook my bed.
    'You can't stop here,' the policeman said –

(*Chorus*)
'You better get born in some place else,
Oh move along, get along, move along, get along,
Go! Move! Shift!'

2.   Born at the tattie-lifting time,
      In an auld bell-tent near a tattie-field.
      The fairmer says, 'The work's a' done,
      It's time that you were movin' on.'

3.   Born on a common near a building site
      Where the ground is rutted wi' tractors wheels.
      The local people said to me,
      'You lower the price of our property.'

4.   Born at the back of a blackthorn hedge
      When the white hoar frost lay on the ground.
      No eastern kings came bearing gifts,
      Instead, the order came tae shift.

5.   Wagon, tent or trailer-born
      Last week, last year, or in far-off days,
      Born here or a thousand miles away
      There's always men near-by who'll say –

Ray Fisher

This was written and composed by Ewan MacColl for one of his *Radio Ballad* documentaries. On the present tape Ray Fisher, who accompanies herself again on guitar, introduces the song, talks about the *Radio Ballads* and continues: 'This one, *The Travellers*, was about tinkers and travellers all over Britain, who have been regarded as social misfits, people who wouldn't conform...the attitude to them has been "We don't want you". Here, the woman is about to give birth in a covered wagon by the side of the road...a police car arrives, the family are told to move on...so the child is born...on the road.'

Remarks earlier on Fisher's style apply equally here: her 'Go! Move! Shift!'

is quietly electrifying, and her occasional vocal rubato is even more free. There are few Scots words here for as she suggests, the song was written about the whole of Britain. The last two verses widen the horizons even further and it becomes a song about the whole world. 'This song has a lasting message,' Ray says, 'always minority groups will be seen as a threat.'

Group 14: The Supernatural

Lizzie Higgins: *Willie's fatal visit* (Child 255)
Aberdeen 1973; rec. S.S. SA 1973/174.

1. Wullie's gane owre yon high, high hills
    An' doon yon dowie dens,
    It is there he met a grievious ghost
    That wid fear ten thousand men.

2. 'Oft hae ye travelled this road, Wullie,
    Oft hae ye travelled in sin,
    Ne'er thocht ye o' my poor soul
    When yir sinful life did end.

3. Oft hae ye travelled this road, Wullie,
    Yir bonny new love tae see.
    Nae mair ye'll travel this road, Wullie,
    For this nicht avenged I'll be.'

4. She has ta'en her perjured love
    And she's rived him frae gair tae gair,
    An' on ilkae side o' Mary's stile
    Of him she's hung a share.

5. Yir father an' mither baith made moan
    Yir new love muckle mair,
    Yir father an' mither baith made moan
    An' yir new love rived her hair.

No-one else can make your flesh creep quite as Lizzie Higgins does in this spine-chilling ballad. She got it from her mother and has honed it down to its stark essentials. Jeannie Robertson's, both words and tune, is the second of Bronson's two versions; Child has only one. Her version has two important additions (verse three above) which confirm the revenant-as-jilted-love hypothesis: 'Your bonny love' becomes 'Your bonny new love', and the last line introduces the revenge declaration. Child's final comment, 'Stanzas 15–17' (in effect verses 2–4 above) 'are...too good for the setting: nothing so spirited, word or deed, could have been looked for from a ghost wan, weary and smiling', suggests that he had not considered this hypothesis, for he would surely have remembered that jealousy is cruel as the grave.

Jimmy Hutchison also sings this ballad, and his comments suggest a further twist to this grisly tale: '...it would lose a lot of its weight if the ghost was not that of Willie's jilted girlfriend seeking her revenge. It does not say in the song how she came to be dead but I would think that Willie himself bumped her off so that he could take up with his new love. This would make a double revenge and twice as sweet maybe? Or she might have died of a broken heart as they did in those days, but I think myself that Willie dunnit.'

Higgins herself adds the final, Hardy-esque touch: '...the sweetheart he murdered was going to have a baby, but I'm very glad to say she avenged her murder by killing him, just as he had killed her without any compassion at all.'

Lizzie Higgins sings this on *Ballad Folk* (BBC REC 293).

Group 15: Philosophical

Adam Young: *If ye only wait a wee*
Kinross 1977; rec. A.P. AM10.

Oh I heard a mi-ther sin-gin' tae her wee slee-py wean, And

oft-times frae the hill-side cam' a soft an' sweet re-frain; But of

all the songs that touch the hairt an' haunt us till we dee, It was

"Din-na get doon-hair-ted, lad-die, learn tae wait a wee".

1. Oh I heard a mither singin' tae her wee sleepy wean,
    And oft-times frae the hillside cam' a soft an' sweet refrain;
    But of all the sangs that touch the hairt an' haunt us till we dee,
    It was 'Dinna get doonhairted, laddie, learn tae wait a wee.'

2. Noo ye dinna get doonhairted though the plains be clad wi' snaw,
    For the sun will still be shinin' and the gentle breeze will blaw;
    Though ye dinna see the mavis or the larks abuin the lea,
    They will set the echoes ringin' if ye only wait a wee.

3. Noo ye canna sail life's oceans 'neath a sky o' simmer blue,
    For there's oft-times stormy seasons that we all maun westle through;
    But there's aye a silver linin' tae the darkest cloud we see
    And yir boat will reach the harbour if ye only wait a wee.

This song creates a powerful impact, due partly to the way it is put over: Adam Young is 'unashamed of soul', yet he eschews any hint of sentimentality. He says, 'This song has a general and sincere meaning of truth in it.' One feels a whole lifetime of experience is being poured out, for he is not a young man and indeed the slightly laboured quality of his voice has perhaps a greater effect here than a young fresh voice could achieve. But it is not only the singer's personality and style that makes this performance moving, the song itself contains the essence of good popular art. The tune has vitality of shape and of form, and the words with their graphic imagery – the iron grip of winter, the desperate situation of a storm at sea – illumine the theme and say more than many sermons or philosophical treatises. The opening verse suggests a kind of universal mother singing to all of earth's children. Adam learned this song when he was at school, and it was recorded on an old 78 record by the late Neil MacLean.

Footnotes

1. Stevenson, 1914, pp. 171–2.
2. *The Concise Oxford Dictionary*, 7th edition, Oxford 1982.
3. *Bothy Ballads*, no. 1 in *Scottish Tradition* series, CTRAX 9001 and CDTRAX 9001, 1993. First published 1971.
4. Descriptive transcription: writing down what has actually *been* sung or played. Prescriptive notation sets down the music *to be* sung or played, with the composer's instructions concerning tempo, dynamics and expression or interpretation.
5. The fourth and last volume contains some more detailed transcriptions.
6. *Scottish Studies* vol. 14, 1970, pp. 35–58 and pp. 155–88, and vol. 16, 1972, pp. 139–59. Also Percy Grainger, *Journal of the Folk Song* Society vol. 3, 1908–9, pp. 147–242.
7. See Karpeles 1987, pp. 31–8; Collinson 1970, pp. 4–10 and 10–21; and Bronson 1959, vol. 1, p. xxviii, and vol. 2, pp. xi–xiii. Also see Marcia Herndon, 'Analysis: the Herding of Sacred Cows?', *Ethnomusicology* vol. 18, 1974, pp. 219–63.
8. Alison McMorland, *The Belt wi' Colours Three*, Tangent TGS 125. This disc includes Sheila Douglas's 'O Mither, Mither'.
9. Hunter 1978, p. 12. See Dobash and Dobash 1992, also *Scottish Women's Aid Annual Report 1992/93* and previous reports.
10. See also Cowan ed. 1980, pp. 48–51.
11. The rhythmic figures ♩ ₃ ♪ and ♪ ₃ are sometimes interchanged here with ♩. ♩ and ♪ ♩. ; this practice is common.

12. Herd, 1776, vol. 2, p. 232.
13. Norman Buchan, 20 August 1977, Edinburgh.
14. MacColl, 1960, p. 32.
15. *The Muckle Sangs*, no. 5 in *Scottish Traditions* series, CTRAX 9005 and CDTRAX 9005, 1992. First published 1975 and 1979.
16. Jane Turriff, 8 November 1976, Fetterangus.
17. Quoted by Woolf, 1945, p. 36.
18. Hunter, 1978, p. 103.
19. Kinsley, 1971, p. 480.
20. Crawford, 1960, p. 239.
21. Collinson, 1970, pp. 1–3.
22. *Jeannie's Merry Muse* disc, EMI 7EG 8534.
23. Belle Stewart, *Queen Among the Heather* disc, Topic 12TS 307.
24. Reeves, 1960, p. 3.
25. MacColl, 1960, p. 14.
26. *The Muckle Sangs* booklet, see n. 15.
27. See Ailie Munro, 'Lizzie Higgins and the Oral Transmission of Ten Child Ballads', *Scottish Studies* vol. 14, 1970, pp. 155–88; and Munro's review of Higgins' disc 'Up an' Awa' wi' the Laverock', *Traditional Music,* no. 6, 1977, Peter Hall's notes on this disc, Topic 12TS 260 and on *The Back of Bennachie* disc Topic 12T 180, Stephanie Smith, 'A Study of Lizzie Higgins as a transitional figure in the development of oral tradition in the Northeast of Scotland', University of Edinburgh M. Litt. thesis, 1975, and Ray Fisher 'Uniquely Lizzie', *English Dance and Song*, vol. 55, no. 2, summer 1993.

Jim Sutherland   Gordeanna MacCulloch   Dick Gaughan

Allan Morris   Cy Laurie   Eileen Penman

Heather Heywood   Peter Hall   Sheena Wellington

Sheila Douglas   Stanley Robertson

V *Folk Revival in Gaelic Song*
by Morag MacLeod

If all the music in the world was cut off, the music of the Western Isles would serve the whole world![1]
Nan Mackinnon, Vatersay

It may have become tedious to quibble at the use of the term 'folk' with reference to a certain category of song, and to quote the clichéd expression of the American who said 'All music's folk music: leastways I never heard of no horse making it,' but when prestigious writers like Hugh MacDiarmid equate 'folk' with 'peasant' (Chapter III), some attempt must be made to set the record straight. Not that one is making a qualitative assessment of any class of society, but one must try to present the facts as they stand. I will generally use the term 'traditional' instead of 'folk' With Gaelic song it is even more important to make the distinction than it is in Scots or English, and in order to explain why, I shall start by relating, as briefly as possible, something of the various categories of song that exist.

As far as culture was concerned, Gaelic society was very much male-dominated. Musicians and poets were professional people attached to the houses of the clan chiefs. These artists, whose offices were hereditary, had to undergo a rigid training and the trained poets used very elaborate metrical systems to make poems about events pertaining to the clan. On important occasions these poems were recited, to the accompaniment of the harp. Harpers could also compose songs. Social stratification was in terms of closeness in kinship to the clan chief. Younger sons of younger sons were lower in the scale, but still part of any social occasion within the clan.

The trained poets composed in a literary language and in a variety of syllabic metres – that is, in metres based on the number of syllables per line – a form that scholars believe originated from early Christian Latin hymns. Untrained poets came to use different kinds of metre with measured stresses rather than syllables. One of these metres, which is sometimes referred to as bardic because of its strong connection with a grade of poet called bards, consisted of a varying number of lines containing x stresses and a final line of x+1 stresses.

Harpers too were known to compose poetry and, judging by surviving examples, this was also of a type which employed regularly spaced stresses. The verses tended (within the poem) to be of the same length, usually of four, eight or sixteen lines. Number 16 in the School of Scottish Studies *Scottish Tradition* series, *Gaelic Bards and Minstrels,* illustrates poems in bardic metre and in the other one used by the harpers, amhran, in their sung settings. The publication contains seventeen examples of one and eighteen of the other, sung by William Matheson.[2]

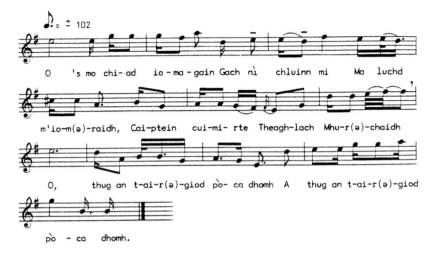

O 's mo chi-ad io-ma-gain Gach nì chluinn mi Ma luchd

m'io-m(ə)-raidh, Cai-ptein cui-mi- rte Theagh-lach Mhu-r(ə)-chaidh

O, thug an t-ai-r(ə)-giod pò- ca dhomh A thug an t-ai-r(ə)-giod

pò - ca dhomh.

My greatest concern
In all that I hear
Of the people I mention,
A handsome captain
Of the family of Murdoch
Who gave me the pocket money.

The largest coin,
Great in value,
Great in profit,
From your comely hand;
And the intrepid men
Who hunted in the high mountains

Happily would I
Travel to your homestead,
Wine and feasting,
Pipes sounding,
Wax candles
And witty sociable young men

Versatile youths
Hardy and vigorous,
Who could fold sails
On a squally day,
They would not be weaklings
Sailing to Stornoway.

Greatly would I like to have
Seaworthy ships
Shod with iron
And ropes steadying them,
And splendid young men
Who were skilful at sailing.

To go to your homestead,
With its firearms,
Your hunting on the mountains,
Your slender deer-hounds,
And your men
Busy roasting wild fowl.[3]

Most types of Gaelic song may be traced back to those three. Musically, syllabic verse seems to have been chanted. Bardic verse seems to have been set to very distinctive melodies, as the form of the poetry itself is distinctive. Melodies attached to the amhran type – the type most commonly used by harpers – have an international flavour.[4]

Even before the break-up of the clan system in the eighteenth century, the professional poets and musicians who had depended on the native aristocracy for their livelihood had already, due to social changes, become reduced to the status of the ordinary people. But there are still people alive who can trace their ancestry back to members of this privileged professional caste of artists – poets and musicians.

While the earlier system still flourished, the trained poets, in common with their counterparts in Ireland, composed in an archaistic and specialised form of Gaelic, whereas the untrained bards and harpers tended to use the vernacular of their day. It was all what could be termed 'heroic' poetry even if the subjects were not invariably serious, especially in the harpers' compositions. Women were not expected to compose such songs, and there are legends regarding some of those who did being buried face downwards. Women of high rank who composed conventional men's verse were tolerated, but regarded as almost immoral. It must, however, have been mainly women – not always aristocratic – who composed choral songs, which were sung by a soloist for the verses while others would join in the chorus. Of such were the work songs, adapted for various purposes such as waulking (that is, shrinking home-woven cloth), milking, churning or reaping, which have come down in oral tradition to the present day.

In the course of the eighteenth century – though there are significant earlier examples – it became common for other poets, not connected with the clan chief in a professional way, to compose poems which described and praised nature, and eulogies and elegies for their chiefs and others. From that time the composition of syllabic verse virtually ceased except for a specific type of eight-line verse; such verse was used by poets until recent times, and there may still be examples of it being produced. It is always sung to close variants of the same melody. (It probably survived for so long because of this. The composers were certainly not consciously following any but the most basic rules of rhyme and were not counting the numbers of syllables very carefully). Bardic verse is seldom heard sung now except in a form with three-line verses. But a large number of songs extant in oral tradition can be dated to the seventeenth century and earlier.

An example of syllabic verse is the Heroic or Ossianic ballad, also sometimes referred to as Fenian ballad. Ossian, the legendary poet of Scottish and Irish tradition, was reputed to have been the last survivor of the Fianna, or Fenians, whose exploits he was believed to have celebrated in song. These ballads – probably medieval in origin – are in syllabic metre and were sung in Gaelic-speaking areas until quite recently. There are ballads from other cycles of Celtic hero tales as well. The oldest written sources for these heroic ballads are manuscripts of the medieval period. And there lies a crucial factor in any discussion of folk songs in Gaelic. A great many Gaelic songs in fact – and not only those very early examples – owe at least some part of their transmission down to modern times, to written sources of one kind or another. The largest corpus which came from mainly oral tradition, with regard to verbal text, belongs to the work-song category, and there are a few others of the amhran type still extant, which may not have been written down until relatively recently.

For the melodies of songs, however, as distinct from the verbal text, we have to rely almost entirely on oral tradition. Most poems were expected to be sung, but most written sources for the melodies are almost negligible. Some are arranged for instrumental performances, and some are written in rhythms and stress patterns that suit the English translation only. All in all, the reader has almost to know the tune already before he can use the written source, and only a few scholars take the trouble to learn the melodies in that way. And yet, even to the present day, melodies can be found for songs that were previously thought to exist only in verbal form.

While verbal texts may have come from written sources originally, they have often been learned through oral transmission. This is natural, as tunes and words would be learned together, although non-singers may sometimes recite songs. You therefore have a situation where large amounts of sophisticated poetry are committed to memory by people of all classes and educational levels – as if dustmen, engineers, schoolteachers, labourers, nurses and doctors could recite chunks of *Marmion, Paradise Lost* or *Morte d'Arthur*. It is only fair to say, however, that there were individuals and families who had a better oral tradition than others.[5]

Where could one hear such songs? One must avoid the danger of presenting an idyllic picture of an entirely musical existence on the croft, but there is no doubt that music – oral or instrumental – played a very important part in people's lives. In more recent times and up until the early 1950s the ceilidh house was a feature of rural and island life. Any house would have potential for a ceilidh – topical discussions, storytelling, singing, reciting poetry – as long as the household was hospitable, but there were some that were more popular than others. Such houses would probably be the venue for tellers of tales, with or without melodies attached, and the syllabic and bardic songs would be sung there, along with songs in lighter vein and recent local compositions of all kinds. Another locale for songs in general was weddings and all the gatherings connected with them. Songs with refrains and a good beat were especially popular at weddings, when the company would stand in a circle holding hands and stamping their feet, endangering the floor boards. It was very important to know a few songs of this kind if you had a reputation as a singer, and I have heard of singers hearing a song of twenty verses or more for the first time, and then singing it faultlessly at the wedding the following day. Women sang at shielings, the temporary dwellings where they lived in the summer months while looking after the cattle. Finally, there were songs for accompanying work and other activities.

People sang to themselves while carding, spinning or weaving, for which any variety of rhythms could be adapted. They sang in stricter rhythm when rocking a baby, or playing with him, and when milking cows. On suitable occasions they sang communally, reaping, rowing, hauling in fishing nets, waulking tweed, (that is, beating it against a board, wet and soaped, in order to wash it and shrink it[6]). Occasionally they sang for dancing.

The culture changed when the social organisation changed and everything that I have mentioned above was subject to this. The introduction of hydro-electric power has probably had the most far reaching effect on the social organisation, combined with improvements in the financial status of people in rural areas. Beautiful light-coloured carpets, which became practical because they could be kept clean by electric vacuum cleaners, are discouraging to courteous visitors who are afraid they might dirty them. With electricity came facilities for television reception, and soon every household had a set. This not only caused people to stay at home instead of going to visit friends, but it discouraged them from visiting because, when they did so, the television set was often not even switched off in the house they were visiting. The ceilidh house gradually became a very rare commodity.

Holding wedding receptions in houses created a lot of work for the families concerned and it became fashionable after a time for them to be left in the capable hands of hotel proprietors. Although weddings in hotels remained a source of opportunity for potential singers, they ceased to be so to the same extent as previously.

These changes came gradually, but were much accelerated by the two World Wars for various reasons, partly because, having served in the armed forces, young people got the taste for a different kind of life. Educational opportunities were improved and alternatives to crofting began to be considered. As there were no opportunities for learning a profession and few for learning a skilled trade within the Gaelic-speaking areas, the tendency was to move south and the population that was left consequently became an ageing one. The emigrants learned new ways, new songs, new stories. They also sent money home, they bought furniture and soft furnishings and generally helped to improve the standard of living in the home they had left behind – hence, in some parts, the carpets, the electric sweepers, the television sets. At the same time, the mills took over the finishing process for any tweed that was made. Engines were well established by then, replacing sails and oars. Gradually, inhabitants of rural areas took to the machine and to an easier life. New ideas about the upbringing of children, smaller families and therefore less help for a busy mother (older girls in large families played a crucial part in the upbringing of their infant siblings) must have put a stop to the singing of lullabies. But, above all, the improvement in communications caused the Gael, who had for so long and for diverse reasons thought that he was no good, to imitate what he saw his Lowland compatriots doing, having learned this through his own travels, through tales brought home by relatives or through radio and television. As part of this improvement in his status, he tended to dismiss Gaelic as a viable language, and many despised everything connected with it. Schools in general encouraged this attitude.

Changes had been taking place long before the two World Wars. Round about the beginning of the century the movement, partly encouraged by Queen Victoria's example, which made it fashionable to travel in the Highlands, had some influence on the islands as well. Writers of travel books and artists 'discovered' the Hebrides and, in their wake, collectors of songs and other traditions descended on the islands. They thought that the old ways were changing so much that the indigenous songs would disappear. The changes were not taking place as rapidly as was to be the case later, but the collectors, most of them from outwith the Gaelic cultural area, thought that rescuing the songs was a matter of great urgency. The most famous of them was Marjory Kennedy-Fraser, (1857-1930) from Edinburgh, and her work with the *Songs of the Hebrides* – the first volume was published in 1909 – was one of the first attempts at reviving an interest in Gaelic songs. Mrs Kennedy-Fraser used a phonograph to record the songs and she and her sister performed them, suitably accompanied and doctored according to urban Victorian tastes. In their chapter on 'Art Versions of Waulking Songs' in *Hebridean Folksongs* (Vol. 1), John Lorne Campbell and Francis Collinson give two significant quotations, referring to Mrs Kennedy-Fraser. First, George Malcolm Thomson, in *A Short History of Scotland* (1929) writes of Mrs Kennedy-Fraser's discovery 'of an exquisite folk-poetry and folk music among the Gaelic-speaking fisherfolk of Eriskay and other Hebridean islands: it is one of the most romantic and fortunate accidents in modern history that this small and lively world yielded up its treasure before it passed away.' Rait and Pryde in Scotland (1934) wrote of the Kennedy-Fraser collection *Songs of the Hebrides*: 'Not only is it clear that the essentials of the originals are generally preserved and that the alterations and additions are improvements; it is even doubtful if in many cases, anything would have survived without the interested labours of these collectors.' It was generally thought that Mrs Kennedy-Fraser had saved Hebridean song from oblivion, whereas the truth is that there is not one of the songs in her collection which could not have been recorded in its original form until recent times, from people who may or may not have heard of her. Not only the tunes – especially the rhythms, tempi and placings of stress – were changed, but the words were 'improved' by her collaborator, the Rev. Kenneth MacLeod. A moral outlook was present at the beginning of the century which resulted in a bowdlerisation of many down-to-earth verbal texts. The language of the songs – English or Gaelic – seems to us now ridiculously flowery. Shielings were traditionally occupied by unmarried girls and were, inevitably, often visited at night by young men whose intentions were probably not honourable. A song composed by a would-be Casanova tells in terms of amusing self-mockery of one such visit where, unfortunately, the girl's mother was present, and she woke up and nearly caught the visitor in *flagrante delicto*, so to speak. In the tradition the song is known as 'I spent last night in a shieling'; in *Songs of the Hebrides* 'An Island Shieling Song'. Musically, the tempo and rhythm are changed so that it becomes suitably sentimental for its new text: 'I spent last night in the shieling/with cattle dripping milk of lulling/the night's dew dripping kindness/on the maidens in the shieling' (my translation). Other verbal texts were changed without even the amount of justification assumed here, merely to corroborate the 'noble savage' idea that was so trendy at that time.

Societies founded by exile Gaels in Glasgow, Govan, Edinburgh and London put on ceilidhs (so called) and grand concerts. The piano began to be used as an accompanying instrument. Choirs were formed using vocal harmony, which was completely new to Gaelic song. It became fashionable for singers to have their voices trained. *An Comunn Gàidhealach* (probably best translated 'the Gaelic Speakers' Association') was formed in 1891 and held its first festival of Gaelic song and literature in Oban in 1892. This became an annual, competitive event known as the National Mod. Unfortunately, since few or no Gaels were musically literate, the music for these competitions was written by outsiders, and the performances were judged by outsiders. It takes a long, long time to learn about a different musical tradition. Those people thought – we are all British after all – that it was easy. Scales and rhythms were adapted to the well-tempered easily assimilated Western European norm. They probably decided that deviations from these were just native errors. A wit from the island of Lewis, writing in the *Stornoway Gazette* in the 1950s, protests none too subtly: 'To win at the Mod, ye singers, leave the natural airs at home, then go to some professor of the musical arts who will train you in Eyetalian airs and the taafetiffes and the doramifasosos till such time as you can hold a note from Queen Street [a railway station in Glasgow] to Mallaig [one of the railway terminals for the Western Isles]. Don't sing like a — [various Gaelic phrases used here] granny with a child because that is too natural, too much like a boorish blackbird or a tone-lazy lark. And if you know any good-old songs, bury them, for of such is not the kingdom of medals. Never mind Gaelic. It can be bought in phrases, unrationed.' (George Morrison, *One Man's Lewis*.)

Until the late 1950s the small Gaelic Department of the BBC in Glasgow encouraged the Mod style of singing Gaelic, with auditions for solo recitals and performances by approved Gaelic choirs. To quote George Morrison again: 'We heartily congratulate the Laxdale choir on their success at the Mod...the folk must live, as Laxdale does, in an area civilised enough to know that there are choirs and there was Gaelic. The two stages on either side are to know (a) that there are no such things as choirs, but plenty Gaelic, or (b) that there are plenty choirs but no Gaelic.' (Originally published 1948.)

Meantime, there were several individuals showing concern about the status of Gaelic singing and of Gaelic culture generally. In the 1850s Frances Tolmie, a Gaelic speaker from Skye, wrote down the songs she heard from women she visited who were knitting stockings for different Highland regiments. Some of her collection was later published by the Folk-Song Society in their journal.[7] She probably did not have conservation in mind, however, although the results of her work should have fulfilled a conservationist's desires. The Folklore Institute of Scotland began to collect and record unpublished Gaelic songs in 1947. The Linguistic Survey of Scotland, operating from Edinburgh University, was collecting Gaelic traditional material as well, before the School of Scottish Studies was itself established in 1951. The Irish Folklore Commission extended its interests to Scotland in 1946 when Calum I Maclean, employed by them, collected in the Highlands and Islands. Of course, the tradition was not dying as people like Mrs Kennedy-Fraser would have had us think, but it was in great danger of becoming so diluted that rescue of its most indigenous elements was seen to be urgent. John Lorne Campbell of Canna and his wife, Margaret Fay Shaw, did a lot of collecting in their own island, but especially in South Uist and Barra.[8] Alan Lomax came from the United States in 1950, commissioned by the Library of Congress and, with the help of Calum Maclean and Hamish Henderson, collected Gaelic songs in the Highlands and Hebrides, publishing some of them later on disc under the Columbia label.[9]

There were occasional broadcasts of traditional singers such as Alasdair Fraser, a schoolteacher from Wester Ross working in Conon Bridge, and Flora MacNeil and Calum Johnston, both from Barra. In 1955 Joan MacKenzie, a young schoolteacher from Lewis, whose style of singing was definitely verging on the traditional, won the Comunn Gàidhealach's premier award, the Mod Gold

Medal. The most recent singer of a similar traditional quality to win the Medal had been Kitty MacLeod, in 1936, but Joan MacKenzie's success marked the beginnings of a change of attitude amongst the Mod judges.

The general folk song revival in Britain was having an effect on Gaelic audiences too. The School of Scottish Studies started in a modest way in 1951 to create an archive of all kinds of oral tradition, Scots and Gaelic. It was fashionable for a time in Edinburgh to hold concerts featuring traditional Gaelic singers, and the organisers were fortunate to have, on the spot, such superb artists as Flora MacNeil and Calum Johnston, Kitty and Marietta MacLeod – sisters from Lewis, Kitty being the same as the one mentioned above – and a few others. One of the series of events that focussed those singers was the People's Festival Ceilidhs described in Chapter III. The reaction to the concerts was mixed. There is always a certain amount of snobbery attached to such gatherings, especially in a culture-conscious city such as Edinburgh.

Flora MacNeil is probably the best known of the pioneers of traditional singing. When she first started to sing in public in Edinburgh and Glasgow, collectors such as Alan Lomax, Norman Buchan and Ewan MacColl took an interest in her songs, and people like Sorley Maclean, his brother Calum and Calum Johnston of Barra were there to boost her own interest; but otherwise she was habitually asked to sing something 'not too traditional'. In Barra, a few were heard to say, 'Flora only sings those unattractive old songs' – 'Cha bhi Fleòrag a' seinn ach na seann òrain ghrànda sin' – and at ceilidhs in Barra itself only the popular songs of the day were sung. Flora refused to compromise, and gradually attitudes changed.

When Fred Macaulay was appointed producer of Gaelic programmes for the BBC in Glasgow, having spent some time collecting traditional material for the Linguistic Survey of Scotland, he may well have been following his own inclinations when he introduced less of the Western European Art Music brand of singing to his public. Or he may have been catering for the taste of a minority that was possibly beginning to increase. There is no doubt, at any rate, that the BBC had the greatest influence on the Gaelic public, and 'ordinary' people who had never left their island and rural homes saw the possibility of having their own repertoires featured on radio. Nothing could be better for the prestige of traditional song. This, in turn, influenced An Comunn Gàidhealach which has been trying in recent years to put more emphasis on the traditional way of singing, and to choose prescribed songs that are more attuned to the indigenous culture. The public is hard to convert, however, and it will be a long time before the adult competition of traditional songs will have as much prestige as the Gold Medal final where the emphasis is on musical prowess of a conventional kind.

Gaelic was not a part of the interest in folk groups that came about in the mid-1950s. A group in Edinburgh, called The Night Hawks, invited Dolina Maclennan, a Gaelic singer from Lewis, to join them around that time, and that was more or less the extent of Gaelic involvement in the folk world then. Folksong societies heard too little of Gaelic singing of the authentic traditional type for its members to be able to judge it with any degree of discrimination. Certain singers, whose intonation was in fact suspect from any point of view, were regarded as good because of a misinterpretation of the subtleties of Gaelic melodic intonation. As is the case with other traditional genres, Gaelic melodies are not always based on either the major or minor scale, and their intonation sounds strange, therefore, to anyone reared on these. For that reason, there were those who showed that they were initiated by their enjoyment of what they thought was the genuine article when the singer was unable to hit the right notes!

Gaelic singers did not really get into the folk scene until An Comunn Gàidhealach introduced a folk group contest at the annual Mod. This brought to the fore groups such as Na h-Oganaich, Na Sgoilearan, Na Siaraich and Sound of Mull, etc. They all had their day. What constitutes a folk group? More than one performer, musical instruments, harmony and traditional songs – a mixture of old and new – fairly strong voices, youth, and preferably good looks. It was difficult to get all those ingredients together. Members of groups tended to be university students, or have recently left school. They tended not to have settled into permanent employment of any kind. Whether the group met in the cities or in island or country districts, there would always be one or two members who were in the area only temporarily. The tendency was, not to continue in the manner of the Seekers as New Seekers, with numerous changes of personnel, but for the groups to disintegrate. One or two, like The Lochies and Sound of Mull lasted well, and the others can still be heard on disc and are very popular on radio request programmes. Folk groups contributed substantially to the revival of Gaelic traditional songs, since they were always looking for something new to add to their repertoire, and because of the years between, when only a limited variety of Gaelic song was heard by the general public, the most unusual 'new' songs were the old ones. A group which had a very high potential in this direction was Am Bradan Breac (The Speckled Salmon) which formed in Edinburgh in the early seventies as a kind of concert party. There were fourteen of them, pipers, fiddlers, dancers, a clarsach player and singers. They sang, danced and played solo and in groups. They could therefore cope with such a variety of material as no ordinary folk group could do. For example, they performed waulking songs in a more convincing way than could most groups of three or four members, especially as those who played the instruments could sing as well. Am Bradan Breac lasted for only a year or two. The difficulties of keeping a normal-sized folk group together were multipied about threefold in this ensemble!

The emergence of Runrig and Capercaillie has been a great boost to Gaelic song. Both started life as dance bands, but Runrig first and, later, Capercaillie saw the potential for an updating of the Gaelic tradition in singing. Both have achieved this without compromising the roots of the tradition to an unacceptable extent. There is, of course, a great difference between the view of a Gaelic speaker and that of other Scots in the question of compromising the roots of the tradition, and both of those bands have a strong Highland background. Perhaps one could go as far as to say that it needs to be in the blood, at the risk of sounding racist!

One musical phenomenon that has not needed much of a revival is the distinctive method of singing metrical psalms that is used in Gaelic-speaking congregations of the Presbyterian church. The method has survived from Reformation times and was in fact initiated by English Puritans in order to overcome the difficulty of congregational singing when people could not read, or there were not enough copies of written texts to go round. The practice was for someone to read a line of the verse before the congregation sang it. Gradually the spoken line must have developed into a chant, but the practice of precenting was given up a long time ago by the majority of congregations except Gaelic speaking ones. It was very rarely that an English or Scots speaking congregation could be heard using it in this century. The Gaels have held on to it stubbornly and have made it their own, using it in church and in family worship, although the ballad metre of the psalms is unknown otherwise in Gaelic, and although no more than one or two of the tunes were composed by Gaelic speakers.

The spoken line is chanted; melody notes have been changed, instinctively, no doubt, to conform more closely with the melodic intervals that were familiar in the Gaelic tradition; and the melodic line is ornamented, the degree of ornamentation varying from place to place. (The Lewis style, for example, is more elaborately ornamental than that of other areas.) As well as all this, the line is sung very slowly, the same gracenotes do not always come together, and the near-discordant polyphony which sometimes ensues creates a tension, so that the sound is very strange and puzzling to the uninitiated. Even among the uninitiated, however, Gaelic psalm singing is often commented on as being strikingly beautiful. Singing with precenting in this way was never in danger of going under in the way that other Gaelic traditional music was, but it is interesting to speculate on what might have happened if the revival had not taken place. In the late 1940s, for example, the BBC was using a small choir for all the Gaelic religious broadcasts from the studio. The choir would sing each note as written, with few if any gracenotes, even when precenting was used. Sometimes it was not used, and the psalms were sung in the Lowland way. From the 1960s onwards, however, recordings of congregational singing have been used for almost all Presbyterian Gaelic religious services on radio. In recent years, interest has been stimulated through the production of cassettes, especially by Lewis Recordings Ltd, Stornoway. One of the Scottish Tradition series by Tangent is called *Gaelic Psalms from Lewis,* and it is accompanied by an explanatory booklet.[10] While the language lives, the tradition is likely to remain fairly strong.

The situation in Gaelic music now is as strange as is the situation of the language. In the places where the language should be strongest, young people prefer to speak English. Children generally speak Gaelic until they go to school, but after a very short time they speak more English than Gaelic and some forget their first language completely. Parents who abhor this state of affairs have been able to do little to counteract it, but some enlightened education authorities now support learning through the medium of Gaelic. Opinions differ as to the efficacy of such a move; sometimes the Gaelic medium child hears no Gaelic in the home, as many incomers to Gaelic speaking areas find the idea socially and politically attractive although they themselves do not speak the language. On the other hand the reverse was true of English for many generations – that is, children had to deal with a language in school which they seldom heard spoken in the home. The decline in numbers of people speaking has got steadily worse since the 1980s, while the interest among learners of all sorts of nationality – American, Australian, English, German, Irish, Japanese, Scandinavian, Scottish and Welsh – has steadily increased.

The taste among young Gaels is for pop songs and the majority would rather listen to Radio One than to Radio Highland. Country and western music is very popular, and groups sing in Gaelic using country and western tunes.

The dependence of the popularity of the rock/pop group Runrig on their Gaelic profile is very difficult to assess. It probably is significant as part of a wider Scottishness that fans do not find quite so apparent in the works of other

Scottish pop groups. Runrig also has a fair element of what could be described as folk in their songs. They sing fewer now of their own adaptations of old Gaelic songs, but their familiarity with such songs seems to have a certain amount of influence on their compositions.

During the summer of 1991 a crowd of 40,000 attended a Runrig concert at Edinburgh Castle, and another concert in 1993 attracted a similar crowd. Many of the early-teenage members of that audience would attend concerts by other popular pop artists, Scottish or otherwise. A sizeable number, however, especially among the students present, would prefer a concert by Capercaillie, a distinctively folk band with a Gaelic singer, to any other band apart from Runrig. Runrig and folk groups have a significant following in common, and the same fans will buy recordings of solo singers such as Catherine Ann MacPhee, Christine Primrose, Arthur Cormack and others.

Local authorities in the Gaelic-speaking areas have appointed tutors in instrumental music, and the Western Isles employs more than one tutor in traditional Gaelic Song. Good instructors are scarce, and those appointed have to cover an area that makes any worthwhile development very difficult, but there has been official support for Gaelic-medium schools over the past decade. It is to be hoped that success in the teaching of Gaelic music will come in the wake of that.

Virtually private enterprise helped to set up the first area festival of Gaelic music, in Barra, but the Western Isles council made funds available for it from the beginning. The first Barra Féis took place in 1981 and was seen as a great success. Other areas soon emulated. Seen as an antidote to competitiveness, which is so much a part of local Mods and the National Mod, féisean have become a movement, and they are now run through the summer months in the Hebrides and the mainland from Thurso to Inverness, at 27 venues in all, to date. They last for a week or a fortnight, and art, drama and dancing are taught as well as instrumental music and Gaelic songs, and follow-up courses are now being established in some of the relevant areas over the winter months.

Féisean are sponsored now by public bodies such as the Scottish Arts Council, Highlands and Islands Enterprise, six regional councils and some television companies, along with the Committee for Gaelic Television. A company has been formed, called Féisean nan Gàidheal (Festivals of the Gael), with charitable status, and it is mainly organised through a Gaelic Arts officer, an appointment made by the Scottish Arts Council in 1987, and drama and music officers appointed between then and 1993.

Each Féis gives an opportunity to improve fluency in the language itself, but many tend to be patronised more for their non-language content. Whatever their aims were at the beginning, only two venues, South Uist and Inverness, insist on Gaelic as the teaching medium. Nevertheless, children from a Gaelic background are being given tuition in their own traditions, and one of the outcomes to which we may look forward could be the better use of accompanying instruments for Gaelic singing.

Opportunities for Gaelic speakers to learn skills in instrumental musicianship have come late, but, we hope, not too late.

There is in the 1990s a fashionable interest in Celtic music, and while 'Celtic' seems to have undefined boundaries, singers who see Gaelic as part of it are taking advantage of its popularity, sometimes with little expertise in the language.

(To those of us who spoke the language from infancy the sounds can be excruciating!) One Gaelic-based group has emerged in recent times, all of its members being well-known Gaelic singers, with Blair Douglas on keyboard and Alison Kinnaird, who also sings, but is better known as an expert on the harp and its history; they call themselves MacTalla or Echo.[11] Other groups such as Sìleas go on using Gaelic material in their repertoire and some solo singers also manage to produce near-authentic sounds in spite of being recent learners of Gaelic. Runrig seem to have moved away from using the language quite as much as they did at first, but Capercaillie, having got into the British Top-Forty charts with a Gaelic waulking song, continue to include several Gaelic songs in their selections, whether on stage or on disc. Several of Runrig's songs have now gone into the tradition,and are sung at ceilidhs and by professional singers. This is a way that the tradition is going forward. One of the negative aspects of the Gaelic song tradition is the tendency to use well-established tunes for any new songs. A tune has to be very strong to withstand this, and it is refreshing to hear songs like those composed by members of Runrig, although their skills as poets will never match those of the more conventional poets of the past. This is mainly because a higher register of the language is not familiar to a younger generation. The Bible and good powerful preaching, songs and daily conversation with an older generation kept this register in people's backgrounds. It is difficult to encounter any of those nowadays, and the poetic language has consequently deteriorated, with many inconsistencies in grammar, for example, although the thoughts expressed in the songs are poetical. The famous poets of the day do not have melodies in mind for their compositions, and this has taken away a rich element from the tradition which it had in the past. Exceptions are, for example, the late Murdo MacFarlane,[12] who composed his own tunes for his poems, and Aonghas MacNeacail, whose poem Breislich (Delirium) has been made famous by Capercaillie in their album of that name.

In order for the tradition to be renewed, clever artists of today have to know their own pasts thoroughly. One way that this may be achieved is through historical societies. Those that exist have produced cassettes of local songs, and this can be regarded as a good source for younger performers. In the 1970s several documentary-type plays were produced by companies such as 7:84, and that encouraged research into songs to illustrate historical events. Singers like Catherine Ann MacPhee, from Barra, have benefited from that time, and songs which had been obscure were heard, given a modern, but tasteful Gaelic treatment. That, together with the Féisean movement and continuing support for traditional music tutors in schools, gives hope for the future.

The School of Scottish Studies was at a disadvantage in the past when songs released from there were given a treatment which offended the original singers of them. A later generation had more confidence in itself and in its own culture, and singers were not willing to accept arrangements produced by those who did not speak the language, as had been the case previously. A heavy teaching schedule makes it difficult for the School to be an effective resource for singers. It needs public funding to provide personnel to cope with public enquiries and to produce popular material for the public market, both in Scots and in Gaelic. Funding for Gaelic television, where the Government has given £9,500,000, has been used in a very small way to enhance the showing of musical programmes, with varying success. The money has been used for a great variety of programmes, and often much time is wasted because of those who jumped in to take advantage of the money with too little background knowledge. The worst ignorance is that of not recognising your ignorance, and there is an arrogance in people who think they can pick up the nuances of this ancient language and its culture when they have heard of it for the first time only recently. It is a terrible indictment of British education that this should be so. Why don't we get on with it ourselves then? Gaels have varied skills like everyone else in Scotland, and not all of them are interested in such matters. (There is, for example, a dearth of young teachers to bring forward the Gaelic medium teaching which has recently been given general approval in educational circles.) The development of Gaelic culture is left in the hands of a very small number out of only about 68,000 people who speak the language.

The revival for Gaelic traditional songs is still going on. 'Celtic' music, as commented previously, is very fashionable and the words are sometimes secondary to the beat and the atmosphere of Celtic and African mist, but there are some singers who are anxious to learn the words and pronounce them properly. Sometimes movements like the present inclination to dress Gaelic songs in a 'World Music' commercial garment urges people to seek the authentic original. It is not too late for the authentic original to get its place, with television coverage, Gaelic medium schools, Féisean, and the general public interest in minority cultures.

Donnie Munro of Runrig has stated that he was 'robbed of my own language through the education system.'[13] If the powers-that-be continue to support Gaelic medium schools, (a slightly faint hope at present; it looks as if the idea is not getting easy approval in its application to secondary schools), then the language may survive. If the language lives, the songs will live, and in time the work of tutors in the Féisean and in schools will bear fruit. Singers are rediscovering the beauty and relevance of the older Gaelic songs, and perhaps some day we will have a government which will give the School of Scottish Studies facilities to make its treasures available to those singers.

Footnotes

1. The late Nan MacKinnon recorded 400 proverbs for the School of Scottish Studies. This was said to her – probably in Gaelic – by the late Donald MacPherson from Barra, who was the first person to record her on tape.
2. Published by Greentrax, (CTRAX 9016D), Cockenzie, East Lothian.
3. From *A Collection of Gaelic Songs,* p. 10, produced for the use of undergraduate students at the School of Scottish Studies. Recorded from Calum Johnston, Barra, by Calum I. Maclean in 1953, SA1953/12. In Scottish Tradition cassette series (Tangent TGM MC 504).
4. For further information see William J Watson, *Bàrdachd Ghàidhlig: Gaelic Poetry 1500–1900.*
5. See *Tocher* 13, 18, 20, 22, 24, 27 etc.
6. See booklet accompanying the LP *Waulking Songs from Barra* (Tangent TNGM 111), reissued on cassette and CD by Greentrax (CTRAX 9003 & CDTRAX 9003).
7. *Journal of the Folk Song Society,* vol. 4, no. 16 (1911), pp. 143–276. See also Ethel Bassin, *The Old Songs of Skye; Frances Tolmie and Her Circle.*
8. Margaret Fay Shaw, *Folksongs and Folklore of South Uist.*
9. Vol. 6 (Scotland) of The World Library of Folk and Primitive Music, Columbia SL

209, 1953, Library of Congress.
10. Scottish Tradition, reissued on cassette and CD (9006) by Greentrax.
11. '...mairidh gaol is ceòl' – Love and music will outlast (the world), Temple Records, Midlothian 1994. The singers are Arthur Cormack, Eilidh MacKenzie and Christine Primrose.
12. 1901–82. His song texts are in *An Toinneamh Dìomhair,* Stornoway, 1973 and a selection performed by himself is on the cassette *Dàin Mhurchaidh,* with booklet, An Comunn Gàidhealach, 1986.
13. From an interview in the *Edinburgh Herald and Post,* 8 August 1991.

Flora MacNeil

Calum Johnston

VI   *The Travelling People*

It's a proud thing to be a traveller.[1]
Jane Turriff

[Referring to a family with eight children]...like all travelling people, they
just had to keep moving. It is only with this sense of freedom that they can
get any joy out of living and they are willing to bear discomfort, even
hardships, to keep that freedom.[2]
Betsy Whyte

Now the life of the traveller is fading into the past.[3]
Duncan Williamson

Travellers used to be called tinkers, but because of the derogatory, even racialist,
connotations it has acquired, the latter term is hated by most of the fraternity. It
will only be used here when speaking of the past. Both gypsies and tinkers were
ancient nomadic castes of metalworkers and other craftsmen. The tinkers were
indigenous to the British Isles; in Scotland the word derives from the old verb
tink, meaning to mend or solder – which is partly onomatopoeic in that it
suggests one of the sounds made when working with metal – and the Scots name
is tinkler. The gypsies on the other hand came from all parts of Europe, moving
into England in the fifteenth and sixteenth centuries and thence northward
throughout Britain, and they themselves encouraged the idea of a possibly more
distant country of origin: India, or North Africa, hence the name, from
'egyptian'. It has been said that in Scotland, 'the two races fused and united in
the sixteenth century because of the similar mode of life'.[4] Some intermingling
certainly occurred, and over the next four hundred years other subsidiary elements were added to the mixture: the dispossessed, resulting from disasters such
as Culloden and the Highland clearances; Irish Romanies and tinkers; and de-
serters, with other 'broken men'. Nevertheless the two groups remained distinct,
and the tinkers had existed for hundreds of years before the arrival of the
gypsies.[5] In mediaeval Gaelic society, skilled craftsmen, particularly metalworkers, shared in the (graded) privileges which that society accorded other men of
arts.

Today most gypsies are to be found in Central and Southern Scotland; in the
Borders and Galloway especially, considerable fusion took place between the
two fraternities. It is the tinkers north of this with whom we are concerned here,
now generally referred to as travellers or the travelling folk. This name may be
accepted in a sense at least partly historical, rather than literal, thus resolving any
contradictions arising from the settlement in houses of a considerable number.
Many of those now settled, for part or all of the year, retain their traveller identity and culture.

What is this culture? Basically it consists of the varied elements in the whole
traditional Scottish culture – songs, instrumental music, stories and customs –
but stamped with the hallmark of the travellers' strongly individualistic style and
content, forged by their hard yet rich lifestyle. They were isolated both socially

(as outcasts from the accepted norm of society) and geographically (as regards camping sites). They were thus thrown back on their own resources for social intercourse and entertainment. Yet during their travels they would pick up tunes and songs from different parts of the country, from other travellers but also from non-travellers whom they met at work: for example, ploughmen and cottars – ploughmen often whistled at their work, and songs would be heard during mid-yokin' breaks. Isolation and travel thus led to a paradoxical combination of cultural inbreeding plus diversity, two factors which helped to build up a distinctive brand of tradition. Belief in fairies, elves and other supernatural beings is widespread, but in a curiously symbolic way, the deeper meaning hovering on the edge of the listener's subconscious. This is evident in the story included below.

It is in the tale *par excellence* that one finds the travellers' imprint: it is a more malleable form than the song, it is not bound up with a tune and so it provides more immediate opportunity for textual recreation, thus permitting infiltration of idiosyncratic touches and of symbolic material which supports and interprets their life experience.[6] Factual and historical material also appears – for instance there are many Burker stories, based on the notorious murders committed in order to sell bodies for dissection. For obvious reasons travellers were unusually vulnerable to this hazard, but in their stories they have built it up into outsize proportions.

Duncan Williamson spoke of the close connection between songs and stories[7] revealed by his research among his own people. His father would tell stories, '...he maintained they were stories, but some parts – he'd sing them.'[8] This may provide a link with the Gaelic tradition. Although the verbal text of travellers' songs, especially the ballads, is often rather fragmentary, it is perfectly comprehensible to listeners who already know the stories. (See notes on *Andrew Lammie*, Chapter IV.)

A quality possessed to a marked degree by travellers, especially the women, is what Betsy Whyte of Montrose described as 'the gift of perception'.[9] She herself could 'read' a person's hand with uncanny accuracy and sensitivity, indicating his or her past experiences, struggles or personality difficulties, but she refused to attempt any foretelling of the future.

Travellers' singing styles vary according to the singer's personality and mood,[10] but one quality almost always appears: they are impassioned, intense, often imparting a sense of hard-won victory and sometimes of grandeur.[11] This is not the same as singing loudly, although volume is always an element in expressiveness. But it has much to do with the ability to show feelings, and with the deep emotion aroused by many songs. The tears may be for someone, now dead, who used to sing that song – as Betsy Whyte said, 'It lets people know that he was important to them. In a way he's not dead as long as his songs are still alive.' MacColl and Seeger comment on the singing style: 'There is an almost heroic quality in the singing of travellers, a desire to declaim, to demand attention, an assertion of oneself as a singer.'[12]

The heroism, the hard-won victory, are those of survivors from a centuries-old persecution and prejudice which still exists to this day. 'Until the end of the sixteenth century gypsies and tinkers, with one or two notable exceptions such as Johnny Faa, who was granted protection by James V, received nothing but punishment from the law.' In fact, the death penalty could be inflicted on anyone merely rumoured to be an 'egyptian'.[13] Musicians and actors also suffered severe harassment in Reformation and post-Reformation Scotland;[14] gypsies and tinkers were often known to be good singers, pipers and fiddlers, so they were doubly penalised. Progress and understanding came at a snail's pace. During the nineteenth century legal measures restricting the use of traditional camping grounds, such as the verges of the old drovers' roads, were stepped up. Even in 1918 the Departmental Committee on Tinkers in Scotland referred to travellers as 'representing a different stage of human development',[15] and in Government reports of the 1980s one finds accounts of continuing ill-treatment by the settled population.

The 1992 report admits 'It is now generally accepted that Travellers should have legal stopping places', but goes on to mention the 'many obstacles' faced by local authorities who try to make this a reality.[16] Then there is the recent phenomenon of New Age Travellers, many of whom do not wish to be on serviced sites. The number of travellers in Scotland in 1992 was an estimated 3,000 on the road, plus 60 households of NATs,[17] and with 10,000 settled travelling people.[18] How can such a small minority be seen as a threat?

To the settled community the travellers' chief faults are, first, they do not have a fixed home, and second, they have no regular job with an employer. Yet travellers take pride in these facts which they see as belonging to the essential nature of their existence. In practice they are not wholly consistent about the first, since there is movement in and out of houses for part or all of the year, and many travellers have become permanently settled though they may take an extended working 'holiday' in the summer. But the housed travellers do not consider themselves any the less 'travellers'. The two groups have an essentially symbiotic relationship. For the mobile traveller the settled families represent contact points, telephones for passing on family news or for possible work contacts, while for the housed traveller those still on the road represent links with continued tradition.

The historical/sociological reasons for the emergence of itinerant peoples lie outside the scope of this chapter, but the travellers undoubtedly filled a social need. The lawmakers, who lived in towns, did not appreciate this fact. The farmers and the rural lairds, however, were generally glad of the travellers' seasonal help, their manual skills and buying and selling expertise, and as a result they usually allowed them to camp on their land and often turned a blind eye to the odd spot of poaching. Travellers going round houses brought news with them – the country people were glad to see them, as it saved them visits to shops; and the tinklers did soldering and other mending, as well as odd jobs around the place. Centuries of nomadic living, in turn, bred within the travellers a need for this life.[19] One of the travellers' defensive measures over the centuries has been the development of their own language, cant; in Scotland there exists both Scots-English cant and Gaelic cant.

The second 'fault' of the travellers is that they have no regular job. The Puritan work-ethic is seen here – there must be something wrong with a man who does not work his seven or eight hours a day, five days a week. But travellers think it is normal and sensible to work only when you need to – seasonal work, anything that needs to be done, their own traditional occupations and skills – and to have more time for chat, for ceilidhing, for the really important things in life. This attitude deserves serious consideration even though it may appear somewhat romantic, and even though another interpretation is that they work at anything that comes up, often very hard, in order to survive the lean winter season. The traveller women – who have always earned money outside the home as well as doing all the work within it – still hawk goods, collect rags or clothes and do seasonal work. Much seasonal agricultural work is in fact carried out by the whole family – men, women and children. During a discussion on unemployment, Sheila Stewart said: 'The country hantle have routine, we never do... Travellers can always turn their hand to something – they'll never be stuck.'

The versatility of travellers is remarkable, but many of their trades are difficult to accommodate in modern urban housing: the used-car trade which replaced the traditional horse-trading, scrap metal activities, basket-making and pearl-fishing materials, plus second-hand goods of all kinds are often unwelcome to neighbours. Important contributions are made to the recycling process, and not only of metals: the collecting and selling process distributes many useful artefacts otherwise destined for rubbish dumps. Conservationists recognise this now, but travellers have been doing it for hundreds of years. Yet full citizenship, minority rights and sometimes even voting rights seem to elude them.

Duncan Williamson, originally from Argyllshire, has been housed since 1980, but lived for most of his life in a traditional bent-boughs tent, also known as a gelly. It is made from saplings – preferably hazel, rowan or birch – which are pushed into the ground, bent over and bound together. This structure is then covered with various waterproof materials firmly tied down. Duncan's tents were more spacious than any caravan and were often warmed by a closed fire, with a circular chimney going up through the roof.[20] He spoke of the satisfactions of the travelling life: 'Ye wake up in the morning an' ye hear the birds singin'...ye've no worries, no one tells ye what to do...you have nothing but you have everything. It's so peaceful...you come and go as you like...no need to keep up with the boss.' (Pause) 'Ye don't *need* these things...'[21]

As the oldest girl of a large family, Jane Turriff was sometimes left to look after her brothers and sisters when their parents went on the road. But she looked forward eagerly to the school holidays:

> Seven weeks holidays...ma father an' mother travelled, an'...we *all* went. Ma mam an' dad was really happy though when they were away travellin', an' so was I. And I loved the horse – ma father had a good horse, an' he'd a lovely big caravan... Travellin' all day...the sun shinin', an' yir face was brown...yir hankie on yir head...an' the bairns was all lovely an' brown. An' the horse was just takin' its time...goin', ye know? – we never ran the horse, we'd *all day* – was nae hurry tae go anywhere, we jist travelled all day... [In the evenings] if it was fine weather, we'd have the fire outside, an' then they started cookin'...my mother did the cookin', when we were out...Oh me, we spent lovely times. An' then, we would've been on the road all day, and we'd mebbe come til a cross-road...an' ye'd see mebbe another caravan comin', approachin', ye know?...I was so happy, I said, 'I wonder who it could be, I wonder who it could be'...an' here was...ma auntie, or ma grandma, or some o' them... That's the life I loved... We loved singin', you should hear the old people singin' in those days, it was great... Some o' them wad jist sit an' play on the chanter...an' some o' them mebbe playin' a tin whistle. Ma granda used to play the tin whistle...an' Davie, ye ken m' uncle Davie?... I think he learned it aff o' him, because that was his father... An' then ye'd have heard them singin'...they were aye singin', there wisnae much music in those days, so they were aye playin' their own kin' o' music...an' singin' round the

camp-fire [at Old Meldrum, Danny Stewart reported, the country hantle would come and listen] an' even on the road, singin', ye know. An' then when we stopped at a place...where we was goin' to stay all night, the girls wad all get together, an' mebbe go away fir milk, tae a farm, ye know, an' I was...though I was lame, I wad go wi' them...I just hopped along on ma crutches... [laughed] ...I was young, an' I was swack! – though I had the crutches, I could go...I walked wi' them, an' enjoyed masel' wi' them, and...aye this singin' was in ma heid...an' then ma friends would say to me, 'You've a bonny voice, you can fair sing!' ...an' they wad a' get singin', thegither...an' we'd come home again and...what happy we was! We loved animals, an' we always had a dog...a haund-dog, an' they used tae catch rabbits for wer supper...an' mebbe a big pot o' potatoes, an'...this stovies, in a great big iron pot...with onions...oh gosh, whit a great feed it was... I didna like hoosin' up, because ye dinna meet in wi' lots o' friends when ye're hoosed up...[22]

It would, of course, be wrong to give too idealistic a picture of traveller life. Persecution has devious effects, and injustices which already exist in a country or community tend to appear in harsher form amongst persecuted groups within that community. Misery and deprivation have led to excessive drinking, leading in turn to fighting and exacerbated feuds between family groups. Considerable male/female violence has been found (very rarely the reverse), together with the double standard of sexual morality for men and for women. These two points were raised by all the travellers I spoke to,[23] only one of whom excused the violence, and they are supported by written testimony.[24] Black as these points are, they do not figure among the usual complaints made against travellers by the settled community, doubtless because many of the latter still do not consider these to be really serious misdemeanours. It is possible that a vicious circle may be at work here – exaggerated reports spread by settled people may have affected traveller men so that they came to regard this type of violence as a necessary characteristic of traveller manhood. There is very little divorce, although this is partly due to the fact that until recently women have had no redress against ill-treatment. The children are cared for with kindness and with considerable lenience.

The two main causes of prejudice – itineracy, and the spasmodic work-pattern – have already been discussed. The other grumbles – that travellers are dirty, they do not send their children to school, they leave litter about, they bring down the value of neighbourhood property – are either simply untrue, coals-in-the-bath-type accusations, or else they form part of the vicious circle initiated by an uncomprehending, uncaring society, and especially that part which seeks a scapegoat for its own unfulfilled needs. Andrew Douglas has pinpointed the worst of this carping attitude as coming from the 'poor white trash' of the settled population and discerns an element of jealousy in it and possible fear of the un-conforming – these people are different, they make us feel our lives are mediocre, some of them are famous and yet they've had less education than we have.

This brings us back to the special gifts of the travelling people. They are among the chief custodians of traditional culture, they form a rich seam in Lloyd's 'submerged world'. Yet so many Scots are still ignorant of the wealth of art and wisdom on their very doorsteps, carried out by the despised 'tinkers'. Once again the stone which the builders refused has become the headstone of the corner.

Evidence has been shown of the invaluable contribution made by travellers to the folk-music world over the past 40 years (extensively recorded by the School of Scottish Studies, Edinburgh University). This contribution should be publicised to the wider community by the media. The BBC television programme *The Stewarts of Blairgowrie;*[25] a documentary film, *The Summer Walkers*, made by Neat and Henderson (1977);[26] and a documentary for Grampian television, *Journey to a Kingdom* (1992), show what can be done. However, far more education and publicity is needed to stem the continuing prejudice which, says Sheila Stewart, has remained unaltered over the last decade. The Scottish Arts Council has helped: as well as grants for book publishing they have supported visits by storytellers to schools, and the Netherbow Forum in Edinburgh. Valuable written accounts of this culture – songs, tales and memorabilia (including recently composed songs) – may be found in issues of *Tocher* magazine, many of which are still in print.

There has been no revival *per se* amongst the travellers themselves. They were at first unaware of the important role they were playing in the folk revival. As Duncan Williamson said: 'We have no need to revive something that has really been there among us all these years.' He also declared that a large majority of travellers 'like to keep the sacred things that were passed to them...they are a bit ashamed tae exploit their forbears' culture to the public', and that there are some songs which will never be passed on to non-travellers. (Cf. the Navaho Indians' belief that 'songs are a form of wealth'.)[27] On the other hand Sheila Stewart believes that 'our language and culture are not secret – or sacred – any longer.'

Looking now at the other side of the coin, what effect has the revival movement had on the traveller community? Although a comparatively small number have been closely involved, the results are more far-reaching than might have been expected. The internal grapevine, always important among travellers, has spread awareness of their possible status as tradition-bearers and as purveyors of age-old truths. 'The travellers were a race of people who kept very much to themselves and were a close community,' says Stanley Robertson.[28] There was always a kind of stigma attached... 'Suddenly they found themselves being sought after by scholars and teachers who were looking to them as a source of information. It made them feel very important and brought them into a new dimension of social intercourse.' Sheila Stewart: 'The revival has taken songs to a wider audience, and taken travellers to places...the songs and the travellers are accepted more... It works both ways, the travellers appreciate their own culture, and the settled community do too.' Betsy Whyte stated that the first reaction to collectors was often, '"They must be awful hard up for songs if they come to the travelling people", but now they realise the value of what they have to give.' Festivals and clubs give great pleasure: 'they meet people there, too, not just the country hantle they met on farms.' Whyte, whose maiden name was Townsley, visited some Edinburgh schools in March 1980.[29] She talked to the children, told them about her book, *The Yellow on the Broom*, told them stories and sang some songs. The teacher of one class later brought to Betsy Whyte a little girl whose name was also Townsley: the child said she had been ashamed before, but now felt proud to be a traveller. So the first effect has been an increased confidence and pride of identity.

The post-1945 years brought many world-wide changes. In Britain the welfare state came into being, and in general a more caring, a broader, more democratic and less class-ridden outlook spread. The folk revival was part and parcel of this new outlook. Stanley Robertson again:

> The folk revival did many things for the benefit of the travellers. It gave them a better public image, and people began to understand that travellers were not the filthy, ignorant creatures they were so often made out to be...they realised that travellers were quite intelligent and had much to offer. The schools began to take a better interest in their children and many long-lasting animosities were being banished. With folks like Jeannie Robertson and Belle Stewart making good names in public circles it set the ball rolling for the improvement of conditions for travellers, especially those who were still living on the road. Many groups and organisations started to help travellers get better deals, and travellers themselves responded by mixing more with the country people. During the fifties many travellers inter-married with country people. On the whole the folk revival did the travelling people a vast amount of good. On the other hand it caused a tremendous amount of jealousy among the travelling people themselves. There were bitter arguments about the songs that were collected because certain families claimed sole rights to certain songs. [Belle Stewart also spoke of this.] Sometimes it caused an intellectual snobbery...a situation arose where travellers were calling each other names. Even up to date many families still bear grudges with each other. The folk revival also brought a new awareness of witchcraft, dope, vice and moral slackness. Traveller people would not participate in certain things but with the influence of the people socially, the revival brought many new hazards. The folk revival opened up the eyes of the travelling people to new dimensions of exploration and exploitation.

Sheila Stewart felt less strongly on one point: 'There was some jealousy among travellers at the beginning, but we've got over it now.' And as Belle Stewart said in another context, 'There's no need to go to the travellers to find that.' The green-eyed monster appears in all human situations. On the exceptional degree of integration of the Stewarts within Blairgowrie, Sheila Douglas comments that this is partly due to their becoming well known through the folk revival.

There is wide recognition among travellers of the pioneering part which Hamish Henderson played in collecting their songs and stories. Bryce and Betsy Whyte: 'Hamish started things...it took courage on his part.' Courage indeed, for he took time to fraternise, to win confidence and trust, to sleep rough in tents. In the fifties, to be on such friendly, equal terms with social outcasts was hardly the way to win friends and influence people of the Establishment, academic or otherwise. The successful collector must first establish a rapport with his or her informant, and this is especially important with travellers, whose history has bred into them a wariness and a suspicion of the outside world. By contrast, in the early years of this century Aberdeenshire collectors Greig and Duncan would seem to have collected very little from travellers.[30]

The feeling for words is another gift shared by many travellers:

> To me, the Scottish balladry, the Scottish folk pipe singin', is the word: magic. Proper, sheer, naked magic... It lay dormant... I hope there's millions will understand and find, in it, what is *there*. It's about human beings, their

loves, their liberty or their broken hearts, the death, the grief, the sorrow, the...cups o' happiness flowin' over – they had everything in life, and they've left this in their songs and balladry – they've left everything there. An' if a person sings it with feeling, inside the inner *them*...they can *feel* this...they dinna need to tak' LSD to get the feeling, they can get it through singin'...the same beautiful, transcending heights, away among the mysterious gods... Ye see, long ago, your great poets...your master painters, your Leonardo da Vincis and a' them...and your great composers of olden days, they *all* felt this *magic* thing, which their painting and their music brought. Well I find the same, as a woman today of forty-seven, 1976, in Aberdeen, I find the same thing...an' any man or woman or teenager or child, can find this...in these ballads and songs.[31] (Lizzie Higgins)

Travellers are not only articulate, they can express themselves with a natural poetry and dignity, in spite of – or because of? – their general lack of formal education. They are in a real sense the aristocrats[32] of the road. Like Jock Stewart they are folk 'you don't meet every day', who will treat you with courtesy and sensitiveness. However, categories tend to overlap, and rigid, hard-and-fast statements can blur important differentials within a group. Travellers are not to be confused with tramps or beggars, and their origin is different from that of the American hoboes, but there are some factors common to all social groups found on the road. The hobo's main objective is to find work – Allsop describes him as 'the unemployed spoil cast aside by a bold and ruthless *laissez faire* system',[33] and he rejects the comfortably vague theory that the hobo is driven by wanderlust.[34] Judging from the numerous statements by these men that Allsop records, it would seem that the primary need – the search for work – can sometimes engender a secondary need amounting almost to an addiction for being on the move, in spite of the hardship and persecution involved. In any case, that primary need involved travel, and for the hobo surrounded by the vast distances of the United States this became the call not so much of the road as of the railroad. Above all, the freight-train was the magnet which over the years drew countless thousands with the hope of free travel, and around which a whole genre of poetry and song has centred. (And as we have seen, by a curious process of cross-fertilisation, songs from American work-fronts, with the freight-train as the central motif, became, during the fifties, the basic material for the British phenomenon of skiffle.) The hate/love felt by the disparaged migratory worker for his hard lifestyle may be set against the ambivalent attitude shown to him by the rest of society: 'the wraith of the adventurer with a bedroll hitting the cinder trail to elsewhere remains the *doppelganger* of the American who lives a steady and relatively anchored life.'[35] This parallels closely the situation of Scottish travellers who have been described as the 'alter-ego of the settled population'.[36]

There is another American connection which was emphasised by all those I spoke to, and that is the travellers' strong predilection for cowboy stories, cowboy films and country and western music. The reasons are not far to seek: cowboys are not settled, they travel and work with horses, they live rough and sleep out of doors, they have their tea in cans, and they sing round an open fire. And with the American expansion: '...they were all travellers, they set off across the West in their covered wagons... But travellers here had no land to do it with, because all the land was already owned before the traveller came on the roads...' This shows the yearning and the contradictions in the traveller syndrome, and I queried the travelling versus settling-down paradox here. 'If the travellers had land, *some* of them would have settled down – that doesnae mean to say they wouldnae have *moved* after…they want to own their piece o' land so they can go and come back, tae have some place to come back tae.' (The Whytes also said they liked a base to return to.)[37] There were many travellers among the emigrants to the New World, 'and there's not one traveller family in Scotland at the present day who hasn't got connections…' (Duncan Williamson).

Danny Stewart: 'When I was a boy, the farm workers, travelling people, sang cowboy songs – Bing Crosby was number one favourite… In Old Meldrum, there were 30 or 40 traveller families…all daft on cowboy series… There are few horses now, yet travellers still like country and western songs and cowboy stories.' Jane Turriff knows a number of such songs, and is fond of yodelling (and good at it), 'but I'm more into old Scottish songs now, and I prefer them.' Belle Stewart said her husband Alec loved country and western songs, had learned them especially during their visit to the States and used to play them on his 'goose'.[38] Stanley Robertson remembers hearing his father sing these songs, as well as Jeannie Robertson, who liked trying to yodel.

Duncan Williamson regards his stories and songs as constituting a more valuable legacy than anything material: 'We're giving our children something that will last them for the rest of their entire life.' He has a large collection of tapes he has made, recording travellers during his journeys round Scotland. Alan Bruford has written: 'When you consider that until 1950 less than 30 international folktale types (Marchen) in Scots or Scottish English were known to scholars, and Duncan alone certainly knows at least a hundred types and can tell many more stories of the same kind unknown to the Arne-Thompson catalogue, you may realise what a debt Scotland's culture owes to the travelling people and to this one exceptional traveller.'[39]

Here is one of Duncan's stories:[40]

The Elf and the Basket-Maker

Old John an' his old wife was an old travellin' basket-maker that travelled the west coast of Scotland, many's an' many's the years…an', he made baskets all over, ye know?…made baskets for everybody, an' mendit baskets, he was very good at his trade. And him an' his old wife…was on the road an' they had a wee donkey an' cart, ye know, for carryin' their stuff from place to place. So, one night, he says tae his auld wife, he said, 'Mary,' he said, 'I think,' he said, 'we'll gae doon,' he says, 'tae this wee campin' place that I know,' he said. 'An',' he said, 'I remember,' he said, 'I used tae cut some nice willows for ma baskets,' he says, 'an' I cut them last year; an' this year,' he said, 'I think,' he said, 'they'll be growin' aboot the nice size noo for cuttin',' he said, 'an' I'll stey there for a couple o' days an' make some baskets,' he says, 'an' there's plenty hooses aboot for ye 'ae dae yir hawkin'.' – see? 'Fine, John,' she says, 'that'll dae fine.'

So they came tae this wee campin' place an' they pit up their camp, an'…they had their tea an' it wis…a nice evenin' so he says, 'Mary,' he said, 'I think I'll go away up,' he says, 'an' cut some o' these wands.' 'Well,' she says, 'I'll take ma basket an' I'll go away up an'…hawk some o' these hooses roon' aboot.' See? So she hawked places, an' peens an' thread an' things, she's through the hooses.

Auld John gets his knife, it...there was a bit, part of a...table knife, cut through the centre, he used for makin' his baskets, ye know? – he hadnae got a good knife. An' away he goes. An' he walks up through this wood, to where...he used tae cut his sticks, he'd cut them every year. That's the wild willows. An' he landed back, up this wee path, through the wood...back tae this wee place where he'd cut these sticks every year. An' as usual, oh they were growin' nice, growin' straight up, ye see. 'Upon my soul,' he says, 'they really did grow,' he says, 'seein' I cut them last year.' He said, 'They're really good stuff.' So he's cuttin' away an' he's leavin' them down, an' cuttin' away, leavin' them doon in wee bunches, when this voice says, 'Well, John, ...ye're busy.'

'God bless me,' he said. 'What was't I heard – is there somebody speakin'?' Th' old man looked around...not a soul to be seen. 'Aye, John,' he says, 'there's nice...condition this year for ye.' An' he looked roon' again an' he couldnae see nothing. The auld man rubs his ears, he says tae his self, 'Am I hearin' things,' he said, 'or whit is it?' So he started to cut some more. 'Aye, John,' he said. 'They're nice stuff,' he said, 'ye've got this time.' An' he looks roon' where the voice cam' fae – an' there, sittin' on a wee...a wee block o' a tree, was a wee elf...a wee elf aboot...six inches. The auld man rubs his e'es. 'God bless me,' he said, 'Are you real or are ye no real?' 'Aye,' he said, 'John, I'm as real as what you are.' 'Well, upon my soul,' said the old man, he says, 'I never seen anything like you,' he said, '*what* are ye?'

He said, 'I'm an elf.' 'Ah, an *elf*,' [scornfully] says the auld man, 'there nae such thing as elves.' 'Well,' he said, 'seein's believin',' he said. 'But,' he says, 'am I seein' things,' he said, 'are you really an elf?' 'Aye,' he says, 'John,' he said, 'I'm an elf.' 'But,' he says, 'what dae ye want frae me?' he said. 'Well John,' he says, 'we ken aboot you,' he said. 'We ken,' he says, 'that you've been comin' here cuttin'...these woods, these sticks,' he says, 'for years. And,' he said, 'I come...for you,' he says, 'to dae a job for me.' 'God bless me,' says the old man, he says, 'Dae a job... I couldnae dae n' job for you,' he said. 'Aye,' he said. 'John,' he says, 'you can dae a job for me,' he said. He said, 'I come fae Elfland,' And he said, 'We ken aboot you,' he says, 'for...numbers o' years,' he said, 'an' we want you to dae a job for us.' 'God bless me,' says the old man, he said. 'I heard ma faither,' he said, 'an' ma grandfaither tellin' stories aboot elfs,' he says, 'but...I've never had the pleasure o' seein' yin in ma life.' 'Well, John,' he says, 'ye're seein' yin noo.'

'But,' he says, 'what could I,' he says, 'me an auld traiveller basket-maker,' he says, 'dae for an elf?' he said. He said, 'you're supposed to hae magical powers an' everything,' he said. He said, 'Ye dinnae need the likes o' *me* tae dae things for ye.' 'Ah, but,' he says, 'John...whit we need you to dae for us, we cannae dae it.' '*What* is it,' he said, 'ye want me tae dae?' He said, 'We want ye...I want ye to mak' me a cradle.'

'A cradle?... God bless me,' he said. '*I* cannae mak' ye a cradle,' he said. 'Aye,' he said, 'John, you can mak' the cradle,' he said. 'But,' he said, 'what dae ye want wi' a cradle?' He said, 'I want the cradle,' he said, 'for tae haud a baby.' 'Whit kind o' baby?' he said. He said, 'An elfin baby.' 'Oh no,' says old John. 'No, no,' he said. 'I cannae dae it for ye.' 'Oh aye, John,' he says. 'You can dae it.' He says, 'Look, are you a full grown elf?' He said, 'Aye, I'm a full grown elf.' He said, 'What size are ye?' He says, 'Ye're no much bigger than that...six inches. What size,' he said, 'is a...baby elf?' 'Oh,' says the elf, 'no very big.'

'Well,' he said, 'hoo dae ye expect me,' he said, 'an old traiveller,' he says, 'to get stuff like that,' he said, 'as thick as that,' he says, 'to mak' a cradle tae haud a baby elf?' He said, 'It's out o' the question.' 'Ah, but John,' he says, 'you can dae it.' Old John, he says, 'I doot,' he says, 'I couldnae dae it for ye,' he said. He said, 'I cannae even believe,' he said, 'that ye're...that such a thing,' he said, 'I must be dreamin'.' He says, 'Ye're no dreamin',' he said. 'Well,' he says, 'there nothing I can dae for ye.' 'Ah, but,' he says, 'th'are...'

So auld John gaithered up his wee puckle o' wan's...the elf jumped on the tap o' the wan's, sat under his oxter...ye ken hoo ye carry somethin' under yir airm. 'Where are you gaun?' says auld John. He says, 'I'm gaun hame wi' ye.' He says, 'Ye cannae come back wi' me,' he said, 'I... I've got a...ma camp.' 'I ken ye've got a camp,' he said, 'an' yir auld wife Mary's away wi' a basket,' he says, 'callin' the hooses,' he said, 'and you're camped the same place as ye were last year. An',' he says, 'ye cut these wan's last year.'

The old man left the wan's doon. 'Well,' he says, 'one thing,' he says, 'we'll have tae get this squared before we go,' he said. He said, 'I'm goin' hame wi' you, John. And,' he said, 'you're gaunnae mak' me a basket.' 'Well,' he says, 'sit doon,' he said, 'an' tell me: how am I gaunnae dae it?' He says, 'You're gaunnae dae it.' 'What dae ye want the basket for?' 'Well,' he says, 'I'll tell ye. Noo,' he says, 'keep this tae yirsel.'

He said, 'In Elfland,' he says, 'we have got a new queen.' He said, 'This year the king has tooken a new queen, an',' he says, 'it's his second wife, an',' he said, 'she's gaunnae have a baby. And everybody,' he said, 'was welcome,' he says, 'tae the weddin'...o' the young queen gettin' mairried. But,' he says, 'they forgot aboot yin...wicked auld...elf...woman...they never gien her an invitation...an',' he said, 'she pit a curse on the new-born baby, when it comes to the world, when it's born...that it'll never be right, unless it's rocked in a human cradle. An',' he says, 'you're to mak' it.'

'No me,' he said, 'I couldnae mak' a cradle for a wee baby infant,' he says. 'John, you'll mak' it,' he said. 'I ken you can *dae* it. Are ye *willin'* tae dae it, if I help ye?' 'Well, now,' he says, 'that's different,' he said, 'if you help me,' he said, 'that's different,' he said. 'Hoo're ye gaunnae help me?' 'Never mind,' he says, 'John – pick up yir wands.' John picked up the wan's, the elf jumped t' the top o' the wan's...pit them below his oxter. Back he goes to the camp.

The auld man's oot o' breath when he gets to the camp. The old woman's back. In these days the auld traivellers hardly used a kettle for makin' tea, they kept one o' these...a can, a tin can wi' a lid on it, ye ken, for makin' tea for the two auld folk.

He says, 'Mary.' She says, 'What?' He says, 'Look what I got.' She says, 'Whit did ye get? Did ye find something?' 'No,' he says. 'Look,' he says, 'what's sittin' on the top o' the wan's.' She says, '*What's* sittin' on the top o' the wan's?' She says, 'I cannae see naethin'.' He says, 'Luik at the wee gadgie,' – meanin' the wee man. She says, 'What wee man?' She says, 'What's wrong wi' ye, were ye drinkin' or something?' 'Aye, *drinkin'*,' he says, 'whaur wad I get a drink in the middle o' a waste wood?'

The old woman looks...and she sees the wee... 'God bless ma soul an' body,' she said, 'what' that?' she said, 'whaur did ye get that?' He says, 'Hello Mary,' he said, 'I'm an elf.' She says, 'Ye're whit?' He says, 'I'm an elf.' 'God bless me,' she said, 'I hear ma granny,' she said, 'an' ma great-granny speakin' aboot elfs,' she says, 'but you are the first elf that ever I seen in my life' – and the wee man cam' in. And the old woman was sittin' there, an' the old man was sittin' – and the elf sittin' cross-legged wi' his legs foldit aside the fire, see? She says, 'Whit dae ye want fae us, for,' she says, 'we never done ye any hairm.' 'No,' he says, the wee elf, 'I ken,' he says, 'ye never done anything...that ye'd dae us nae hairm,' he said. 'I only come,' he says, 'for John,' he says, 'to dae a wee job for me.' 'But God bless me,' says the...auld woman, she says, 'what could John,' she says, 'an auld tinker man,' she says, 'dae,' she says, 'for you – an elf,' she said, 'fae Elfland,' she says, '(ye've) got all the magical powers: youse can get onything in the world.' He says, 'Aye true,' he said, 'we're woodland elfs,' he says, 'we can dae a lot o' things, but,' he says, 'we cannae dae the thing that we needed done...but,' he says, 'John can dae it'... '*What* is it?' He said, 'I want him to mak' me an elfin cradle...for an elfin baby.' 'Oh God bless me, maister,' she says, 'my aul' man couldnae mak' ye an elf's cradle,' she said, 'he can mak' *cradles*,' she says, '...for a *big* wean.' She says, 'What size would the elfin wean be?' 'Oh,' he says, 'aboot...three or four inches high.' 'Ah no,' she says, 'it's impossible.' She said, 'He couldnae get the stuff.' 'Well,' John said, 'I was tellin' him that,' he said. 'That I couldnae get nae stuff...thin enough for tae mak' a cradle fir a wee baby, elfin baby.' 'Aye,' he says, 'Mary...John can dae it.'

'Well,' said the aul' man, he says, 'if I'm gaunnae dae it I suppose I'll have to dae it.' He says, 'Gie him some tea.' Noo, the wee elf was that wee...th'auld woman had tea in a can, so...she hadnae got a cup big enough for [to suit] the elf tae haud, so she took the lid o' the can and she holdit the lid like that tae him, and the wee elf held it in his two hands an' he...drunk up the tea. Eh? 'Very good,' he said. 'That was good.'

He says, 'Mary, are you willin',' he says, 'tae help a wee babbie...get a cradle?' the elf said. 'God bless me, wee maister,' she said, 'I'm willin' tae help,' she says, 'ony wee wean,' she says. 'God never gave me...th' blessin',' she said, 'o' ony weans o' ma ain.' She said, 'I dinnae even hae a grand-wean or nothin',' she said, 'and,' she says, 'I like wee weans,' she said. 'I wad dae anything in the world tae help a wee babbie...even suppose it's a wee elf-babbie.'

She said, 'I want tae help – I'll dae onything in the world,' she says, 'tae help him.' 'Weel,' he said, 'wad ye let...auld John,' he says, 'have some o' yir hair?' She says, 'He can have a' the hair he wants,' she said. 'He can get the lot,' she said, 'I'll give the lot, if it's ony guid gae him.' This auld man, he says, 'I cannae mak' (a) cradle wi' human hair.' 'Ah, but,' the elf says, 'wi' my help ye can,' he says, '– let me pull the hairs.' The wee elf got up on th' auld woman's knee an' climbed up th' aul' woman's shouther...an' he pit his two hands tae yin o' th' aul' woman's hairs an' he gien it a pull...pull't a single hair oot...and he handit it tae auld John...an' aul' John pit his hand up an' catched it, and there was the beautifulst strip of fine, thin cane that John had ever saw in his life...thin as a human hair that ye could tie in roon' yir...finger in knots. 'Well, upon my soul,' says the auld woman, she says, 'I never seen the likes o' that.' 'Nor me,' says th' auld man, he says. He said, 'I cuid dae anything wi' that,' he said... 'I could do anything wi' that.' 'Well,' says the wee elf, 'you're gaunnae get plenty o' it,' he said. An' he kept pullin', an' he kept pullin', an' he kept pullin', an' got... 'n' left it doon till he'd a bunch that size.

An' he pulled some more, an' he made it a wee bit thicker, for the ribs. 'Noo,' says the elf, 'I'm goin' off,' he says. 'An',' he says, 'I'll be back,' he said, 'when that cradle's ready.' 'Well upon my soul,' says th' old man, he said. 'I've never seen the like o' that,' he said, 'in all my days – noo,' he says to her, he said, '...if you ever mention a word o' this to ony other human being,' he said, 'I'll kill ye deid.' He says, 'Never you say a word to no human being,' he said. 'John,' she says, 'I couldnae tell naebody,' she says, 'aboot that, because,' she said, 'naebody in the world'll ever believe us.' 'Well,' he says, 'a' the better,' he said, 'if naebody believes it,' he says. 'We don't want nobody (t') ken about it.' He says, 'That wee man'll be back,' he said, 'an' if it's no made,' he said 'a jijim-ant'll follae us the rest o' oor days.' Meanin' bad luck.

So the old man got busy an' he sets...to work an' he workit an' he workit an' he cut, an' he made the beautifullest cradle...it wasnae mair than three inches long, with a hood on it...an' he cut two nice pieces o' wood an' he pit lovely wee rockers on tae it. He says tae th' auld woman, he says, 'Hae ye got ony bits o'...cloth aboot ye?' he said. She said, 'The only thing that's in there, John,' she said, 'in ma basket is a roll o' red ribbon,' ...a bit broad ribbon...she was sellin', to the hooses. And the auld man took the ribbon an' he wove the ribbon inside it, an' made the beautifullest thing ye ever saw in yir life...fit fir any elfin wean.

'There,' he said, an' he pit his finger to it on the floor an' it rocked back an' forrit like that – hood an' everything on it – ken? – miniature, that size. He said, 'That should please that wee man when he comes back.' So th' auld man turned his back tae light his pipe, an' whit did th' auld woman dae? The auld traveller women used tae carry a big pocket roond their side at one time, ye ken...a big leather, a big pocket, that's (th') thing. She put her hand in her pocket, an' she took oot a wee silver thrupenny piece, and she dropped it into the cradle when th' old man wisnae lookin. See? – this is to hansel a new-born baby, ye see – solid silver.

But early in the mornin' th' old man's up; th' auld woman had their wee cup o' tea in the mornin' but they're nae sooner up...in comes the elf. 'Good morning, John,' he said. 'Oh good morning,' says John...to the wee...to the wee elf. 'Good morning, Mary,' he said, 'Ha ha,' He said, 'I see ye got ma cradle finished. An',' he said, 'it's a good yin it is.' 'Aye,' says John, he said. 'There it is,' he said. 'It's ready for ye.' The wee elf put his finger tae it – 'Oh,' he said, 'it's in first class order.' He says, 'John, you'll be repaid for this.' An' he luiks again – the wee man was gone, cradle an' a'. See?

'Well, upon my soul,' says...th' auld man, he says, 'I never seen the like o' that.' See? So, the old man an' woman, th' old man went aboot his wey, th' auld woman went away and she took two or three baskets th' auld man had made but she hadnae gone tae the first hoose till the woman bought four o' them at once there – she wasnae minutes awa'. She come back. He said, 'Ye're no back a'ready?' says the old man. 'Aye,' she said. 'Yir four baskets is gone,' she said, 'an' I've an order for another two or three.' 'Well, upon my soul,' he said. 'I'll have tae try an' get them made.' So they sat doon; the day passed by.

The next mornin' the old man got up, an' he took to break two or three sticks to start his fire, an' sittin' ootside at the top o' the stane was his wee cradle.

He says, 'Woman.' 'What?' she said. He says, 'Come 'ere.' He said, 'Look – I tellt ye, I said I couldnae mak' a cradle for an elf wean.' She says, 'What wey?' She said, 'it was the best cradle ye ever made in yir life,' she says, 'suppose it was wee,' she said. He said, 'Luik, sitin' oot there on the top o' the stane.' He said, 'It's back.' He said, 'I tellt ye it was nae use.'

Th' auld man goes an' he brings it in an' he luiks intae it and then he luiks at the aul' woman. He said, 'Mary,' he said, 'whit did you dae?' She said, 'I never...' He says, 'Whit did ye dae?' She says, 'I never done nothing.' He says, 'What's that in the cradle?' 'Ah,' she said, 'a wee thrup'ny bit,' she says. 'I pit intae't, for tae hansel the young wean.' 'Curse you, woman,' he said. He said, 'You done it.' He said, 'You ken fine,' he said, 'ye should never offer a elf silver, in no way,' he said. She said, 'I didnae mean nae hairm.' 'Well,' he said, 'bad luck upon us now,' he said. 'You done it,' he said. 'Ye should never've put that threepenny bit,' he says, 'into the cradle.' He said, 'It's a good job,' he said, 'that I ken what tae dae...or,' he said 'we'd have bad luck the rest of our days.' He said, 'Look,' he said, 'get me ma tools oot.' The aul' man had a big box o' tools for makin' his tin. 'An',' he said, 'you get aboot yir business,' he said, 'An',' he said...an' he kin'led up his fire. She says, 'What're ye gaunnae dae?' 'Never you mind,' he said. 'what I'm gaunnae dae,' he said. 'I ken what I'm gaunnae dae,' he said. 'You get aboot yir job,' he says. 'Only for you,' he says, 'I wadnae need, to have to dae all this trouble. You pit me,' he said, 'in this trouble, with you and,' he said, 'yir silly cairry-on,' he said, 'wi yir hanselling new-born weans,' he said, 'that's an elfin wean, no a traveller's wean ye're hansellin'.'

The old man got his files oot, an' he kin'led the fire up red an' he took the silver threepenny bit an' he put it in the fire an' he made it red-hot till it was red. An' he took his tin cutters, and he sat and he cut an' he cut an' he cut it in thin strips. Th' old woman sitting watching him. 'What're ye daein'?' she said. 'Never you mind,' he said, 'what I'm daein',' he said, 'it's your fault onyway,' he said, 'that I wad need to dae this. You get aboot yir business,' he said. 'Oh well,' she said, 'I'm no gaun any place today,' she said. 'I'm bidin' hame.' 'Well,' he says, 'bide at hame but,' he says, 'keep oot o' my road, don't come near me,' he said, 'it's your fault.'

He sat...and he soldered an' he hammered an' he hammered an' he choppit an' he hammered an' he hammered an' he solder't an' he hammered an' he polished an' he cleaned for a good strucken hour.

He says, 'Wumman. Have you any peens in yir basket?' She says, 'Whit?' He says, 'Peens.' (*Pins*, y'know?) 'Aye,' she said, – y'know the auld traiveller women in the olden days that used to hawk the hooses, they kept wee bunches o' wee...yon wee brass pins, ye ken? He says, 'Gimme yin o' the pins.' She says, 'Whit're ye gaunnae' – 'Never you mind whit I'm gaunnae do wi' it,' he said, 'it was yuir fault onywey. Gimme it. Never you mind what I'm gaunnae dae wi' it,' he said, 'I ken what I'm daein'. Curse upon you,' he said. 'You're the cause o't,' he said, 'ma wee cradle wasnae taken awa' wi' the...elves.'

He polished an' he cleaned an' he soldered, an' the old woman's lookin' over his shoulder – 'Dinna be luikin',' he said, 'it's your fault.' An he held it up tae her, efter he's finished, he says, 'Luik at that.' An' there it was, Ailie...the bonniest silver butterfly ye ever saw, miniature butterfly, soldered on t' the pin. A solid silver butterfly, made from the thrupenny piece; legs, wings; as if it was just...made it annoled, soldered on to the pin. He took it, an' he pinned it in the side o' the wee cradle, and' he took the wee cradle in his hand, an' away he went.

She says, 'Whaur are ye gaun?' 'Never you mind,' he said, 'where I'm gaun,'

he said, 'it's your fault. No your business.' 'Will you be long till you're back' –
'I don't know when I'll be back,' he said. 'I don't know when I'll be back, but
I'll be back sometime.'

Away he goes, back to the same bush where he met the elf. An' he takes the
wee cradle an' he sits an' he has a good luik at it, his ain sel', – an' he felt sad,
ye ken. An' he places it on the wee block where he had seen the elf, wi' the silver...butterfly pinned to the side o' the cradle.

Back he comes...over tae the front of his tent, an' he sits doon, an'...she says,
'Whaur were ye?' 'Never you mind where I was,' he said, 'nae business o' yours
where I was,' he said, 'you done it,' he says. She said, 'I didnae mean any
hairm.' 'Well,' he says, 'forget aboot it onyway,' he said. He said, 'I think I
managed to right it...to right the wrong now,' he said. 'I'll tell ye the morn,' he
said. 'I'll be better pleased tomorrow,' he said, 'when I...see what happened.'

So the night passes by, an' the next mornin' th' old man got his breakfast an'
away he goes...back to the block where he left the cradle, but when he arrives
there the cradle's gone. [Spat.] He spat on his hands. [Rubbed hands.] He comes
home, he's...dancin' and singin' comin' home to the old woman...the old
woman says, 'What's adae wi' ye, are ye gaun mad?' 'No,' he says, 'I'm no
gaun mad,' he said, 'Mary,' he said, 'the cradle's away,' he said, 'it's been accepted.' 'What,' she says, 'John.' – He says, 'It's been accepted,' he said. 'Aye
well,' she said. An' he said, 'It's no nae fault o' yours,' he said, 'no wi' your
help.'

So...I'm going through ma story...the cradle was gone an' he luiks up in the
bush, where he was cuttin' the wands – the cradle was gone, an' there pinned to
the bush, where he was cuttin' the wan's, was the most beautifullest pocket knife
that ever he saw in his life. Solid, inlaid with silver an' mother o' pearls...stuck
clasped to the tree where he'd cut the wan's, ye see?

Noo, in the olden days, to possess a good pocket knife...among basket-makers was just tae be out of this world, ye ken? Because they couldnae get a good
knife, and if you had a good knife in these days they came fae all parts tae see it,
and everybody, when the basket makers met...together, to show off this knife
was just like showin' off a Rolls Royce at the present day, ye know? An' when
this old man saw this knife stickin' to the tree, he said, 'Ah-h- it's for me,' he
said. Ye ken? He said, 'Never in my days,' he said. 'have ever I saw a pocket
knife like this,' he said – it was juist out o' this world for him.

He took it, and he closed it an' he put in his pocket. It was silver an' ivory, inlaid wi' mother-o'-pearl, an' a four-inch steel blade, an' he went up an' he
touched one o' the wee willows an' it just went...sailed through it, ye know?
'God bless me,' he said, 'that was left for me,' he said, 'by the wee elf,' he said,
'in payment for ma cradle...for ma cradle.'

Back he goes – pits it in his pocket, an' he's going skipping back the road. He
couldnae wait tae get intae his tent an' tell his auld wife. 'Well, John,' she said,
'what happened?' 'Well,' he says, 'the cradle...ma cradle was accepted,' he said,
'the elfs have got it, an',' he said, 'I hope it helps the wee babbie.' 'Well thank
God,' she says, 'for that.' 'An' it's nae help o' yours,' he said, 'mind it wasnae
your help. But,' he says, 'look what I got in return for it, Mary.' Th' auld woman
looked, 'God bless me,' she said. 'In all my days,' she said, 'John,' she said,
'that is a knife,' she said, 'that is a real knife,' she said. 'That's what ye call a
pocket-knife,' she said, 'an' mony's the body that'll be wantin' that fae you' –

'Ah but,' he says, 'it's mony's the body's no going' to get it fae me.'

'That,' he said, 'is a gift...an',' he said, 'a gift it'll be...tae me for the rest o' ma days.'

So...that knife done old John all his days, an' he became one o' the greatest basket-makers in the country, an' his fame o' makin' baskets spread far an' wide, an' every basket that was ever made wi' that knife was sold as quick as it was made. An' that knife passed doon, when old John died it passed tae his son,[41] and when his son died it passed to his grandson and so on right through the family, an' that knife could still be in circulation yet. Among the generation o' travellin' basket-makers was the Burkes...an' the Burkes...was my ancestors, because they were Williamsons...because there were Burkes...was Williamsons now...and Johnstons...among the travellin' people...and that knife could still be among some o' the family yet but naebody likes to talk aboot it. An' that's the last o' ma story.

* * * * *

As with the other arts, storytelling is best heard – and seen – in the flesh. A good narrator can exert a near-hypnotic effect on a large roomful of people, so that nothing else seems to exist for the story's duration. Travellers again are among the leading spell binders – Stanley Robertson is another noted virtuoso in this field.

Traveller culture receives little mention in official reports and academic theses, as they are concerned primarily with social and community problems, and the search for practical solutions to these problems. Culture has thus been a side issue in all these studies. The value and interest of the travellers' way of life, and their contribution in various fields is only now – if belatedly – being recognised.

Among younger travellers a process of acculturation is at work, and Betsy Whyte reported that some of them despise the 'silly old songs and stories'. As we have seen, this is very much what happened earlier in the wider, settled community.[42] Among those who reject this material, there is a feeling that it was part of the bad old days: 'Some travellers are afraid to appreciate the old culture because they were so held down in it.'

The huge increases in both unemployment and homelessness during the past decade have driven some hitherto settled people, especially the younger couples, to take to the road – witness the small but increasing number of New Age Travellers. The Criminal Justice and Public Order Bill, with its draconian – and conceivably anti-traveller – powers in England and Wales, may push more NATs northwards to Scotland. But Jane Turriff, of the older 'ethnic' travellers (their preferred distinguishing adjective) reports, 'There are fewer people travelling around now...there used to be lots of visiting between families.'

Sheila Stewart, who was for some years a member of the Secretary of State for Scotland's advisory committee on travellers, reports on recent developments. Partly owing to her pressure, the law regarding traveller children's schooling has been rewritten: they need not attend in the summer months provided they complete 200 half-days in winter. Of the NATs she says: 'They've made local authorities sit up and *see* their plight – ethnic travellers were always so timid...'; and of the travellers' culture: '50 percent has gone during this last decade...the outside world is seeping in, it edges its way in...my generation will be the last to care...'

Stanley Robertson is one of three travellers whose writings have taken their culture, stories and life-experience to a wider audience than ever before.[43] He still sings, and he feels strongly and creatively about the singing tradition:

> When a race of people lose their culture then a kind of genocide takes place. The travelling People of Scotland were great tradition bearers of story and song. Names like Jeannie Robertson, Lizzie Higgins, Belle Stewart and Jane Turriff came to the front because of the folk song revival and they started a great interest in ballad singing amongst the Scaldie and travelling populations. During the fifties the big muckle ballads were being sung especially within the traveller families. The sixties also attracted some more travelling people to continue to render the ballads but another influence was starting to interfere with the natural oral succession flow. It was mainly the social structure which changed dramatically, and the travellers, now mostly settled, began to surrender their inheritance for a non-culture. It became apparent that the old ways and customs were being eradicated from their lives and a more contemporary ideology replaced their culture. The ballads were no longer being transmitted orally and the younger generations were succumbing to modern ways. To most of the young folks the old ways carried with them a stigma and any associations with these things were to be shunned.
>
> Fortunately a few settled travellers still instilled within their children the awesome responsibility that they were tradition bearers. The issue brought forth a small surge of male and female singers who took a pride in their oral culture with a great emphasis in the big ballad.
>
> Over the last ten years (in my opinion), the girls are more faithful in their stewardship as perpetuators of the lore than the men. Both my daughters Nicole and Gabrielle have a passion for the ballads and they do sing them privately as well as in public. My son Anthony also has expressed a desire to learn more of the muckle sangs and this gives me lasting pleasure.
>
> Somehow here in the north-east of Scotland the bothy ballad has had a revitalisation but the classical traditional ballad has not.
>
> Though I teach my family through the medium of the oral tradition, most bothy ballads are being sought after through books. They are very pleasant songs but they do not have the important authenticity and powerful aura of the classical ballad, such as 'Johnie o' the Brine', 'My Son David' or 'Glenlogie', which are more suited to the oral tradition.
>
> Personally I would like to hear more of the big ballads sung at the festivals by the men because the girls have been faithful in singing the ballads. With the untimely death of Lizzie Higgins last year [1993] I felt a deep sense of remorse because I knew that such a traditional stalwart was completely unreplaceable. Therefore I stated to my own daughters that they were only a handful of the people who were left with the awesome task of keeping alive this wonderful rich heritage that was their legacy from their ancestors, who guarded this treasure of ancient lore from a sacred cache of gems.[44]

Footnotes

1. Jane Turriff, 30 November 1980, Mintlaw. Within a few days of this date I visited travellers Betsy and Bryce Whyte at Montrose; Jane Turriff and Danny Stewart at Mintlaw; and Belle Stewart, Sheila Stewart and her son Ian, with their relatives Willie and Bella MacPhee, at Blairgowrie. Unless otherwise stated, their quoted comments were made at this time; also, from the same time, comments from Sheila and Andrew Douglas, who are closely involved with travellers.

2. Whyte, 1990, p. 183.
3. Williamson, 1983, p. 16.
4. L. Spence, 1955; quoted by Gentleman and Swift, 1971, p. 9.
5. Duncan Campbell, 1910, p. 24.
6. Many folk festivals now include classes in storytelling.
7. See Briggs, 1970, part A.
8. Duncan Williamson, Lochgilphead site, 26 September 1980. Unless otherwise stated, all subsequent Williamson quotes are from this interview.
9. Betsy Whyte's comments were noted from conversations, Montrose, 1981–82.
10. For further comments, see Chapters III and IV and Appendix on the singing of Jeannie Robertson, Lizzie Higgins, Belle Stewart, Sheila Stewart, Jane Turriff, Stanley and Anthony Robertson, 'Old' Davie Stewart and Duncan Williamson. For recordings, see the eponymous tape accompanying this book, Scotsoun, SSC 076; see also *The Muckle Sangs*, Scottish Tradn. Series, CTRAX 9005 and CDTRAX 9005, 1992; more than half the singers are of traveller stock.
11. Betsy Whyte was an exception. She did not think of herself as a singer, but her more reserved and inward style was meltingly persuasive.
12. MacColl and Seeger, 1977, p. 21.
13. Gentleman and Swift, 1971, p. 10.
14. Farmer, 1947, part 2, chapter 2.
15. Gentleman and Swift, 1971, p. 10.
16. *Scotland's Travelling People*, sixth term report by the Secretary of State's Advisory Committee; introductory letter by Harry M. Garland, chairman, 1992.
17. *Counting Travellers in Scotland*, the 1992 census report by the Advisory Committee, p. 66.
18. *The Scotsman*, 29 March 1994.
19. In addition to Gentleman and Swift 1971, there are six 'term reports' and the Census – see notes 16 and 17. All these give a picture of the practical problems and the search for solutions, but only one – 1971 – makes a (scanty) reference to the culture of the travellers, on pp. 44, 58, 60 and 73. There is no reference at all to the best-selling books by travellers (Betsy Whyte, Duncan Williamson, Stanley Robertson) nor to the honours bestowed on Jeannie Robertson and Belle Stewart.
20. See Williamson, 1994, pp. 116–17, for sketches of different kinds of tents.
21. Duncan Williamson, camp near Cupar, Fife, 19 September 1977.
22. Jane Turriff, 8 November 1976, Fetterangus. See also James Porter, 'The Turriff Family of Fetterangus', *Folk Life* 16, 1976, pp. 5–26.
23. Several said violence used to be considered as proof of love, and Betsy Whyte had often heard 'He disnae think much o' her: he's never laid a hand on her since they were married.'
24. Gentleman and Swift, 1971, p. 59; Whyte 1979, pp. 1, 20–21, 104.
25. Presented by MacColl and Seeger, 24 September 1980.
26. Can be hired from Timothy Neat, Duncan of Jordanstone College of Art, Dundee.
27. Quoted by Merriam 1964, p. 83, who adds, 'Music…is conceived as wealth in the form of intangible goods in many societies.'
28. Letter from Stanley Robertson, 18 November 1980.
29. These visits were organised by Edinburgh Folk Festival.
30. See Ailie Munro, *Folk Music Journal*, vol. 6, no. 2, 1991, p. 158.
31. Lizzie Higgins, 9 November 1976, Aberdeen.
32. To be called an aristocrat by a traveller is a real compliment.
33. Allsop, 1972, p. 30–31.
34. Ibid, p. 164.
35. Ibid, p. 270.
36. Timothy Neat, 'The Summer Walkers', *Seer* 2, Dundee Art College magazine, p. 48.
37. See Gentleman and Swift, 1971, p. 112.

38. Goose: small practice pipe, with no drones.
39. *Tocher,* no. 33, p. 150. This issue contains a special feature on Duncan Williamson.
40. Duncan Williamson, recorded at Cupar, 19 September 1977. A problem in transcribing spoken tales is whether to include all occurrences of 'he says', 'she said', etc. To the listener, they act as a kind of oral punctuation: they are often spoken very rapidly, and they are not obtrusive. If they are removed from the written transcription, the whole style is altered.
41. Although this couple had no children of their own, Duncan pointed out that they might adopt an orphan, or a child from a large and poverty-stricken family. This was a common practice among travellers, especially among the childless.
42. This cycle of rejection followed by later revival is found in many different fields of human endeavour – it is connected with fashion in the widest sense of the word.
43. See Robertson 1988, 1989, 1990, 1992, 1993 and 1994; Whyte 1979 and 1990; Williamson 1983, 1985, 1987A, 1987B, 1989, 1990, 1991, 1992, 1994.
44. Stanley Robertson's letter, July 1994, Aberdeen.

Betsy Whyte

Duncan Williamson

VII *Signposts to the Millennium*

Rather than say 'the folk is dead' and attempt to keep folksong alive as
something quaint, antique and precious, let us say 'the folk is changing – and
its song with it', and then help whatever it is changing into – which may be
the whole people welded into one by the new media of communication – not
to be ashamed of its ancestors, but to select the makings of a new, more
universal idiom for the more stabilised society that we may hope is coming
into being, from the best materials available, whether old or new.[1]

Charles Seeger

To me, anything is acceptable. If it works, it will be absorbed; if not,
rejected.[2]

Dick Gaughan

The standards that we believed in [during the 1960s] drew a *line* of some
kind. I believe that...you have got to define the standards...and *action
change* in a thinking way. We will make mistakes in doing this, but unless we
are prepared to do it I think that we run the risk of fossilising our heritage on
the one hand, and on the other, we will forever have modern songs, albeit in
the 'idiom', that cannot really be integrated with the tradition.[3]

Ron Clark

Although the word 'revival' became, willy-nilly, a necessary part of this book's
sub-title (see second preface), the word has become somewhat ambivalent and is
now used in two different ways. First the usual meaning, and that which is
assumed throughout all the preceding pages, refers to the movement for
rediscovering folk/traditional music, in particular the post-Second World War
stage of rediscovery and re-creation. If we accept this meaning, we must ask
whether the reviving process, after close on 50 years, has succeeded? *Or*, the
continued use of the word can imply that revival music is not the real thing, is
not perpetuating the real traditional stuff enshrined for instance in the School of
Scottish Studies.[4] This arises because of the tremendous changes which have
taken place in that music and its performance. But 'change [is] ineluctably
bound to folk music tradition'.[5] It is just that the *pace* of change has been so
much faster during the last 50 years – a change which has been described as 'the
fundamental shift in consciousness which lies at the heart of the folk revival'.[6]
So in sticking to the first meaning I shall make no distinction between
perpetuation and revival. They are too closely intertwined by now. Instead, I will
try to describe and evaluate the chief developments in the folk scene during the
last dozen years.

The main thrust has been towards dispersal, infiltration or spreading through
the community, rather than increased attendance at those centres favoured by the
cognoscenti. Four examples are:

1. The Theatre

The 7.84 Company's productions; during Glasgow's 'Cultural Capital of

Europe' year (1990), *Jock Tamson's Bairns* and *The Ship*; and Tag Company's recent dramatisation of Grassic Gibbon's *A Scots Quair*.

'Now it is quite common to have a band or singers as an integral part of theatre performances.'[7]

2. The Media

Although *Macgregor's Gathering* was cut in 1992, Jimmie Macgregor himself continues, with detailed reports on the revival and other broadcasts. *Travelling Folk, Celtic Connections, Folk on Two,* and *Reel Blend* cover much ground on national radio, and folk music is included in many different kinds of programme. Local radio also makes a valuable contribution. Television offerings are meagre; both television and the press tend to concentrate on the big names. Linked with media coverage is the vast number of cassette tapes and compact discs now available.

3. The literary establishment

The Association for Scottish Literary Studies, for instance, hosted a wide-ranging Folksong Conference in Aberdeen during 1993.

4. Country Dancing

There has been a widespread resurgence in the popularity of various traditional forms of dancing.

The five primary areas of development, however, have been in song; storytelling; instrumental music; protest song; and the influence on education and the wider community. Other topics which will be commented on are: TMSA; world music and *Folk Roots*; clubs, festivals, magazines; art music; and the School of Scottish Studies.

1. Song

There has been a noticeable reduction in the singing of the big ballads, the muckle sangs. There are take-offs, yes – such as Tich Frier's enjoyable 'Matty Groves'[8] (based on Child Ballad 81). Parody can be regarded, in part at least, as a tribute to the original,[9] but it can also betray a kind of psychological block: far from being 'unashamed of soul', some singers now do seem rather ashamed of this commodity. Late in 1990, at a ceilidh in the wee back room of Glasgow's Scotia Bar on the evening of MP Norman Buchan's funeral (which had been attended by over a thousand mourners), I felt a yearning for a long tragic ballad as a kind of catharsis at the end of that day. It would have been a fitting tribute, too, to the one-time teacher of English, whose first hearing, in 1951, of the traditional *singing* of ballads (up to then he had taught ballads as poetry only) was a revelation of Damascus Road proportions, and who became one of the pillars of the revival in Scotland. But all we got that evening in the Scotia Bar were comic songs, old music-hall ditties, one bothy-type song, and a few old blues snatches from a man well on in the drink. (Another traditional recourse: first, do not get serious; second, get drunk.)

There has, however, been a flood of new songs and new settings, and some wonderful new singers. Here are a few of the good songs written within the last decade or so (out-of-date recordings are in brackets):

Recording or Publication	Author and Title	Content
Sung by Ed Miller *Border Background* Folk Legacy C115 (1989)	Matt Armour: 'Generations of Change'	Change within four generations of a family.
The Sang in the Bluid Scotsoun, SSC077 (1986)	Sheila Douglas: 'Chernobyl Lullaby'	Humanitarian.
Sunsets I've Galloped Into Greentrax CTRAX 020 (1988)	Archie Fisher: 'The Great North Road'	Love, and longing for home.
Sung by Ed Miller *Border Background* Folk Legacy C115 (1989)	Jack Foley: 'A Bottle of the Best'	Convivial.
	Tich Frier: 'Bloody Charlie'	Historical/political: a bitter comment on the Bonnie Prince Charlie legend.
A Different Kind of Love Song Celtic CMC 017 (1985)	Dick Gaughan: 'Think Again'	A powerful anti-war song.
In *Folk songs of Scotland* bk. 2, Jarrold (1981)	Jimmie Macgregor: 'Jinkin' Jeannie'	Love.
Disc: *Glasgow Horizons* LIFL 7018, Lismor Recordings (1990). Also on cassette	Geordie McIntyre: 'Inveroran'	W. Highlands. Gaeldom and the urban Scots' roots.
Singing Land Dunkeld (1985), Dunc 004	Dougie MacLean: 'Rescue me'	Cultural claustrophobia.
Words, Words, Words Greentrax CTRAX 013 (1988)	Adam McNaughtan: 'Oor Hamlet'	Story of Hamlet in Glasgowese and other linguistic sources. (*Health warning:* should not be listened to by those of a nervous temperament or a tendency to hysteria.)
Border Background Folk Legacy C115 (1989)	Ed Miller: 'At Home with the Exiles'	Defined by the title – internationalism.
Essential, Eclectic ECL CD9103 (1992)	Rod Paterson: 'The Auld Toon Shuffle'	About Edinburgh.
Rhyme and Reason Gallus, Gal 104 (1990)	Nancy Nicholson: 'Cuddle'	Make love not war.
I Saw the Wild Geese Flee Springthyme SPRC 1015 (1984)	Jim Reid: 'The Wild Geese' and 'Rohallion'	Sensitive traditional settings of Violet Jacobs poems.

Sung by Tich Frier on *The Morigan*, Celtic Music CM C052 (1989)	Ian Walker: 'Hawks and Eagles fly like Doves'	A peace song.
Springtime Music (1990)	John Watt: 'Muchty & the Brig'	Joint celebration of the Forth Bridge 100th anniversary and Auchtermuchty Festival's 10th.
Clearsong, Dunkeld DUNC 005 (1990)	Sheena Wellington: 'Julia's Song'	Welcome to the World for a new baby.

Older Influential Songs

[Disc: *Unity Creates Strength* NEV R007]	Danny Kyle: 'Great Iron Ship'	Industrial, in support of the Clydesdale ship building workers' struggles of the 1970s.
Scottish Songs Ross Records, CDGR 092 (1986)	Stuart MacGregor: 'Coshieville'	Conflict between love and money.
[Disc: *Claddagh* CCA7 (1979)]	Hamish Henderson: 'Freedom Come-all-ye' (see p. 43–4)	A vision of humankind's struggle for liberation.

Other songwriters include Eric Bogle, Dave Goulder, Andy Hunter, Robin Laing, Iain Macdonald, Brian McNeill, Rab Noakes, Eileen Penman, Craig and Charlie Reid, Davie Steele, Ken Thomson; and Michael Marra's brilliant songs *with piano accompaniment* have helped to make this unique instrument more folk-acceptable.

Singers not yet mentioned who have come to the fore, or stayed there over this period, include:

Cilla Fisher and Artie Tresize, with Gary Coupland: their *Singing Kettle* concerts and tapes for children[10]
Maureen Jelks: always a pleasure to listen to[11]
Jean Redpath: Volume 6 of *The Songs of Burns* shows her continuing excellence (now an MBE)[12]
Heather Heywood: a superb singer of classical mould[13]
Janet Russell and Christine Kydd: with fine two-part arrangements and performance[14]
Eileen Penman: a versatile and dexterous singer (see below for recordings)
Andy Hunter[15] and Rod Paterson (see below).

Ray Fisher; Hamish Imlach; Christine Primrose; Karen Matheson of Capercaillie; Donnie Munro of Runrig; Sara Grey; Ian Walker and Ian Bruce (Glasgow based) and Ian Macdonald (formerly of Lewis).

Glasgow's year as Cultural Capital of Europe in 1990 saw the well-timed appearance of recordings of Glasgow songs. *I was born in Glasgow*[16] contains deathless Will Fyffe ditties, 'Twelve and a tanner the Bottle' ('How can a fellow be happy, When happiness costs such a lot?') and 'I belong to Glasgow' complete with its rarely heard verses.

McGinn of the Calton[17] (the book) is an unfinished autobiography, whilst the tape has excellent performances of McGinn's *sui generis* songs, only slightly marred by some overkill from Adam McNaughtan as commentator. This is in sharp contrast to Matt himself on *Revival in Britain*[18] – he always manages to sound exuberant yet relaxed at the same time; but even he is overshadowed by Enoch Kent's quietly seductive singing of his own songs, and by Charles Parker's wonderful 'No Room at the Inn'.

In 1990, *One Singer One Song*[19] was also published, featuring 50 songs plus the words of many more verses scattered throughout the 'stories'. Much carefully researched local and indeed national history is contained within these pithy accounts; in particular the story of the folk revival in Glasgow is told in the detail it deserves. (Let's hope similar accounts from other parts – Aberdeenshire, the North-West, the Islands, the Borders – will soon appear whilst memories at least are still alive.) A pity the music transcriptions are not quite up to the same standard: McVicar seems uncertain as to the difference between 3/4 and 6/8 time.

The Sang's the Thing: Voices from Lowland Scotland[20] is an important collection of memories from farm-workers, tradesmen, travellers and fishermen, with two or three songs from each contributor (some tunes are not faultless, though). These memories give a vivid picture of life in the early and middle parts of this century, and so are at least as much 'the thing' as are the songs.

Lastly, the publication of *Alias MacAlias*[21] has provided essential reading for anyone who wants to understand the revival. An anthology of writings by Hamish Henderson – poet, folk collector, songwriter and activist – it spans 50 years, and includes essays on people, folktales, literature and politics as well as folksongs. Henderson's influence has already been described in Chapter III, and no-one has been a more congenial follower of the democratic muse. He is also in frequent demand as a singer... so his book fits in nicely under SONG, although it covers so much more besides.

2. Storytelling

One of the most ancient of folk arts but the most recently revived, this has caught on over much of Europe. As suggested in Chapter VI, the travellers have led the way in this rediscovery (they themselves never lost the art): Duncan Williamson, Stanley Robertson, Willie MacPhee, and the sadly-missed Betsy Whyte.[22] But many 'country hantle' artists have also appeared, including Sheila and Andrew Douglas, David Campbell, Robin Williamson and the Americans Barbara McDermitt and Linda Bandolier.

There are some quite surrealist elements in this art – subliminal echoes from the powerful world of the unconscious – as well as more readily perceived symbolic material which supports and interprets life-experiences. For instance in the 'Silly Jack' stories, Jack, usually the younger brother, is lazy (unmotivated) and stupid, but when he is driven by dire need (no money, no food) to go on a journey (a symbol for life itself) he turns out to be both brave and shrewd, is often shown to be more caring and unselfish than his older brothers and hence receiving more help from people, animals, birds etc. met on the way, and in the end is highly successful in his quest.

At storytelling events you will usually find one or two singers and/or instrumentalists included in the programme, and there are now week-long conferences and festivals, occasional radio or TV broadcasts, and visits by storytellers to junior schools. The value of the latter in particular can hardly be over-estimated. I have undying memories of Friday afternoons in my own primary school days when a Miss Rivington – the name seemed entirely suitable for I was always totally riveted – told us stories of Norse gods, of Beowulf and Grendel and suchlike. She did not read them, she *told* them. She was tall and dark, she had an arresting voice, and it was the high spot of the week. Not that I couldn't read – I was an early reader – but stories *told direct* have a special gripping quality for children.

A ten-year-old boy wrote to Duncan: 'I really liked your visit...I would like you to come every week... You are as good as Roald Daul [sic].' Linda Williamson, who pioneered the Traditional Storytellers Agency, once declared: 'We are not performers but educationists...this is, for want of a better term, religion.'

Present-day creation within the tradition has appeared: witness Dolina MacLennan's fine tape of Highland stories written and told by herself.[23]

3. Instrumental Music

The instrumental explosion of the 1970s has now become more like a volcanic eruption. Singer Cy Laurie, mine host of Glasgow's Riverside Club and initiator of other thriving ceilidh-dance centres in Edinburgh, remarked in 1991 that young people seeking a national identity through music enthusiastically embrace the tunes and through them the dances, but have difficulty with the songs; he pointed to the popularity of Gaelic groups such as Runrig who play to huge audiences with only a small minority understanding the words.

Various world influences can be traced – including the omnipresent Irish – but the strongest is that of jazz. The strict time structure of harmony changes in jazz accords well with the country-dance structure of most tunes chosen by instrumental groups; in both, a basic number of time-units (or bars) is repeated. This influence started in the 1930s when, Tom Anderson recalled,[24] out-of-work Shetland musicians used to listen to recordings of jazz greats such as the gypsy guitarist Django Reinhardt. They studied his time-and-rhythm style, as in 'Sweet Sue',[25] and tried to adapt it to their own music; Willie Johnson, a guitarist, took on the piano's traditional role of accompanist.

In the 1980s, Johnson and other Shetlanders were living in Edinburgh beside young Jim Sutherland, who played various instruments. Guitarists Jack Evans and Rod Paterson were with Jock Tamson's Bairns. Influenced by the Shetlanders, and with the avowed aim of 'Scottish rhythm and swing', Evans, Paterson and Sutherland started The Easy Club; Paterson sang 'Black is the colour of my true love's hair'.[26] Encouragement for new ventures came from Billy Kay of the *Odyssey* broadcast series. In 'Lord Gordon's Kitchen Boy' (Child 252)[27] Jack Evans is joined by Lowland piper Hamish Moore and jazz saxophonist Dick Lee. The jazziest playing of Scots country dance music I have heard·is the Gaelic group Capercaillie's 1989 'Argyll Reel', with other reels[28] – achieved by syncopation, strong off-beat accenting, subtle bodhran percussion and strict 4-bar or 8-bar structures. Of those attempting to fuse Scots traditional song with rock music accompaniment, the most successful group is 5-Hand Reel: Bobby Eaglesham sings in 'I'll lay ye doon'[29] (see version of this song in Chapter IV). Two more very successful Gaelic groups incorporating jazz are Ossian and Runrig.

Groups which steered clear of jazz are The Battlefield Band and Silly Wizard; the latter's notable associates have been singer-songwriter Andy M Stewart, and virtuoso accordionist and composer Phil Cunningham.

There was no jazz influence either on the clarsach-playing duo Sileas of Mary McMaster and Patsy Seddon,[30] who also sing well. Alison Kinnaird, an established player and a pioneer for this instrument, has produced two books: a collection *The Harp Key*, and a tutor *The Small Harp*. Another noted clarsach player and composer is Savourna Stevenson (see below). Improvements in clarsach construction, which have opened the door to more new music for it, have been made by Mark Norris of Peebles.

The Best of Ross and Cromarty[31] consists of two cassettes of traditional music, with many more instrumental than vocal items; it has been produced by Ross and Cromarty District Council, which is 'committed to developing all types of music, at all levels'. Half the musicians are under the age of 21. There is virtually no American or jazz influence, but exquisite, small-is-beautiful singing from Kirsteen Lewis, Tamsin Jamieson and Jane Calder, a slow relaxed account of 'Come all ye tramps and hawkers' from Norman Stewart, and a haunting song 'Homeland' from Ivan Drever.

Jim Sutherland is making, or 'discovering', folk-linked music. He believes linear treatment is the best way to develop Scottish instrumental music, 'to work not chordally but contrapuntally...the strands sounding together.' His music for three female voices, 'Time Quines', shows intriguing antiphonal treatment, while for the Gaelic film *From the Island* he is a 'soundscape artist'.[32] Somotherland is his experimental group.

The Whistlebinkies would require a whole article to do justice to them and to their chief composer, flautist Eddie McGuire. I wrote about them in the first edition of this book, so will restrict comment here to McGuire's more recent work. He bestrides the worlds of folk and art music. He studied first in Glasgow, then in London, then later in Stockholm where he remembered his Scottish roots. His *Spirit of Flight* (1991) is the first ballet music for Scottish folk group and orchestra, and *Riverside* (also 1991) is the first symphonic work for folk group and orchestra. But *Inner Sound*[33] is for the Whistlebinkies alone (though the link with art music is retained by composer James MacMillan singing his own setting of Soutar's 'The Tryst'). The title piece was composed for a film about Scottish coastal oil exploration: in this you can hear the authentic ebb and flow of sea on shore.

Many original dance tunes in traditional style appear in McGuire's work, notably a fiendish strathspey for Captain Hook in the *Peter Pan* ballet music.[34] (I always felt strathspeys were potentially threatening, with their double-dotted rhythm, and the Scots snap sounding like a stamped foot.) While in Hong Kong for a performance of *Peter Pan*, McGuire was invited to meet composers and musicians in Beijing; there he arranged an exchange of folk ensembles between Scotland and China for the following year. So the Whistlebinkies became the first Scottish folk group to tour in China. They were warmly received, and found surprising musical links between the two countries.

Other groups include Gaberlunzie, Harness, Wildfire, The Dougie MacLean Band, The Boys of the Lough, Wolfestone, Foundry Band, The McCalmans, and now Clan Alba and Old Blind Dogs. Among duos are the well-established Brian Miller and Charlie Soane.

The TMSA's competition for new melodies in traditional style led to the publication of *The 90s Collection* with over a hundred tunes. Many folk instruments have surfaced during the last twenty years: Lindsay ('Twanger') Porteous has a large collection which he takes on visits to schools, for him to demonstrate and the children to try out (they love it). The tiny jew's or jaw's harp is one of his specialities – and storyteller Duncan Williamson invariably takes one with him.

Instrumental playing has become so popular, it has led to what has been called 'a plague of fiddlers'; in Dunoon, '...they did a monster take over with their ninety-mile-an-hour reels and jigs, and no-one else got a look in'.[35] Some festival organisers have been driven to label a room 'For Singers Only'. The cliché 'too much of a good thing' springs to mind – and in more senses than one, for often the same (dance) tune is repeated over and over again, usually *forte*: not infrequently there are textural differences in instrumentation, but no melodic and very little harmonic variation. This is fine if you are dancing (or if you are playing, it seems) because the musical event is thereby transformed; but if you are sitting listening, the repetition can become positively tedious. One sometimes feels the players are enjoying themselves more than the listeners are. But to listen to a good instrumentalist playing with a group, in 'concerto style', with the added textural and antiphonal interest thus afforded, can be really interesting: one thinks of Simon Thoumire (concertina), of Kathryn Tickell (pipes), and of fiddler Aly Bain, the genius who – solo or accompanied – can enchant his listeners with everything from a reel to a slow air or lament. There are also 'listening tunes', for example 'Niel Gow's lament for his second wife'.

In the last decade several works have appeared which show a new approach. They are types of programme music, with descriptively titled movements, written for groups of instruments but without a conductor, as in chamber music or jazz; they are longer (over half an hour), and performed in a concert rather than ceilidh situation. Eddie McGuire's work has already been mentioned. William Jackson's *Wellpark Suite*[36] and his later *St Mungo: a Celtic Suite for Glasgow*[37] and Freeland Barbour's *Killiecrankie*[38] (different instruments are overdubbed for the last); these show imaginative and affectionate use of original material in traditional style, though the themes in their wholeness seem sacrosanct, and again there is much repetition. Savourna Stevenson's suites *Tweed Journey*[39] and *Cutting the Chord*[40] are far freer, the themes are less restricted time-wise – the latter has 10/4 and 10/8 sections – and it is multi-cultural; this music is going places, above all it is refreshingly *new*. In *Tweed Journey* the contrast of different musical sources fits the image of a river accepting all intake as it sweeps its way to the sea.

The most *exciting* work I have heard is the suite *Savage Dance*,[41] played by the Cauld Blast Orchestra and originating in Communicado Theatre's show *Jock Tamson's Bairns* for Burns Night January 1990 and the start of Glasgow's 'Cultural Capital' year (this group's original intention was to merge folk and jazz). The third piece in the suite, also called 'The Cauld Blast', opens with a version of 'Lenox love to Blantyre', the traditional air to which Robert Burns wrote 'O went thou in the cault blast'; this, his last song, was inspired by Jessie

Lewars, the young girl who nursed him through his final illness. After the air, played slowly and *rubato*, the jazz style takes over, with spasmodic outbursts – the first spatterings of rain and growls of thunder – the storm builds up relentlessly until suddenly cut off in a dramatic silence (possibly signifying death). Then come musical comments, a kind of sad instrumental recitative which seems on the point of articulate speech; then after another frenzied turmoil the 'Lenox love' air is heard again, and dies away. To me, this piece is about Burns in the last year of his life. Commenting on the suite, composers Wimhurst and Kettley say: 'It's about *struggle*, a journey through Scotland, and state-of-the-nation...it's hard-hitting.' The Cauld Blast Orchestra's work is not always so successful, but – in a different direction to Stevenson – they also are going places.

4. Protest Song

The word 'struggle' provides a link to this next group. Protest was an important element in the fifties and sixties. It became less fashionable in the seventies, but by the eighties the increasing polarisation of rich and poor, unemployment, apartheid, the women's movement, the nuclear threat, pollution and other national and world topics, produced many new songs in this genre.

We will start with women's protest, because it is the newest and most striking issue to come forward on the folk scene. This took two forms: first, the appearance of more events and more groups for women only, and second, new songs written about women.

Singer Eileen Penman explained the need for the former: '...because the folk scene was very macho, with concerts and clubs dominated by male organisers, musicians and singers'.[42] This despite the accepted fact – a curious contradiction – that women have often been the main transmitters of folk song and culture. Another well-known singer, Janet Russell, has pointed out that these women tradition bearers passed on their songs *within the family circle*, or *round the camp-fire*, but not in the performance arena; that is why women-only events became necessary, to give women more confidence in performing to bigger audiences.

These women's events were wide-spread: Women 'Live' months in 1982 and 1983, in Edinburgh; concerts at certain folk festivals, notably Auchtermuchty; in Glasgow, which saw the formation of the women's choir Eurydice, and the women's Mak Merry festivals in the month of November; in Aberdeen also with Women's Festivals; in Dumfries, with the group Stravaig forming after Sheena Wellington's first women's weekend (and in Fife, the Palaver group); and in Dundee and other centres. Gordeanna MacCulloch, the leader of Eurydice, stresses that she supports equality between women and men, 'the positive rather than the negative emphasis'. Other women's groups are The S/he Bearz (Glasgow), Fabulamas (Aberdeen) and Blo-na-Gael (Dundee). Jae Austen, of Blo-na-Gael, has news of two women's drumming groups: the 50-strong Shebang (Glasgow) and another in Dundee.

The group whose repertoire is most explicitly feminist is Sisters Unlimited;[43] four fine women singers one of whom, Janet Russell, is a Scot. They always receive an enthusiastic welcome when they perform in Scotland.

Second, the new songs about women. Few have appeared in Scotland as yet, but four examples are: Penman's 'Time for the Women' (anti-war) and a stronger one 'I've been a wife'; 'Strong women rule us all' a song about Flora MacDonald; and the delightful 'They sent a woman' by Nancy Nicholson. But most of the more overt songs come from south of the border and show which way the wind is blowing – it is blowing northwards. In Peggy Seeger's song 'B-side'[44] she addresses men as if the situation were reversed, so that women were the more powerful and aggressive sex and men must be warned to be careful: a highly entertaining and thought-provoking *tour de force;* the title of an earlier disc is *Different Therefore Equal.* Then Sandra Kerr's 'We Were There'[45] is perhaps the most moving song of the decade, for any woman with any sense of history; '...women have a hidden yet vital history to uncover, relate and celebrate,' says Kerr. The disc sleeve has a photograph of a suffragette being frog-marched by two burly policemen.

Mention of suffragettes reminds one of violence against women, highly topical now. In June 1994 the Scottish Office, in consultation with Scottish Women's Aid, initiated a media campaign against domestic violence, on four television channels, with posters around the country. COSLA recommended that more than 700 refuge-houses for women are needed throughout Scotland: at present only 239 exist. *CHANGE*, a programme of talks and study, was devised to help men convicted of domestic violence, and to give local courts another option when sentencing them. Other men's groups exist, not necessarily connected with violence but filling a need. Larry Butler, who works in this area says, 'There are interesting groups popping up all over Scotland.'[46]

Continuing male/female violence is directly linked with the struggle *against* patriarchal attitudes and *for* equal rights. The events and the songs described above are helping to cure the feminism-phobia which still exists in Scotland: 'I'm not a feminist but...' often precedes remarks even in the smallest degree supportive of women. This is caused partly by a simple semantic error (see any reputable dictionary) regarding the meaning of the word feminism. One well-educated, male correspondent, who normally uses words correctly and even writes about folk song, actually wrote to me, 'Feminism demeans women'. You might as well say that the Civil Rights movement in the USA demeans black people. Seeger's title *Different Therefore Equal* sums up the aim of both movements.

Of one thing I am quite certain: in a hundred years' time the rantings of present-day feminism-phobists will be as laughable as are the press-cuttings of men writing about the women's suffrage movement early this century. (A selection of these were on display in an exhibition at Glasgow's People's Palace museum during the 1960s – an ideal place to go if you felt low and in need of a good laugh.) This may be why some feminism-haters today are reluctant to have their spoken or handwritten effusions put into cold print.

Many protest songs have appeared on other topics, including a series of three cassette tapes called *Songs from under the bed;* also *Songs from under the Poll Tax*; and a cassette of songs and poems by Morris Blythman (*aka* Thurso Berwick) entitled *Aa Breenge In*[47] on the highly topical nationalist issue but from the republican viewpoint. The ninth issue of *Political Song News* became the first Scottish issue, with more of Blythman's still highly relevant songs and writings. Other songs on particular issues include Ivan Drever's 'Close it down'[48] (closing of mines and shipyards); Adam McNaughtan's 'The Glasgow Councillor' (the 'new' socialism);[49] Andy Barnes's 'The Last Leviathan' (slaughter of whales); Nancy Nicholson's 'Woe is me' (sea pollution); Jim Ferguson's 'Radiation Blues' (against Cruise missiles); and Penman's 'Poll Tax Dodger' (the last three are in *Songs from under...* tapes).

The SNP (Scottish National Party) seems not to use songs much in its campaigns: the only examples in use during the last decade were 'Letter from America' (on Highland Clearances) and 'Cap in Hand' both recorded by The Proclaimers; the Corries' 'Flower of Scotland' (also sung at rugby and football matches); and Burns's 'Scots wha hae' sung at the end of every SNP conference.[50]

5. Influence of the Revival

On Education

Great progress has been made, both in schools and in Glasgow's Royal Scottish Academy of Music and Drama (RSAMD) which trains music teachers. All secondary school pupils now, at some point in their course, learn something about Scottish folk music, and it is an integral part of the Standard Grade music exam. And most students at the RSAMD are exposed to traditional music of various kinds, in courses given by Peter Cooke (mainly 'world' music) and Jo Miller (Scottish music, now as a consultative teacher and planner). (As regards university music students, Cooke's pioneering work at Edinburgh has had a distinctly broadening effect; the course now covers indigenous world music, including African, as well as western art music.) Teachers are supplied with a valuable book – *The Music of Scotland*[51] – with an accompanying tape, in which the importance of live performance is stressed and which encourages teachers to invite folk musicians to their schools. Thus, doors are opening for many schoolchildren who might otherwise have little chance of hearing their own musical heritage.

An important development at the RSAMD is planned for September 1996: a new three-year degree course, BA Scottish Music, will centre on traditional music of Scotland. The course will be half practical – with tuition in singing, clarsach, fiddle, pipes, accordion – and half academic, with co-operation on archival material from the School of Scottish Studies, Edinburgh University.

Still in Glasgow, Alison McMorland and Jo Miller were jointly appointed from 1990 to 1992, by Strathclyde Regional Council, as facilitators or enablers: both noted singers and communicators, they co-ordinated work done in the traditional arts by different bodies. Ever since the early seventies McMorland has been concerned with art as a medium for change, in particular the transforming influence of the whole folk ethos on the lives of ordinary people. She has worked with children[52] and on inter-generational projects. She now works on community care projects throughout Scotland. Under the title of 'Living Arts', and with the co-operation of dancer Richard Coaten, she has initiated new methods of training staff for elderly and residential care. This kind of work is now an accepted part of social responsibility.

There are a few traditional performers teaching in schools: fiddle in Orkney (Ivan Drever) and Caithness (Ian Sinclair), and ballad-singing for a while in Grampian region (Elizabeth Stewart).

On the Wider Community

So many activities have developed, and so many reports have come to me from every region of Scotland, that it is necessary not only to be selective but to summarise these interesting accounts. A clockwise 'tour' of the regions follows, starting at the South-West, with some comments from residents.

Dumfries and Galloway

Instrumental music has caught up with unaccompanied singing. There are several fiddle clubs; the Strathspey and Reel Society joined forces with one of the four Fiddle and Accordion Clubs. Local radio station *West Sound* has a two-hour weekly folk programme. Local pipe-bands teach youngsters. There are folk clubs in Gatehouse of Fleet, Thornhill and Stranraer, and three local festivals including one near Whithorn (where St Ninian landed from Ireland). In 1995 a festival is planned in Carlisle.

Strathclyde

Glasgow

There was much local support, both regional and district, for the 1990 Year of Culture, including the appointment of an administrator, Ellen Morris, for the Glasgow Folk and Traditional Arts Trust. The biggest 1990 event, *Glasgow's Glasgow* exhibition covered 1,000 years of history. *The Tryst Festival* had programmes specially designed for schools.

The Riverside Club became a centre for the renaissance of country dancing, with crowds of young people queuing outside. The owner Cy Laurie, a fine singer himself, has built up this club, and an Edinburgh ceilidh club as well. Successful TMSA ceilidhs took place at the Riverside.

Brendan McLaughlin revived the Scotia Bar, an important centre for folk and poetry. He gave me a copy of *Workers City,* subtitled *The Real Glasgow Stands Up,* a collection of stories, poems, and essays; the editor claims that the 'culture tag' of the 1990 celebrations had 'nothing whatever to do with the working – or workless – class poor of Glasgow but everything to do with big business and money'.[53] A group has formed around the *Workers City* ethos: they occasionally perform for *Soundhouse* productions. McLaughlin notes the split between the trends, the 'cores', of Irish and Scottish nationalisms.

Allan Morris, remembering the 1984 miners' strike says 'through the participation of singers like Dick Gaughan and Hamish Imlach many political activists were exposed to folk song for the first time'.[54]

Ewan McVicar set up a company *Gallus Music* for publishing music and recording tapes; during 1990 he wrote for a free sheet *Culture City.*

Two of the revival's longest-serving figures, Robin Hall and Jimmie Macgregor, continued their careers 'on the other side of the microphone', with Radio Clyde, BBC Scotland and the World Service. For his services to Scottish heritage and culture Macgregor was awarded the MBE in 1994.

In the same year a superb Political Song Concert at the Tron Theatre presented protest songs from 1950 onwards: on the three main protest situations in

Scotland (the Stane, EIIR and Polaris – see Chapter III) and on international issues: South Africa, apartheid and Mandela; Chile and Victor Jara; and the Black
Civil Rights movement. *The Eskimo Republic* script was by Gordon McCulloch;
the songs are still astonishingly relevant. Hall and MacGregor were among a
great bunch of old hands.

Dunoon

Here is part of Alison Duncan's account: 'Many functions use folk and traditional performers now; this tendency is also apparent in material chosen for
competitions at Tighnabruaich annual music festival. Flute, singing, fiddle and
accordion workshops have been held, and women's singing weekends. The
Cowal games, a huge annual Highland affair – "a punters' gathering" in contrast
to Balmoral – ends with a truly memorable folk session.'[55]

Highland Region

'There has been a great revival...in traditional music and song among the
younger generation,' writes Angus Grant, a distinguished fiddler and teacher of
the Highland style. Festivals, Fiddle and Accordion Clubs, Strathspey and Reel
Societies and summer schools are responsible, and 'The TMSA must take great
credit; it gives a platform for musicians etc. who previously had never been seen
outside their native area.' Grant taught for twelve years at the Heritage of
Scotland Summer Schools at Stirling. 'The rock group Runrig gave a big boost
to Gaelic music...the top young Highland band Capercaillie emerged from
Taynuilt district... Lochaber has the biggest 'feis' (Gaelic festival)... Oban...
Inverness (folk club)... Glencoe... Lochleven... Dingwall... young people taking up pipes and clarsach... Glenfinnan... Glencoe.' Grant himself has 20 fiddle
pupils; his daughter and two sons carry on the tradition. 'There are lots of
Highland groups such as Wolfstone.'[56]

Ross and Cromarty

Rob Gibson and Rita Hunter organise the annual Highland Traditional Music
Festival in Dingwall. There are workshops at *Feis Rois* with follow-up classes.
Ullapool has the Canvas Ceilidh and the Ceilidh Place. Instrumental music is being taught in schools, with piping the most popular. Glenuig and Skye festivals... Radio Highland and Moray Firth Radio give local exposure... 'We have
experienced a most invigorating upsurge during the past decade...no offshoot of
a Central Belt approach but a continuation and reinvigoration of Highland tradition...using electronic media as elsewhere.'[57]

Orkney

The Folk Festival is now in its fourteenth year and occasional folk nights are
held during the year. Northern links continue, with contingents arriving from
Scandinavia. There are some fine instrumentalists. Ivan Drever presents a radio
slot.[58]

Shetland

Fiddle music, helped over the years by outstanding masters Tom Anderson and Aly Bain, continues as a living tradition. Young people are tending to stay, with job opportunities from the oil boom. There is an annual folk festival in fourteen venues on different islands.

Grampian Region

Entertainment events (fund-raising, old peoples' concerts, etc.) often employ folk song and music. Peter Hall stresses how important this is for the continued life of the tradition – it ensures the best environment for development of local singers.[59]

Events with a rather higher profile include the Keith and Strichen festivals and a bothy ballad competition in Elgin. Revival singers are The Gaugers (Tom Spiers, Arthur Watson, Peter Hall), Danny Cooper, Janice Clark and Aileen Carr. Other contributions come from song and verse writers, strathspey and reel societies, fiddle and accordion clubs, and dance bands of young musicians. Lizzie Higgins said '...the people do not have time for the big ballads'; and Stanley Robertson comments, 'The bothy ballads overtook the traditional classical ballads...I have written books of stories...I go round schools with stories but not with songs.'[60] Aberdeen City Libraries have produced a tape of these stories, which is available from the usual outlets.

Tayside Region

Annie Bell of Blairgowrie comments that singers now choose the more credible and easily understood ballads: 'Instrumental winners get younger and younger...', diddling and oral whistling are still the forte of her age group (the seventies).[61]

Charlie Murray of Forfar felt that festivals were now more for big farmers and media personalities, and the big ballads less sung... 'the old street singers are a thing of the past...'[62]

Andrew Douglas from Scone has plans to publish his poems. He has made many video-recordings of singers and storytellers over the years. Sheila Douglas has observed changes during the last decade – including 'the big name syndrome – singers and groups who encourage people to buy records and tapes, and to *listen* rather than sing themselves'. The press and television also seem interested in big names only, but radio is best because it includes folk in all kinds of programmes – as a proper category of music – '...this recognition has increased in the past three years'.[63]

Fife Region

Citty Finlayson, Newport-on-Tay, comments that attendances have decreased at folk clubs, increased at festivals, and also that the *number* of festivals has increased. She has praise for women's concerts, children's workshops at the Auchtermuchty Festival, family ceilidh dances mainly for locals, and concerts and ceilidhs spreading throughout Fife. Sheena Wellington on Radio Tay provided good coverage; she is a well known and very good singer, songwriter and activist. Wellington particularly praised Glenfarg folk club ('many good singers'), Kirkcaldy (with Chris Miles) and Forfar (Maureen Jelks and young Scott Gardiner); and also the BBC's radio output, with singers like Jean Redpath and Dougie MacLean. Blairgowrie festival receives a black mark from her.

The Scots Language Society have started a National Resource Centre in the AK Bell Library, Perth.

John Watt of Kinross writes as a (relatively) old-timer – his memories go back to the early sixties, when there were seventeen folk clubs in Fife. Today there are only two, but many more festivals and *informal* sessions, mainly in pubs. His second letter was in an unashamedly nostalgic mood:

> Folk music was a common bond...you thought nothing of knocking on some-one's door in say Derbyshire...he would certainly put you up and feed you even though he had never set eyes on you before... Where are the thousands of people now in their forties who were teenagers then? They are now respected members of society... Where are the children of these ex-folkies? ...a minority have followed their parents' interests...but it's a very sizeable minority...there are now more people than ever before singing, playing and reciting...and more folk music on tape...[part of] testimony to the fruits of the folk revival... P.S. I would not have missed it for anything![64]

This chimes with Jimmie Macgregor's reminiscences of London days in the fifties: 'happy days – sleeping on floors, but hearing and performing – for next to nothing...the beginning of something new'.[65]

Lothian Region

Irene Riggs writes that the big ballads are sung less often, though more people are writing songs. John Barrow comments that 'We're well used now to highly complex input to our brains from...television in particular...perhaps unaccom-panied singing is therefore too simple...is below some stimulus level.' Jean Bechofer, a stalwart of Edinburgh Folk Club, relates: 'It's a capital city...people would not come to hear what they could hear in pubs...so the club books only the best artists.' A non-purist attitude to 'cross-over' music (that is, not strictly folk) has paid off. And the big ballads? – 'Don't worry, they're still around and will come back!'

The Borders

This region seems very much of an entity. Kenny Spiers reports a 'network' of people attending either folk clubs or informal sessions, in Peebles, Innerleithen, Stow, Lauder, Ancrum, Denholm, Melrose and Galashiels. Something of a di-vide exists between grassroots activities and the council-funded activities with big names, but the arts festivals now include folk music. Young people are turning away from pop bands to the more accessible acoustic music. A recent development is JAM (Junior Acoustic Music), a group of young people and children that meets in Galashiels. The yearly Common Ridings continue; and Judy Steele reports on the Rowan Tree Company, Selkirk, which mixes traditional music, storytelling and theatre.

A View from Outwith Scotland

Singer Ray Fisher, who lives in Tyneside but comes from Glasgow, says that songs on 'wider issues' (environment, human rights etc.) have 'a higher acceptance level'. 'The big ballads certainly did not feature prominently in the last decade, but some singers did continue to sing them...Martin Carthy and myself...the ballad has a timeless quality... The blossoming of instrumental music...development of the Northumbrian small-pipes (helped...by my "guidman's"[66] efforts)...the Scottish small-pipes or cauld wind pipes...Hamish Moore.'[67]

6. The Traditional Music and Song Association of Scotland (TMSA)

Though comparatively small in the number of paid-up members, the TMSA is active and influential: it has eight branches, and publishes a quarterly newsletter with short articles, and a useful annual calendar of mainly affiliated festivals. Its organisation is at present under a short-term voluntary review by a senior manager from industry (BP Exploration) which will result in a handbook defining roles and responsibilities. The Heritage Arts Regeneration Project (HARP) is a joint venture between the TMSA and NE Scotland Heritage Trust; it concentrates on work with the under twenty-fives. Jane Fraser, formerly TMSA National Organiser, is on the executive committee of the Voluntary Arts Network (VAN), whose theme is the contribution of amateurs to national culture. A development officer was appointed in 1993 for Grampian Region.

Many more folk festivals have sprung up in the last decade – there are now some 60 in Scotland. In competitions at the festivals affiliated to the TMSA the entrants' choice of songs and tunes is still limited to 'Scottish'. This enthusiasm for competitions and for national content is close to the Irish model: Irish *fleadhs* have many competitions, with invariably Irish items. This is in marked contrast to English festivals, where the number of competitions have dwindled over the years and there is no 'English' restriction. (There is a common Scottish and Irish need for assertiveness as well as excellence.) A curious, and at present unavoidable, contradiction is that competitions are themselves *de facto* linked with the 'star system' so disliked by many of the best folk enthusiasts. But they do provide one – or even the only – way in which unknown performers can be heard; comments from experienced adjudicators also provide an educative element.

Ceilidhs run by the TMSA try to keep the content at least 'traditional', but in Glasgow, the largest and probably the most multi-cultural city in Scotland, '...the branch is not as traditional...it encourages Americans and Irish for instance to sing'. Other Glasgow branch activities include country dancing with a caller (so invaluable to the less experienced), 'hoose' ceilidhs, and workshops, including one by Danny Kyle who is 'keen on participation'.[68]

A struggle within the Association is epitomised by the Glasgow branch's attitude to tradition. 'If you want this universal participation, you do have to loosen up a bit as to what you say folk music is,' said Janet Foley. Georgina Boyes has put it this way: 'In arbitrarily dividing active and passive repertoire into traditional and popular categories, there is a considerable danger that songs of significance to performers will be ignored because of their theoretical unsuitability.'[69] Jack Foley spoke of 'the stuff you used to keep quiet about – *suddenly it's acceptable* – for example, in a pub down the road here, there was an old guy...started singing some old music-hall, working-class...Scots stuff – and I came out with a few I knew and he was *amazed*. He said "oh, oh..." He suddenly realised he wasn't a vulgar old bugger any more.'[70]

In 1991 the TMSA celebrated its Silver Jubilee. It has fought hard for more recognition and more funding for traditional music, and many tributes to its work came from people I spoke to around the country. A recent venture by the Auchtermuchty branch in October 1994, a conference on 'Songs and Singers', was extremely interesting and well attended.

7. World Music and *Folk Roots*

The quarterly magazine *Southern Rag*, started in 1979, always showed an interest in exotic music. In July 1985, when the influx of records and artists from abroad had become a steady stream, the journal changed its name to *Folk Roots* and began to appear monthly, with continuing success. Published in London, it has both reflected and aroused an increasing interest in the indigenous music of different parts of the world. Choice of subjects depends mainly on which artists happen to be in Britain at the time, but occasionally writers temporarily abroad will send in accounts of music in the countries visited. Many of these countries make little if any distinction between pop, traditional and art music. *Folk Roots* also prints news about folk events throughout the UK, as well as articles on UK artists.

Foreign artists visiting this country are usually the *crème de la crème* of their country's talents; and in line with the *Folk Roots* policy of presenting the very best, its UK articles also concentrate mainly on the big names. These facts tend to bolster the star-system tendency.

'There's absolutely nothing between the pages of that magazine to encourage anyone to participate,' said Janet Foley. 'I find this disturbing because I come from the States, from a place where your folk singers are literally *roped off* from the public... When I came over [in 1986] the first thing that struck me was how unlike that it was here...at a singaround, everybody would be there, and the people who couldn't sing well would still have something to contribute.'

Here we have the continuing tussle between democratic participation (a *sine qua non* of the folk revival) and the highest possible artistic standards (also essential – look at Jeannie Robertson, look at Ewan MacColl). Both are necessary.

Another kind of exotic music, originating in the USA in the 1960s, is minimal music (other descriptions – repetitive or meditative music, and acoustical art). 'However, "minimal" means are just as much a characteristic of Indian, Balinese and West African music.'[71]

The influence of world music has reached many folk clubs and can be heard in folk-based compositions of the last two decades.

8. Clubs, Festivals and Magazines

In many ways folk clubs have been the backbone of the revival. The regularity of meetings provides a contrast to the *ad hoc* nature of other folk events; they provide a social centre where people can meet, can listen to different kinds of artists, and can sometimes contribute themselves; it is still mainly an amateur movement and its professionals all started as amateurs. Genuine amateurs in any field love experiencing the art of professionals, enjoying it and learning from it.

The conflict between democratic participation and the highest standards has just been noted. An important factor here is money, and market principles infiltrate here as elsewhere: in a pub or a private house, the music is free, the atmosphere relaxed, and you are more accepting.

Some hints as to the style of a club may be gleaned from their entries in *The Scottish Folk Arts Directory*.[72] Glenfarg, Dunoon, Girvan, Stonehaven, Edinburgh, and Stow all have enticingly worded entries. A decline in the number of clubs and their attendance figures has been in part compensated for by an increase in the number of festivals. Eye-catching entries in the Directory include Islay (Feis Isle), which has 'whisky tasting'; Keith (TMSA) has 'Song and tune sessions [not to mention drinks] in every nook and cranny'; Strathaven has 'the very first ever Harry Lauder look-alike, sound-alike competition' (the fashion for parody has already been noted); Auchtermuchty is 'a lovely family festival for grown-ups and young kids'; Acoustic Music Centre, during Edinburgh International Festival, has 'great crack and a great meeting place'. The TMSA's *Survey of Scottish Folk Festivals* (1990) produced some interesting facts and figures.

Let us look at clubs in four of the chief Scottish cities: Glasgow, Inverness, Aberdeen and Edinburgh. The usual present-day folk-club procedure is common to all – floor singers to start, then the main performance(s); after the interval this is repeated – but there is variation in the number and quality of the floor singers.

Glasgow

(Scotia Bar.) Guests are booked well in advance, some from as far away as Chile; audiences include delegates from trade union and university conferences; there is a writers' prize donated by the host, Brendan McLaughlin.

Inverness

Has alternate singers' nights but floor singers encouraged at both, 'It's not the singer but the song.' A strong Gaelic element, and Dingwall's great annual festival is held nearby.

Aberdeen

Peter Hall notes that this is typically British, with very little regional character. The smaller Stonehaven club has more native material. During 1990, nineteen of the 44 guest nights were Scottish.

Edinburgh

Tends more to formal presentation, with a high standard. There is an annual song writing competition. Purely instrumentalist evenings are becoming more common.

Folk Journals: successively, *Sandy Bell's Broadsheet, Broadsheet, Broadbeat,*

Scottish Folk Diary, ScAN, Scottish Folk Gazette; and in 1993 *The Living Tradition* a UK magazine but produced in Kilmarnock, a larger bi-monthly with articles, reviews and information on events.

9. Art Music

Concerning developments since 1980, David Johnson wrote the following: 'Scotland is now abreast of the times. Moreover, modernism has gone out of fashion everywhere, so that no prizes are awarded *automatically* [my italics] to composers using innovative styles. The whole question of musical language is no longer rigidly defined: writing an easily approachable work for school orchestras, a new Scots fiddle tune or a memorable theme for a film score is as artistically valid as creating esoteric synthetic sounds in an electronic studio. With this new freedom many Scottish composers are now exploring traditional music as a powerful source of inspiration.'[73]

In the last six years, these Scottish composers and their tradition-related works have become better known, or – in the case of Ronald Stevenson – *even* better known. In spite of, or just possibly because of, his close concern with his own roots, Stevenson's musical and artistic interests are global, his output all-embracing, and he is internationally recognised. His *Scots Suite* for unaccompanied violin (1984) contains a Pibroch-fugue, and an 'inebriate' jig which, at its first complete performance, the composer christened 'A Drunk Man looks at the Fiddle'! The piano quartet (1985) entitled *Alma Alba* (the soul of Scotland) – 'the most dazzling recent coalescence of Scots and European themes'[74] – has a final Quodlibet in which a strathspey, a reel and a jig are played simultaneously in exuberant polyphony; in the *Violin Concerto* (1979) – first performed in 1992 – these three idiomatic dances are juxtaposed rather than superimposed. His *String Quartet* (1990), commissioned and performed by the Edinburgh String Quartet, contains Bach-ian figures with folk idioms.

Stevenson's passionate concern with international as well as national issues, together with his belief that music can express and indeed influence these concerns, are shared by Edward McGuire, whose work for folk musicians has already been looked at. In 1979 McGuire declared his wish to 'express in music the struggle for survival and revolution on both the emotional and social levels'.[75] More recently his themes appear a mite more peaceful, in works which include an opera, *The Loving of Etain* (1994), *Glasgow Symphony* (1990) and *Scottish Dances* for orchestra and choir.

A third composer with what one might call an ethical core to his work is James MacMillan. He feels that something of inspiration has been lost to people today, 'There is so much bubblegum music, trivial stuff.' He feels 'a responsibility to open windows on the Divine', and to attempt to 'recapture the soul of Scotland in music'. After reading an account of a woman wrongly accused of witchcraft in the seventeenth century, who under torture confessed to many strange things,[76] he composed a tone poem *The Confession of Isobel Gowdie* as a 'retrospective gesture of compassion'.[77] This almost unbearably expressive piece, acclaimed at the 1993 Edinburgh Festival and at the Proms in 1994, is seriously topical, both as a testament to human rights (torture is practised today in many countries including China[78]) and as a reminder of the deeply-rooted superstitions about intelligent women which cast long shadows even up to the present day. Other more directly folk-related works are his achingly beautiful setting of Soutar's *The Tryst* (1984), already referred to, and – based on this – *After the Tryst* for violin and piano (1988) and *Tryst* for orchestra (1989); also *Variations on Johnny Faa'* and *Scots Song*, both for soprano and chamber group.

Other composers using or influenced by folk music are Judith Weir, whose many works include *Scotch Minstrelsy*, a cycle of five songs which uses Scottish ballad texts and musical idioms;[79] William Sweeney, whose orchestral *Air, Strathspey and Reel* was commissioned by the *Glasgow Evening Times* for the opening night of the 1990 SNO Proms;[80] and David Johnson, whose opera *Thomas the Rhymer* was performed in Edinburgh and who is now writing a set of preludes and fugues for piano.

10. The School of Scottish Studies

This department saw a triple launching in 1971: the first undergraduate teaching course; the *Scottish Tradition* disc series, which later included cassettes and CDs; and the informal magazine *Tocher* (the more scholarly journal *Scottish Studies* had started in 1957). Further undergraduate courses followed in 1977, and honours courses in Scottish Ethnology in 1985 and 1987. Students number nearly 100 for first year, eighteen for second and later years, and postgraduates between ten and fifteen. The Sound Archive now contains about 6,000 hours of tape recordings, not counting those of the Place-name Section or the Linguistic Survey; there have also been donations, such as the John Levy collection of tapes, chiefly of Asian music. The Will Forret bequest is the nucleus of a collection of popular music and folk scene recordings. There is a Photographic Archive and a Tale (Transcription) Archive (Gaelic and Scots). In 1970, equipment for 16mm sound filming was acquired, and other laboratory facilities and techniques expanded to meet the needs of disc/cassette publication and of increasing numbers of postgraduate students, some of whom have made notable contributions in fieldwork and recording. Video-recording began in 1978, and equipment was purchased for the high-speed duplication of tapes.

Regrettably, invitations to tradition-bearers to come and address the students are becoming less frequent. The big annual ceilidh now musters only one visiting artist (university finances are tight these days) but students and staff also contribute music and storytelling items.

Over more than 40 years, changes in the School were inevitable; it is now chiefly a teaching department of ethnology. In 1981 an appeal fund was set in motion, and more funding is badly needed to use and to make more acccessible the vast library of tapes. Fieldwork continues but at a greatly reduced level. Postgraduate students provide the main provender to the tape archive.

The publication of the Greig-Duncan collection of Scots folk songs continues under Emily Lyle as general editor, with a group of associate editors, each undertaking one volume. These associate editors are all well-known revival singers and performers, but their formal qualifications are literary rather than musical. To balance this, there are several music advisers for the series.[81]

Concluding Thoughts – Whither?

In 1968 Ronald Stevenson wrote: 'I think all great art aspires beyond national-ism, as an exploraton of occult regions of experience. But I am convinced that a people's culture cannot get beyond nationalism until it has *realised* it. Scotland hasn't.'[82] Since then we have begun this process of realisation, but there is still a long way to go.

Language is the primary ingredient of a culture, and Scots has a strong case to be considered a language.[83] Originally used by all sections of society, after the unions with England it gradually descended in the social scale. Scots words be-came 'incorrect' as well as lower class; within living memory children who spoke Scots or Gaelic at school were punished.

The folk song revival has helped the movement for re-acceptance of Scots language. 'Language and culture cannot, of course, be equated, but one is a clear index to the other.'[84] Now you can use the wonderfully expressive *verbal* lan-guage of the ballads, for instance, without sticking to the four-square metre they are couched in; it has been used for prose, for drama, for free verse – any literary form. Bartok and Vaughan Williams used their native *musical* language, the dis-tinctive *idioms* of it, with equal freedom, in many different music structures. Composers today are getting interested in *the Scottish language of music*, a lan-guage in which Stevenson par excellence has made himself fluent. (He is also a dedicated contrapuntist – cf. Sutherland's choice, earlier, of 'linear treat-ment...the strands sounding together'.)

Art music is also an important part of our heritage, but 'learned music' as Lloyd called it, demands professional, full-time attention – it cannot be created by the amateur (part-timer). So art music has been, and still is largely, an upper-class affair – Stevenson is one of the few composers from a working-class fam-ily. Folk music was once an alternative music which everyone, 'kings and ploughmen',[85] could take part in; but after the advent of literacy it too, like the Scots tongue, came to be identified with the lower classes.[86]

Today, the alienation apparent in the whole puzzling picture is underlined by two facts:

a. '...the bulk of SAC's budget is absorbed by art forms – ballet, contemporary dance and mime, classical music and opera – which at least 85 percent of the population never attend at all, and in every area of attendance of cultural events, except rock concerts and the cinema, the major factor determining likely participation is social class'.[87]

b. Close on £8 million was spent on music by the SAC (Scottish Arts Council) in 1993–94. Of this, £85,200 was spent on traditional music (for any TMSA readers, this *includes* song) development: 'The emphasis of this scheme is on educational work – employing musicians to pass on skills...therefore, these funds are primarily spent on musicians fees.' In addition, sums expended by Combined Arts were: £38,500 on the TMSA, £27,500 on Traditional Arts festivals, and £29,839 on Gaelic Arts Feisean. This brings the SAC's total expenditure on traditional music in that year to £181,039,[88] which does not include the few thousands spent by Literature on related projects.

Even allowing for the expense involved in such areas of art music such as op-era, ballet and orchestral concerts, there is still a gross disparity here; it has been called the *democratic deficit.*[89]

'Utter the word democratic,' said Whitman. The key word in the above state-ment about the bulk of the SAC's budget is the word 'attend'; the four art-forms mentioned are chiefly non-participatory, they are events one passively *attends*, spectator arts. Composers today are writing more works for amateur orchestras and choirs, but these commissions are not the SAC's big spenders. Folk music and dance involve more participation than any other art forms mentioned in the SAC's recent survey.[90]

Nevertheless listening is an important part of music making – there must be an audience. As I see it, instrumental folk music at present is chiefly for *playing with* or *dancing to*. The instrumental eruption of the 1970s and 1980s, with a repertoire of mainly dance tunes, was followed by the resurgence of country dance, with obvious connections. Archie Fisher spoke of the tedium, at a Fiddle and Accordion club, of 'listening to what is basically dance music', and sug-gested a thrawnness in the listeners' Scottish character: 'We're going to sit here and enjoy ourselves even though we're miserable.'[91] My reservations concerning the new instrumental suites (with several exceptions) have already been stated; but they have some lovely new themes, with much tone-colour variation including the use of bagpipes, the scale having been modified in pitch when played alongside other instruments. They are, at least, breaking away from the mould. (Eddie McGuire and Savourna Stevenson have both had full professional training and study; Karen Wimhurst has studied composition at an American university, and Steve Kettley had a composition bursary from the SAC.)

Pete Heywood, editor of *The Living Tradition*, writes that he is very confident about the future for music (he means instrumental music), but he continues: 'I am less confident about song…sessions are providing a forum for learning tunes. Where will the song tradition flourish? [Another] area of concern is the number of organisers who are giving up…we are in danger of losing the structure that provided a place to learn for so many people – the folk club.'[92] This may be connected with the 'star system' tendency which has crept in, the lessening of democracy in pursuit of high quality. Also, while some instrumental teaching was always accepted as necessary, vocal teaching was frowned on as 'arty'; however in recent years voice workshops have been held by such as Frankie Armstrong, Alison McMorland and Christine Kydd. No new emphasis, this goes back to the mid-1960s, to the voice-training work of MacColl, Seeger and Lloyd in their London club; MacColl refers to 'the mistaken belief that folk singing re-quires no special skill'.[93] Many of us still think, with MacDiarmid:

> Better a'e gowden lyric
> Than onything else ava.[94]

The original source singers of the revival had no vocal training but, learning from their models since earliest childhood, their voices became flexible instru-ments able to express what they wanted. Most of these singers are now dead, so there are fewer such models for other singers. But many of the new generation of revival singers and players may in fact *be* source artists because they learned the songs and tunes *in the family circle*: their parents and grandparents were perhaps revival pioneers some 30 years ago and they in turn may be considered source artists by their young descendants. Some oral transmission still goes on, amid all the confusing changes.

A word about the three quotations which introduce this chapter, uttered respectively in 1953, 1981 and 1994. Seeger is both optimistic and prophetic – but how do we 'select' the makings of his 'new, more universal idiom'? Gaughan's prophecy may – eventually – come true, but what does not 'work' in the end may be absorbed for quite a long time before it is finally, if ever, rejected. But Clark's 'drawing a *line* of some kind' is surely part of Seeger's selecting process: perhaps we should be more selective *now* rather than leaving it all to blind posterity. The pervasive jazz influence, together with traditional dance tunes, is leading alarmingly to the tyranny of the beat. Of course most music contains some beat, but does it have to be such a tyrant?

Unaccompanied singing escapes this tyranny; it can bend and stretch with the singer's interpretation, and with true rubato. This is demonstrated perhaps especially by traditional Gaelic singing. But it does not have to be either solo or unaccompanied singing which shows this freedom; two outstanding examples in church music come to mind. First, the eerie, soul-stopping beauty of Gaelic unaccompanied ornamental psalm singing, where each member of the congregation is free to decorate the tune lavishly, with the resulting musical anarchy resolved here and there by what seems almost like telepathy. Second, the psalm singing of both the Scottish Episcopal and the Anglican churches, in which the words are chanted in unison to a repeated musical substructure and the organist waits until the moment is arrived at for harmonic change and resolution; the words determine the timing, and there is no regularly recurring beat. (A whiff of this is found in the singing of the Lord's Prayer in Church of Scotland services.) And in the film *Lorenzo's Oil* – which was based on fact – the African summoned to the sick boy's bedside sang him a species of free chant which had great healing properties. Most of Clark's 'modern songs, albeit in the "idiom"' (the last word's quote marks speak volumes), have instrumental accompaniment with a regular beat, and many seem far out on the very fringes of folk. And a long-term folk activist is uneasy at the number of evenings spent in folk clubs 'without hearing anything that could accurately be called a folk song'.[95]

My experience of fifteen years in the School of Scottish Studies caused me, contrariwise, to lean in the direction of Bohlman's 'change is inevitable' stance. I still think this, but when both Scots and Gaelic music now seem endangered by the bludgeonings of the beat and other distortions of tradition, perhaps more study and thought is called for. This should come from various directions – including the academic ('the Scots have the liveliest folk tradition of the British Isles, but paradoxically, it is the most bookish'[96]). Much study and thought can be found, for instance, in the six volumes of the Greig-Duncan collection;[97] in addition to words and tunes of over 3000 songs plus many variants, this work contains essential scholarly notes by editors, most of whom are also revival singers. (Is this then an example of that kind of 'highfalutin scholarly treatise' and 'discussion' dismissed scornfully by John Moulden as putting 'ordinary people at a distance'?[98]) The publication of this collection, sponsored by two universities, was undoubtedly a leading factor in persuading Edinburgh Festival to put on, in 1995, a series of 21 nightly events entitled *Folk songs of North-East Scotland: from the Greig-Duncan collection* – a 'first' for folk music, hitherto relegated to the Fringe.[99]

A first step from the folk movement itself could be in the direction of more conferences along the lines of the recent TMSA one on 'Songs and Singers' (see

p. 173), and following MacColl's suggestion about 'hearing the maximum amount of the official depositories of tape, and hearing the maximum amount of discussion that can take place around it'.[100] A second step, from outside, would be the recognition that folk music in Scotland needs more money and more official help from the SAC and other bodies.

The third possible step is wider and more universal in its application (and also more paradoxical, considering previous comments). One of the most important lessons of the folk music revival was that you do not need to have a 'trained' voice to sing folk songs (such a voice *can* be, though is not *necessarily,* a positive drawback). You do not even need to have a 'good' voice, as long as you can, with practice, hold the tune. Cy Laurie believes passionately that *'everyone* should sing, because it's not always the "good" singers who carry the good songs. It's the song that matters not the singer.' If a song moves you, if it expresses something deeply important to you, then why not try learning it and singing it. We might even entertain the idea that singing is a basic human activity, like speaking; you do not have to be an actor with a trained voice to recite a poem that you love. We might also revive the old DIY kind of social evening, with guests encouraged to contribute their 'party piece', be it poetry, or prose, or instrumental music, or singing – a real mixture of different genres, ranging from high art to 'popular', with folk a vital part of the whole spectrum. The present continuing folk revival – more widespread and truly demotic than any earlier revivals (see Foreword) – has made such a mixture possible, by helping to break down the barriers caused by artistic chauvinism of any kind.

All things considered, we may conclude, the folk music revival is secure; indeed the music will always be with us – always provided we help to keep it going.

Footnotes

1. Charles Seeger, 'Folk Music in the Schools of a Highly Industrialised Society', *Journal of the International Folk Music Council,* vol. V (1953), p. 44.
2. Dick Gaughan, from 'Revival: The Tradition of the Future', talk at Edinburgh Folk Festival, 25 March 1981.
3. Ron Clark (co-founder of the Grand Hotel folk club, see p. 36), 12 December 1994, Glasgow.
4. The School has only recently started to record, document and photograph revival artists.
5. Bohlman, 1988, p. xviii.
6. Robert Cantwell, Rosenberg ed., 1993, p. 57.
7. Letter from singer/actress Dolina MacLennan, April 1991, Blair Atholl.
8. Tich Frier, *The Morrigan,* Celtic Music CM C052.
9. See Ian Russell, 'Parody and Performance', Pickering and Green, 1987, pp. 70–104.
10. *The Singing Kettle,* nos. 1 to 4, Kettle KOP 10, 15, 19 and 21.
11. Maureen Jelks, *First Time Ever,* Dunkeld, Duncas 006 (1988).
12. Jean Redpath, *The Songs of Burns,* vol. 6, arranged by Hovey, Greentrax CTRAX 006.
13. Heather Heywood, *Some Kind of Love,* Greentrax CTRAX 010 (1987) and *By Yon Castle Wa',* CTRAX 054 (1993).
14. Russell and Kydd, Greentrax CTRAX 011 (1988); *Dancin', Singin',* CTRAX 077 (1994).
15. Andy Hunter, *A Sang's a Sang for aa that,* Scotsoun SSC 071 (1983).

16. *I was born in Glasgow*, Gallus GAL 102 (1990).
17. *McGinn of the Calton*, Greentrax CTRAX 034 (1990); the book, McGinn 1987.
18. *Revival in Britain*, vol. 1, Greentrax CTRAX 033 (1990).
19. McVicar, 1990.
20. Douglas, 1992.
21. Henderson, 1992. (See also Munro, 1991.)
22. For books of stories and autobiography see Whyte 1979 and 1990, Williamson 1983–94, and Robertson 1988–94.
23. *Wait Till I Tell You*, Heartland Radio, Blair Atholl (1990).
24. Communicated to Vic Smith by Tom Anderson in conversation, circa 1971.
25. *Djangology*, Music for Pleasure MFP 1054 (1937).
26. *Chance or Design*, REL RELS 479 (1985).
27. *Smiling Waved Goodbye*, Greentrax TRAX 016 (1985).
28. *Sidewaulk*, Green Linnet, SIF 1094 (1989).
29. *A Bunch of Fives*, Topic 12TS 406 (1979).
30. *Beating Harps*, Green Linnet SIF 1089 (1987).
31. Rowan Records RCDC 1 and 2 (1989, 1990).
32. Jim Sutherland, 25 March 1994, Edinburgh.
33. *Inner Sound*, Klub records, ZCLOC 1063.
34. *Peter Pan*, Scottish Ballet SB001.
35. Letter from Alison Duncan, December 1990, Dunoon.
36. *Wellpark Suite*, IONA IRC 008 (1985).
37. *St. Mungo*, Greentrax CTRAX 041 (1990).
38. *Killiecrankie*, Lapwing Records LP, LAP 126.
39. *Tweed Journey*, Eclectic ECL 9001 TC (1990).
40. *Cutting the Chord*, Eclectic ECL TC 9308 (1993).
41. *Savage Dance*, Eclectic ECL TC 9002 (1990); also *Durga's Feast*, Eclectic ECL TC 9410 (1994).
42. Letter from Eileen Penman, July (1991), Edinburgh; *see* also Boyes 1993, p. xii.
43. Sisters Unlimited, *No Limits*, Harbour Records, HARC 013 (1991).
44. From *Familiar Faces*, Blackthorn Records BR 1069 (1988).
45. *We were There*, Pukka Records YOO PO8 (1987).
46. Larry Butler, 26 August 1994, Glasgow.
47. *Songs from under the bed*, SFUTB 1–3 (1988–89). *Songs from under the Poll Tax* (1991). *Aa breenge in*, Gallus GAL 109. From John Greig, 20 Glen Street, Edinburgh EH3 9JE.
48. Wolfstone, *The Chase*, Iona Records (1992).
49. *Glasgow Horizons*, Lismore Recordings LIFL 7018 (1990).
50. From enquiries at SNP office, Edinburgh, 15 August 1991 and 12 January 1995. But see Brand, 1978.
51. Jo Miller, *The Music of Scotland*, in Assocation with Music Advisers in Scotland, 1988. *See* also her M. Litt. thesis, *Traditions of Music Making in Glenkens, Galloway*, chapter 6, in School of Scottish Studies library.
52. See McMorland, 1975; with tape.
53. McLay ed., 1988, p. 1. *See* also its successor McLay ed., 1990.
54. Allan Morris, 30 August 1990, Glasgow.
55. See n. 35.
56. Letter from Angus Grant, 1 December 1990, Fort William.
57. Letter from Rob Gibson and Rita Hunter, 17 August 1990, Dingwall.
58. Conversation, Johnny Mowat, June 1991 and August 1994, Orkney.
59. Letter from Peter Hall, January 1991, Aberdeen; includes later Hall quotes.
60. Letter from Stanley Robertson, January 1991, Aberdeen, and from Lizzie Higgins, Aberdeen.

61. Letters from Annie Bell, 14 December 1990 and 21 January 1991, Blairgowrie.
62. Letter from Charlie Murray, February/March 1991, Forfar.
63. Letters from Sheila Douglas, February 1991 and July 1994, Scone.
64. Letters from John Watt, October/November 1990, Fife.
65. Letter from Jimmie Macgregor, 29 October 1990, Glasgow.
66. Colin Ross, a noted piper.
67. Letter from Ray Fisher, 22 January 1991, Whitley Bank.
68. Babs Finlay, 3 September 1990, Trades Hall, Glasgow.
69. Georgina Boyes, 'New Directions – Old Destinations', in Russell ed., 1986, p. 13.
70. Jack and Janet Foley, 31 July 1990, Hamilton. All subsequent Foley quotes are from this interview.
71. Mertens, 1988, p. 12.
72. From *Blackfriars Music*, 49 Blackfriars St. Edinburgh EH1 1NB.
73. 'A New Musical Language' by David Johnson, in *The Story of Scotland*, vol. 4, part 51, 1988, *The Sunday Mail* (Scotland).
74. MacDonald, 1989, p. 100.
75. Quoted by Richard McGregor, *Musical Times*, June 1979.
76. Smout, 1985, p. 191.
77. James MacMillan, quoted from BBC2 programme *The Score*, 14 August 1994, and from conversation, 21 August 1994, Glasgow.
78. See *Detained in China and Tibet*, Human Rights Watch, London/New York, 1994.
79. See 'Judith Weir', in Morgan ed., 1988, pp. 23–50.
80. The Scottish Music Information Centre, 1 Bowmont Gardens, Glasgow G12 9LR, provides a wealth of detailed information.
81. See Munro, 1991, for many more facts about the School in relation to the Revival.
82. MacDonald, 1989, p. 95: a profound comment, with political implications. 'Realise' also includes the musical meaning.
83. See Alexander Fenton, 'Scots Language Culture', no. 21, *Arts for a New Century*, SAC, 1991, pp. 9–10.
84. Fenton, ibid., p. 8.
85. Sheila Douglas, 'Traditional Arts/Folk Arts', no. 20, *Arts for a New Century*, SAC, 1991, p. 2.
86. *See* Buchan, 1972, chapter 20.
87. *Charter for the Arts in Scotland*, HMSO, 1993, pp. 50-51.
88. SAC Annual Review, 1993-94, SAC Annual Report, 1993–94; and letter from Helen Jamieson, Music Officer, Performing Arts Department of SAC, 19 January 1995.
89. Sheena Wellington, 'The Traditional Arts', *Chapman* 77, 1994, p. 7
90. See 'Participation in and Attitudes Towards the Arts in Scotland', a survey commissioned by the SAC, 1991, figure 1.
91. *Travelling Folk*, BBC Radio Scotland, 10 March 1994.
92. Letter from Pete Heywood, 2 September 1994, Kilmarnock.
93. MacColl, 1990, pp. 298, 305–6.
94. For Ronald Stevenson's heart-stoppingly beautiful setting of this, see *A 'e Gowden Lyric,* Bardic edition, Aylesbury, 1990.
95. Sheila Douglas, *The Living Tradition*, issue 10, 1995, p. 22.
96. Alan Lomax, quoted by Hamish Henderson in sleeve notes for *The Muckle Sangs;* see Chapter IV, footnote 15.
97. See Shuldham-Shaw and Lyle, 1981–95.
98. John Moulden, *The Living Tradition,* issue 11, 1995, p. 20.
99. A CD *Songs from the Greig-Duncan collection,* CDTRAX 5003, is available from Ian Green, Cockenzie Business Centre, Edinburgh Road, Cockenzie, East Lothian, EH32 0HL.
100. Ewan MacColl, 9 December 1988, Beckenham, Kent. Also quoted in *Folk Music Journal* 1991, volume 6 no. 2, p. 159.

Appendix

As an extension of Chapter IV, and as a comparative study, transcriptions of four versions of each of four songs are given below. Music transcriptions for each song are of those verses included by all four of the singers, numbered according to the order in which they are sung. Complete verbal texts are given separately, plus notes on each set of performances. Each song belongs to one of the groups outlined in Chapter IV, as follows:

He widna wint:	*Group 3*, COMEDY AND MUSIC-HALL
Willie Macintosh:	*Group 4*, FEUDS AND WAR
Banks o' red roses:	*Group 5*, SEXUAL VIOLENCE AND SEDUCTION
Johnnie my man:	*Group 1*, LOVE

(Comments by the singers in Chapter IV and in the Appendix were made in 1981/82, so the author's comments have also been left as at that time; any changes are in the main abbreviatory. See p. 54 for names of recorders.)

He widna wint his gruel

183

cruel   Oh the ve-ry first nicht that he got wed   He

cru-el,oh, For the ve-ry first nicht that he got wad   He

cruel   For the ve-ry first night that he got wed   He

cru ------ el   The ve-ry first nacht that he got wad   He

sat   an' grat for gruel. He wid-na wint his gruel,   He

sat an' he grat 'for gruel. He win-na wont his gruel,No he

sat an'he grat for gruel. He sat an'grat for gruel,Aye he

sat an' he grat for gruel. He wud-na wont his gruel,Oh he

wid - na wint his gruel, Oh the ve-ry first night that he got wed He

win-na want his gruel, Oh the ve-ry first nicht that he got wad He

can - na wint his gruel, Noo the ve-ry first night that he got wed He

wud - na want his gruel, Oh the ve-ry first nacht that he got wed He

sat an' he grat for gruel. (V.2) "There's nae a pot in

sat an' he grat for gruel. "There's no a pot in

sat an' he grat for gruel. "Noo there's nae a pot in

sat an' he grat for gruel. "Oh there's nae a pot in

can-na wint ma gruel, Oh the wa-shin'pot it-'ll dae wi' me For

win-na want his gruel, "Oh the wa-shin'pail it' ll dae for me For

can-na want ma gruel, Och the wa-shin'pot it-'ll dae wi' me For

can-na wint ma gruel, Oh the wa-shin'pot it- 'll dae for you For

I maun hae ma gruel."(V.3)"There's nae a spoon in a'the hoose That

I maun hae ma gruel." "There's no a spuin in a'the hoose That

I maun hae ma gruel." "But there's nae a spoon in a'the hoose For

I maun hae ma gruel". "Oh(ho)there's nae a spuin in a'the hoose That

you can sup yer gruel"; "Oh the gair-den spade it-'ll dae wi'me For

ye can sup yer gruel"; "Oh the gair-den spade it-'ll dae for me For

ye tae sup yer gruel"; "Och the gair-den spade it-'ll dae wi' me For

ye can sup yer gruel"; "Ah the gair-den spade it-'ll dae for me For

I maun hae ma gruel. For I maun hae ma gruel, I can-na wint   ma

I maun hae ma gruel".He win-na want his gruel,No he win-na want his

I maun hae ma gruel. For I maun hae ma gruel,Aye I   can-na want ma

I maun hae ma gruel. For I maun hae ma gruel,Oh I   can-na want ma

gruel, Oh the gair-den spade it-'ll dae wi'me For I maun hae ma

gruel, "Oh the gair-den spade it-'ll dae for me For I maun hae ma

gruel, (S)o the gair-den spade it-'ll dae wi'me For I maun hae ma

gruel, Oh the gair-den spade it-'ll dae for me For I maun hae ma

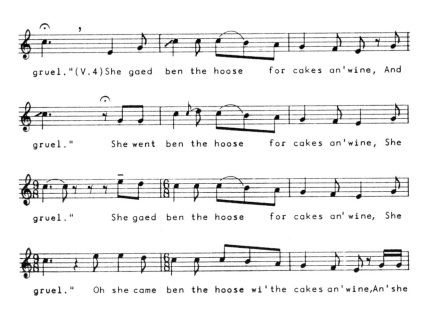

gruel."(V.4)She gaed ben the hoose for cakes an'wine, And

gruel." She went ben the hoose for cakes an'wine, She

gruel." She gaed ben the hoose for cakes an' wine, She

gruel." Oh she came ben the hoose wi'the cakes an'wine,An'she

gruel, Oh gy-a - wa'gy-a-wa'wi'yer fal-de-rals For I maun hae ma

gruel, "Gae a - wa'gy-a-wa'wi'yer fal-de-ral For I maun hae ma

gru-el, Gy-a - wa'gy-a-wa'wi'yer fal-de-rals For I maun hae ma

gruel, Ah gy -a - wa'gy-a-wa'wi'yer fol-de-rols For I maun hae ma

gruel." (V.5) Come all young las - sies take my ad-vice And

gruel." So come a' ye las - sies where-ere ye be An'

gruel." You, come a' young las - sies tak' my ad-vice An'

gruel." Oh come all young las - sies take my ad-vice An'

ne-ver mair-ry a wea-ver,   The ve-ry first night that he got wed He

ne-ver   mar-ry   wea-ver For the ve-ry first nicht that ye get wad He'll

ne-ver mar-ry a   wea-ver For the ve-ry first night that he got wed   He

ne-ver mair-ry a wea-ver,   The ve-ry first nacht that we got wad He

sat   an' grat for gruel. He wi-(hi)d-na wint his gruel,   He

sit an'he'll greet for gruel. He win - na   want his gruel, No he

sat an' he grat for gruel. He sat   an' grat for gruel, Aye he

sat an' he grat for gruel. He wud -na want his gruel Oh he

wid-na wint his gruel, Oh the ve - ry first nicht that

win - na want his gruel, For the ve - ry first nicht that

can - na wint his gruel, Noo the ve - ry first night that

wud - na want his gruel, Oh the ve - ry first nacht that

he got wed He sat an' he grat for gruel.

slightly slower

he gets wad He'll sit an' he'll greet for gruel.

slower

he got wed He sat an' he grat for gruel.

getting slower

he got wad He sat an' he grat for gruel.

Jimmy MacBeath. SA 1960/109, Aberdeen 1960 Rec. H.H.

1. There was a weaver o' the North
    An' oh but he was cruel
    Oh the very first nicht that he got wed
    He sat an' grat for gruel.
    > He widna wint his gruel,
    > He widna wint his gruel,
    > Oh the very first night that he got wed
    > He sat an' he grat for gruel.

2. 'There's nae a pot in a' the hoose
    That I can mak' your gruel;'
    'Oh, the washin' pot it'll dae wi' me
    For I maun hae ma gruel.
    > For I maun hae ma gruel,
    > I canna wint ma gruel,
    > Oh the washin' pot it'll dae wi' me
    > For I maun hae ma gruel.'

3. 'There's nae a spoon in a' the hoose
    That you can sup your gruel';
    'Oh the gairden spade it'll dae wi' me
    For I maun hae ma gruel.
    > For I maun hae ma gruel,
    > I canna wint ma gruel,
    > Oh the gairden spade it'll dae wi' me
    > For I maun hae ma gruel.'

4. She gaed ben the hoose for cakes an' wine,
    And brocht them on a too'el;
    'Oh gy-awa' gy-awa' wi' your falderals
    For I maun hae ma gruel.
    > For I maun hae ma gruel,
    > I canna wint ma gruel,
    > Oh gy-awa', gy-awa' wi' your falderals
    > For I maun hae ma gruel.'

5. Come all young lassies take my advice
    And never mairry a weaver,
    The very first night that he got wed
    He sat an' grat for gruel.
    > He widna wint his gruel,
    > He widna wint his gruel,
    > Oh the very first nicht that he got wed
    > He sat an' he grat for gruel.

Heather Heywood. AM2, Rec. A.P. Kinross 1977

1. For there was a weaver in the North,
    An' oh but he was cruel, oh,
    For the very first nicht that he got wad
    He sat an' he grat for gruel.
    He winna want his gruel,

No he winna want his gruel,
Oh the very first nicht that he got wad
He sat an' he grat for gruel.

2.   'There's no a pot in a' the hoose
      That I can mak' yer gruel;'
      'Oh the washin' pail it'll dae for me
      For I maun hae ma gruel.'
      He winna want his gruel,
      No he winna want his gruel,
      'Oh the washin' pail it'll dae for me
      For I maun hae ma gruel.'

3.   'There's no a spuin in a' the hoose
      That ye can sup yer gruel;'
      'Oh the gairden spade it'll dae for me
      For I maun hae ma gruel.'
      He winna want his gruel,
      No he winna want his gruel,
      'Oh the gairden spade it'll dae for me
      For I maun hae ma gruel.'

4.   She went ben the hoose for cakes an' wine,
      She brought them on a towel;
      'Och gy-awa' gy-awa' wi' yer falderal
      For I maun hae ma gruel.'
      Oh he winna want his gruel,
      No he winna want his gruel,
      'Gae awa' gy-awa' wi yer falderal
      For I maun hae ma gruel.'

5.   So come a' ye lassies where'er ye be
      An' never marry a weaver
      For the very first nicht that ye get wad
      He'll sit an' he'll greet for gruel.
      He winna want his gruel,
      No he winna want his gruel,
      For the very first nicht that he gets wad
      He'll sit an' he'll greet for gruel.

Willie Mackenzie. AM5, Rec. A.P. Keith 1976

1.   Noo there lived a weaver in the North
      An' oh but he was cruel
      For the very first night that he got wed
      He sat an' he grat for gruel.
      He sat an' grat for gruel,
      Aye he canna wint his gruel,
      Noo the very first night that he got wed
      He sat an' he grat for gruel.

2.   'Noo there's nae a pot in a' the hoose
      For ye tae mak' yer gruel;'
      'Och the washin' pot it'll dae wi' me

For I maun hae ma gruel.
For I maun hae my gruel,
Aye I canna want ma gruel,
Och the washin' pot it'll dae wi' me
For I maun hae ma gruel.'

3.   'But there's nae a spoon in a' the hoose
For ye tae sup yer gruel;'
'Och the gairden spade it'll dae wi' me
For I maun hae ma gruel,
For I maun hae ma gruel,
Aye I canna want ma gruel,
(S)o the gairden spade it'll dae wi' me
For I maun hae ma gruel.'

4.   She gaed ben the hoose for cakes an' wine,
She brocht them on a too'el;
'Ach gy-awa gy-awa wi' yer falderals
For I maun hae ma gruel.
For I maun hae ma gruel,
Aye I canna wint ma gruel,
Gy-awa' gy-awa' wi' yer falderals
For I maun hae ma gruel.'

5.   You, come a' young lassies tak' my advice
An' never marry a weaver
For the very first night that he got wed
He sat an' he grat for gruel.
He sat an' grat for gruel,
Aye he canna wint his gruel,
Noo the very first night that he got wed
He sat an' he grat for gruel.

Tommy Truesdale. AM12, Rec. A.P. Kinross 1978

1.   Oh there was a weaver o' the North
And oh but he was cruel
The very first nacht that he got wad
He sat an' he grat for gruel.
He wudna want his gruel
Oh he wudna want his gruel,
Oh the very first nacht that he got wed
He sat an' he grat for gruel.

2.   'Oh there's nae a pot in a' the hoose
That I can sup ma gruel;'
'Ah the washin pot it'll dae for you
For I maun hae ma gruel.
For I maun hae ma gruel
Oh I canna wint ma gruel,
Oh the washin pot it'll dae for you
For I maun hae ma gruel.'

3. 'Oh (ho) there's nae a spuin in a' the hoose
    That ye can sup yer gruel;'
    'Ah the gairden spade it'll dae for me
    For I maun hae ma gruel.
    For I maun hae ma gruel,
    Oh I canna want ma gruel,
    Oh the gairden spade it'll dae for me
    For I maun hae ma gruel.'

4. Oh she came ben the hoose wi' the cakes an' wine,
    An' she brocht them on a too'el;
    'Ah gy-awa' gy-awa' wi' yer folderols
    For I maun hae ma gruel.
    For I maun hae ma gruel,
    Oh I canna want ma gruel,
    Ah gy-awa' gy-awa' wi' yer folderols
    For I maun hae ma gruel.'

5. Oh come all young lassies take my advice
    An' never mairry a weaver,
    The very first nacht that we got wad
    He sat an' he grat for gruel.
    He wudna want his gruel
    Oh he wudna want his gruel,
    Oh the very first nacht that he got wad
    He sat an' he grat for gruel.

This is a bothy song. It was collected by Hamish Henderson from several farm workers of pre-First World War vintage, including Jimmy MacBeath himself, who found the bothy life so harsh that he determined not to return to it after the war. Instead he became an itinerant singer, and a highly successful one. This was one of his favourite songs; the other three singers above all learned it from him – two of them directly, and Heather Heywood indirectly – and it is still very popular.

Jimmy MacBeath's performance of this song makes it quite clear that he appreciated the satire as well as the comedy of its theme. His rich, gravelly voice changes as he acts out the parts of bewildered, anxious-to-please bride and domineering, petulant husband, the latter's part rising to high G at the end of verses 1, 4 and 5 as if to underline the final world 'gruel'. In bar 11, the repeated plea 'widna wint his gruel' or 'canna wint ma gruel' is broken up by rests, these breaks suggesting an ironic pseudo-pathos; and a gleeful chuckle or slide accompanies some of the more bizarre remarks. It's not just a pretty song; the satire is savage enough even to hint that he's got cold feet about the whole business of consummation, and seizes every chance of postponing it. Not surprisingly, the only direct comment on all this is the word *cruel* (the perfect rhyme for gruel) – comedy often includes cruelty as an ingredient. MacBeath adopts a relatively slow tempo, leaving time for the performance details mentioned, and so blending serious satire with high comedy.

Heather Heywood, of Kilmarnock, says that at the time her recording was made she felt much sympathy for the woman here. This sympathy is shown in the slow pace she adopts – the slowest of these four versions – and in the *caveat* that issues from her use of the future tense: first, 'he winna...', twice in each verse (with a rhythm which fits the word), and then in the last verse where she addresses her female listeners directly: '...the very first nicht that *ye* get wad *he'll* sit an' *he'll* greet for gruel' (my italics). In other words: 'Watch out, or this will happen to you!' She prefers a curve of stepwise links in the melody, rather than a leap. This is exemplified in bars 7 and 15 of each verse, and also in bar 10 and the second half of bar 9. This last variant is also found in Tommy Truesdale's version. Heather Heywood adds this comment: 'I think the man in the song shows his determination to have what he wants no matter how much he is tempted. (Typical stubborn man!)'

Willie Mackenzie, from Elgin, has the lightest approach. He sees this simply as a 'nice wee catchy song,' and goes no deeper. He adopts the fastest pace of these four, and gives more chuckles than MacBeath. He says the theme is 'It's the belly that keeps up the back.'

Tommy Truesdale from Girvan, now living in Glasgow, takes it at a relatively fast pace, second only to Mackenzie's. His is a robust and fairly straightforward interpretation, but like MacBeath he combines comedy with irony. He comments: 'The way to a man's heart is through his stomach. It could be a dig at the importance of gruel in the daily diet of most Scots at that time, and that a man would prefer his gruel before love. I know of some men who would prefer, not so much gruel, but other pleasures in life before their wives.'

These three singers keep fairly closely to Jimmy MacBeath's tune-model, and melodic and rhythmic variations are slight. Singers sometimes make slight slips in words, but it's usually easy to spot these.

Willie Macintosh (The burning of Auchindoun) (Child 183)

If ye burn Au-chin-doun Hunt-ly he will heid ye."

If ye burn Au-chin-doun Hunt-ly he will heid ye."

If ye burn Au-chin-doun Hunt-ly he will heid ye."

ye burn Au-chin-doun For Hunt-ly he will heid ye."

(V.3)"Heid me or hang me, It will ni - ver grieve me:

"Heid me or hang me, That will ne - ver fear me:

"Heid me or hang me, That will ne - ver fear me:

"Heid me or hang me, Hunt-ly he'll nae fear me: For

I'll burn Au-chin-doun Al-though the life'ud leave me."(V.4) As

Usual speed

I will burn Au-chin-doun Though the life leaves me." And as

I will burn Au-chin-doun Though the life will leave me." As

I'll burn Au- chin-doun Though a' the breath shall leave me." As

I gaed doun by Fid-dich-side on a May mor - nin',

I gaed in by Fid-dich-side on a May mor - nin',

I came in by Au-chin-doun on a May mor - nin',

I gaed in be Fid-dich-side on a May mor - nin',

Au-chin-doun was in a bleeze An hour be-fore the daw - nin'.

Au-chin-doun was in a bleeze An hour be-fore the daw - nin'.

Au-chin-doun was in a bleeze An hour a-fore the daw - nin'.

Au-chin-doun was in a bleeze An hour be-fore the daw - nin'.

(V.5)"Craw-in',craw-in', For a' yer crouse craw - in', I

"Craw-in', craw-in', For a' yer coorse craw - in', They

"Craw-in', craw-in', For a' yer crouse craw - in', Ye've

"Craw-in', craw-in', A' yer grouse are craw-in', I've

brunt yer crops an' tint yer wings An hour be-fore the daw-nin'."

burnt yer crops an' tint yer wings An hour be-fore the daw-nin'."

brunt yer crops an' tint yer wings An hour a-fore the daw-nin'."

burnt yer crops an'I've tint yer wine An hour be-fore the daw-nin'."

Madeleine Taylor. SA 1971-243, Rec. P.C. Kinross 1971

1. As I gaed doon by Fiddichside
    On a May mornin',
    I met wi' Willie Macintosh
    An 'oor* before the dawnin.'

2. 'Turn again, turn again,
    Turn again I beg ye,
    If ye burn Auchindoun
    Huntly he will heid ye.'

3. 'Heid me or hang me,
    It will niver grieve me:
    I'll burn Auchindoun
    Although the life 'ud leave me.'

4. As I gaed doon by Fiddichside
    On a May mornin',
    Auchindoun was in a bleeze
    An 'oor before the dawnin.'

5. 'Crawin', crawin',
    For a' yer crouse crawin',
    I brunt yer crops an' tint yer wings
    An 'oor before the dawnin'.'

*The word 'hour' is spelt here as it is pronounced by the four singers.

Dick Gaughan. SA 1971/192, Rec. F.K. Edinburgh 1971

1.   As I came in by Fiddichside
   On a May mornin',
   I spied Willie Macintosh
   An 'oor before the dawnin'.

2.   'Turn again, turn again,
   Turn again I bid ye,
   If ye burn Auchindoun
   Huntly he will heid ye.'

3.   'Heid me or hang me,
   That will never fear me:
   I will burn Auchindoun
   Though the life leaves me.'

4.   And as I gaed in by Fiddichside
   On a May mornin',
   Auchindoun was in a bleeze
   An 'oor before the dawnin'.

5.   'Crawin', crawin',
   For a' yer coorse crawin',
   They burnt yer crops an' tint yer wings
   An 'oor before the dawnin'.'

Allan Morris. SA 1973/109, Rec. P.C. Kinross 1973

1.   As I came in by Fiddichside
   On a May mornin',
   I spied Willie Macintosh
   An 'oor afore the dawnin'.

2.   'Turn again, turn again,
   Turn again I bid ye,
   If ye burn Auchindoun
   Huntly he will heid ye.'

3.   'Heid me or hang me,
   That will never fear me:
   I will burn Auchindoun
   Though the life will leave me.'

4.   As I came in by Auchindoun
   On a May mornin',
   Auchindoun was in a bleeze
   An 'oor afore the dawnin'.

5.   'Crawin', crawin',
      For a' yer crouse crawin',
      Ye've brunt yer crops an' tint yer wings
      An 'oor afore the dawnin'.'

Anthony Robertson. SA 1977/4, Rec. K.C. Aberdeen 1977

1.   As I gaed in be Fiddichside
      On a May mornin',
      I spied Willie Macintosh
      An 'oor before the dawnin'.

2.   'Turn again, turn again
      Turn again I bid ye,
      If ye burn Auchindoun
      For Huntly he will heid ye.'

3.   'Heid me or hang me,
      Huntley he'll nae fear me:
      For I'll burn Auchindoun
      Though a' the breath shall leave me.'

4.   As I gaed in be Fiddichside
      On a May mornin',
      Auchindoun was in a bleeze
      An 'oor before the dawnin'.

5.   'Crawin', crawin',
      A' yer grouse are crawin',
      I've burnt yer crops an' I've tint yer wine
      An 'oor before the dawnin'.'

This ballad is based on a historical incident, but two different characters with the title-name are confounded in it. The possible incidents are dated 1592 and 1550. The terrain is Banffshire, near Dufftown. Bronson gives only the above tune, recorded by Ewan MacColl who learned it from his father. Once again MacColl is the revival source – Anthony Robertson got his version from his own traveller family. The words are very similar to Child B, but the last verse has been changed now to a final taunt, addressed presumably by Willie Macintosh to Huntly's clan, in the continuing feud which was started by the murder of the 'Bonny Earl of Murray'. The meaning of this taunt is not obscured by the slight variations in the words above: only Allan Morris has MacColl's 'Ye('ve) brunt yer crops' (meaning 'you've brought this on yourself'), two have 'I('ve) brunt/burnt...' and Dick Gaughan has 'They burnt...'

Maddy Taylor's is the most dramatic and extrovert statement. She sings with contained urgency in a loudish voice with an edge to it ('a good song for exercising the lungs!' she says), and she keeps the potentially fierce strathspey rhythm. A touch of *parlando* style, in the last syllable of the second line, verses 1, 2, 4 and 5, heightens the drama. She draws out the first line of verses 1 and 4, 'As I gaed doon by Fiddichside', into two bars instead of one, thus giving it a more declamatory air, as if introducing both parts of the story. Anthony Robertson does the same. Maddy Taylor, who was raised in Perthshire, has been a professional singer and guitarist for some years. She learned this song from the singing of Mike Whelans, and notes that several words have become altered (compared with the MacColl version). She describes the song as '...a wee story, a narrative, it speaks for itself', and takes it at a pace considerably faster than the other three.

Dick Gaughan's interpretation is also highly dramatic, but in a more personal way, as if he is re-living the events as Willie Macintosh himself, risking his life yet hell-bent on revenge. By postponing the first appearance of the note G, in bar 1, to the first syllable of 'Fiddichside', he is able to end this line on the dominant note, A: an 'open' ending, which affects the beginning of the next line also. The strathspey rhythm is again pronounced. This singer is a master of fleeting, delicate ornamentation – which goes well with the slight but fast vibrato in his voice – and is capable of a beautiful *sostenuto*. The tempo is slower, more reflective, and the timing flexible. Gaughan is of mixed Highland and Irish blood, and has lived most of his life in Leith, just north of Edinburgh. He cannot remember where or when he learned this song, and he describes its theme as 'evidence of a particular phase of barbarity in the evolution of human society'.

Allan Morris's rhythms are less dotted than the first two singers', but the drama comes over in his strong, positive voice and in the sense of more objective involvement which he projects – as the storyteller this time, the observer. His emotion, if not recollected in tranquillity, is at least tempered by distance. The tempo is the same as the last singer's. Morris learned this from Ewan MacColl's recorded singing, in the late sixties or early seventies. He likes it because of the terse words, because it has something to say about Banffshire four centuries ago, and because 'its vengeful mood allows you to "cut loose"'. Asked what he felt was the theme, he replied, 'Using words alone, I would say, a revenge theme.'

Anthony Robertson of Aberdeen learned this when he was about ten, from the singing of his father (Stanley Robertson) and grandfather. He has never heard anyone else sing it. As always in oral transmission, changes in words are unlikely to occur unless they make sense, even if the sense is changed, and the two words in verse 5 here, which differ from the other three versions, are: 'A' yer *grouse* are crawin',' and '...I've tint yer *wine*...', but they are at least as likely to be the words of a version older than the other three. (Stanley Robertson thinks that tint means destroyed, or blighted, as used at the end of his version of 'Davie Faa', Child 200.) Anthony takes this at the slowest tempo, his voice is rounder, and he makes the ballad sound almost lyrical. In the first bar of verses 2, 3 and 5, the note B is avoided; the tune goes up to high D, and then leaps rapidly from C down to G, the Scots snap here coming most effectively on the word 'turn'.

Although there are some differences in words and tune amongst these four versions, they are not extensive and there are no fundamental differences in interpretation.

The banks o' red roses

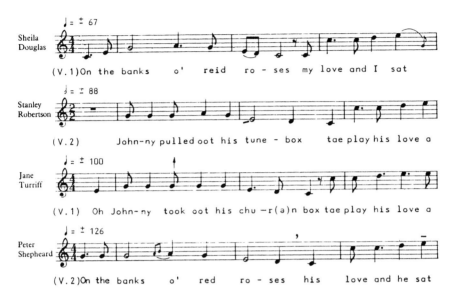

play his love a tune. In the mid-dle o'the tune   she

she stood up an cried,   "Oh   John-ny dear, oh John-ny dear,

l'ove sat doon an' cried, In the mid-dle o'the tune his.......his

play his love a tune. In the mid-dle o'the tune   oh   she

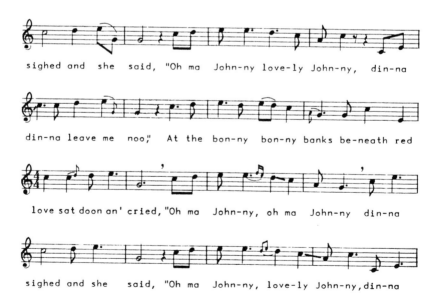

sighed and she   said, "Oh ma John-ny love-ly John-ny, din-na

din-na leave me   noo," At the bon-ny bon-ny banks be-neath red

love sat doon an' cried, "Oh ma   John-ny, oh ma   John-ny din-na

sighed and she   said, "Oh ma   John-ny, love-ly John-ny, din-na

leave me." (V.2)   When I was a wee thing and ea-sy led a -

ro - ses. (V.1)   When I was a wee thing I heard ma mo-ther

leave me." (V.2)Oh when I wis a young thing I heard ma mam-my

♩ = ± 116

leave me." (V.1)   When I was a wee thing an' easy led as-tray

stray   A - fore I wad work I wad rai - ther sport and

say,   A - fore I wad work I wad rai - ther sport an'

say, 'At be - fore I wad work I wad rai - ther sport an'

——   Be - fore I would work I would   ra - ther sport and

play,   Aye a - fore I wad work I'd rai-ther sport and

play,   A - fore an'I wad work I wad ra -ther sport an'

play,   Oh be - fore I wad work I wad ra-ther sport an'

play,   Be - fore I would work I would ra-ther sport and

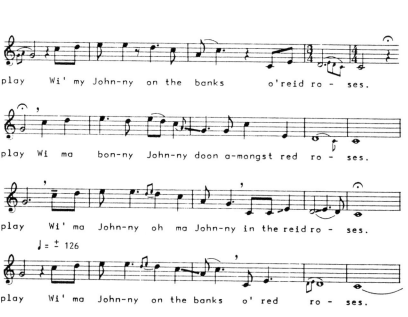

play Wi' my John-ny on the banks   o'reid ro - ses.

play Wi ma   bon-ny John-ny doon a-mongst red ro - ses.

play   Wi' ma John-ny oh ma John-ny in the reid ro - ses.

play   Wi' ma John-ny on the banks   o' red   ro - ses.

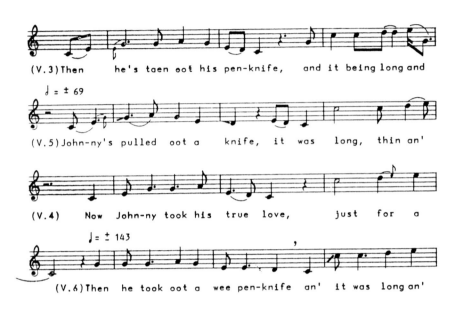

(V.3)Then he's taen oot his pen-knife, and it being long and

♩ = ± 69

(V.5)John-ny's pulled oot a knife, it was long, thin an'

(V.4) Now John-ny took his true love, just for a

♩ = ± 143

(V.6)Then he took oot a wee pen-knife an' it was long an'

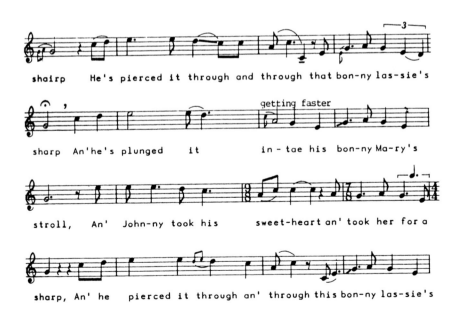

shairp He's pierced it through and through that bon-ny las-sie's

getting faster

sharp An'he's plunged it in-tae his bon-ny Ma-ry's

stroll, An' John-ny took his sweet-heart an' took her for a

sharp, An' he pierced it through an' through this bon-ny las-sie's

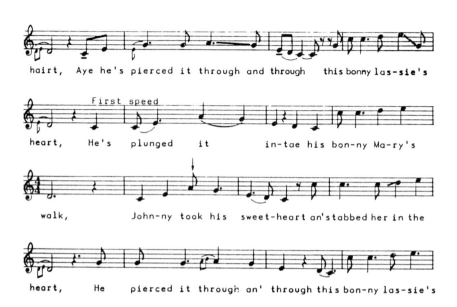

hairt, Aye he's pierced it through and through   this bonny las-sie's

First speed

heart,   He's   plunged   it   in-tae his bon-ny Ma-ry's

walk,   John-ny took his   sweet-heart an'stabbed her in the

heart,   He   pierced it through an' through this bon-ny las-sie's

hairt And he's left her ly-in' there a-mang reid ro - ses.

heart An' he   left her ly-ing   low be-neath red ro - ses.

heart An' he's left her ly-in' there   'neath reid ro - ses.

heart An' he   left her ly-in'   low   'mong   red   ro - ses.

Sheila Douglas. SA 1971/243, Rec. P.C. Kinross 1971

1. On the banks o' reid roses my love and I sat doon,
   And he's taen oot his chairm-box tae play his love a tune.
   In the middle o' the tune she sighed and she said,
   'Oh ma Johnny lovely Johnny, dinna leave me.'

2. When I was a wee thing and easy led astray
   Afore I wad work I wad raither sport and play,
   Aye afore I wad work I'd raither sport and play
   Wi' my Johnny on the banks o' reid roses.

3. Then he's taen oot his penknife, and it bein' long and shairp
   He's pierced it through and through that bonny lassie's hairt,
   Aye he's pierced it through and through this bonny lassie's hairt
   And he's left her lyin' there amang reid roses.

4. As verse 1.

Stanley Robertson. AM2, Rec. A.P. Kinross 1975

1. When I was a wee thing I heard ma mother say,
   Afore I wad work I wad raither sport an' play,
   Afore an' I wad work I wad rather sport an' play
   Wi' my bonny Johnny doon amongst red roses.

2. Johnny pulled oot his tune-box tae play his love a tune,
   An' in the middle o' the tune she stood up an' cried,
   'Oh Johnny dear, oh Johnny dear, dinna leave me noo,'
   At the bonny bonny banks beneath red roses.

3. Johnny's took her tae his hoose an' he treated her to tea
   Sayin', 'Arise my bonny Mary an' come awa' wi' me,
   Arise my bonny Mary an' come awa' wi' me
   Tae the bonny bonny banks beneath red roses.'

4. Johnny's gaed owre the high road, diggin' wi' a spade,
   Johnny's gaed owre the high road, diggin' at a grave,
   Johnny's gaed owre the high road, diggin' wi' a spade,
   And the bonny bonny banks beneath red roses.

5. Johnny's pulled oot a knife, it was long, thin an' sharp
   An' he's plunged it intae his bonny Mary's heart,
   He's plunged it intae his bonny Mary's heart
   An' he left her lying low beneath red roses.

6. Come a' ye bonny lassies, a warnin' tak' o' me,
   For it's never let a young man in yer company,
   For it's never let a young man in yer company,
   Wi' ma bonny Johnny doon amongst red roses.

Jane Turriff. AM12, Rec. A.P. Keith 1978

1.   Oh Johnny took oot his churn-box tae play his love a tune,
      In the middle o' the tune his love sat doon an' cried,
      In the middle o' the tune his...love sat doon an' cried,
      'Oh ma Johnny, oh ma Johnny dinna leave me.'

2.   Oh when I wis a young thing I heard ma mammy say,
      'At before I wad work I wad raither sport an' play,
      Oh before I wad work I wad rather sport an' play
      Wi' ma Johnny oh ma Johnny in the reid roses.'

3.   As verse 1.

4.   Now Johnny took his true love, just for a stroll,
      An' Johnny took his sweetheart an' took her for a walk,
      Johnny took his sweetheart an' stabbed her in the heart
      An' he's left her lyin' there 'neath reid roses.

5.   Now Johnny took the high road, howkin' wi' a spade,
      An' Johnny took the high road, howkin' at a grave,
      Johnny took the high road, howkin' wi' a spade,
      An' he's left her lyin' there beneath reid roses.

Pete Shepheard. AM12, Rec. A.P. Keith 1978

1.   When I was a wee thing an' easy led astray
      Before I would work I would rather sport and play,
      Before I would work I would rather sport and play
      Wi' ma Johnny on the banks o' red roses.

2.   On the banks o' red roses his love and he sat doon
      And he took oot his fiddle for tae play his love a tune.
      In the middle o' the tune oh she sighed and she said,
      'Oh ma Johnny, lovely Johnny, dinna leave me.'

3.   Noo they walked and they talked till they cam' untae a cave
      Where all night long her Johnnie had been digging at her grave,
      Where all night long her Johnnie had been digging at her grave
      By the bonny bonny banks o' red roses.

4.   'Oh Johnny, lovely Johnny, oh that grave is not for me;'
      'Oh yes, my lovely Jeannie, that your bridal bed shall be,
      Oh yes, my lovely Jeannie, that your bridal bed shall be
      By the bonny bonny banks o' red roses.'

5.   As verse 2.

6. Then he took oot a wee penknife an' it was long an' sharp,
    An' he pierced it through an' through this bonny lassie's heart,
    He pierced it through an' through this bonny lassie's heart
    An' he left her lying' low 'mong red roses.

7. Noo as he was comin' homeward his heart was filled with fear,
    For every face he met he thocht it was his dear,
    For every face he met he thocht it was his dear
    Lyin' cold upon her bed 'mong red roses.

8. As verse 2.

Of the four examples chosen this song shows the greatest differences within the four versions: differences in the words, in the details and the interpretation of the story, and in the musical interpretation. The versions of the tune itself show but slight variation. All start with the same two verses, but in differing order. In the music transcription all the related verses are aligned, including the murder verse, and only the three which correspond to those in the first version are shown. (The same procedure is followed in *Johnnie my man*.)

Where the theme of the girl murdered by her boyfriend appears in western folk song, it is generally understood that she is pregnant, even when this is not explicitly stated.

Sheila Douglas regards this as a story which ends in tragedy, and she shapes the song accordingly. She sings very slowly, with a sad lyricism and with deep feeling, and one feels the seeds of tragedy are there from the very beginning. 'It is the love that is doomed,' she says, and there is no anger or harshness in her singing. She finds sexual symbolism in the second line of verse 1, and so does Pete Shepheard. Except for the ending, the two halves of the melody are almost identical, and the rounded, soaring voice unites words and tune into an artistic whole. 'I love the beautiful long-drawn phrases of the tune, and the way it rises to a climax and falls so expressively down at the end. The words have that dramatic intensity and economy of all great ballads. It seems to me to be about the way all-consuming sexual passion can wreck people's lives and bring about tragedy and death.'

Stanley Robertson of Aberdeen, a nephew of Jeannie Robertson, treats the song very differently. His fuller version of the words, and Pete Shepheard's, makes it clear that the murder was calculated. This is the fastest account, sung at more than twice the speed of Sheila's. On the occasion of this performance, Stanley's introductory remarks included the following: '...a song my mither used to sing – I've heard it sung a lot in the folk scene – it's usually sung slow – I've heard Heather Heywood sing it awfa bonny...but I'll have to sing it the wey't I kenned it frae my mither, which is mair – a serious song, but it had – a pleasant *wey* to think o' the serious... and ye *do* think o' the seriousness o' the song because of the pleasantness o' the tune... "The banks o' the red roses"...for me it's something pleasant.' He has since described it as 'a horror ballad – if sung slow, it's too much; the tune is euphemistic and puts it over in a digestible way.' He is very hard on the woman: 'In the song the girl admits she is loose –

"Before I wad work I wad raither sport an' play wi' ma Johnny..." She obviously becomes pregnant and the young man feels trapped. He could cope with fatherhood but not with her constant nagging.' The only reason he gave in support of the 'constant nagging' charge was that she had interrupted her lover in the middle of the tune he was playing her, having always taken the 'tune-box' line literally. As for the 'sporting and playing' he evidently regards this as all the woman's fault, and he says 'wee thing' can refer to an adult. Once when he sang this, '...a lady started to cry. I thought she was moved with the song but on investigating further I found out that she had a daughter murdered in the same fashion. Many travellers used this song to teach their daughters the dangers and perils in breaking their moral standards, and that the aftermath could bring much suffering and heartbreak.' (It seems it was not used as a warning to sons.) His aunt Maggie Stewart also sang this: 'It was one of those songs that always seemed to crop up at travellers' parties and gatherings.' His cousin Lizzie Higgins also sang it, but slowly.

The chief difference in Robertson's version of the tune, also found in Jane Turriff's, is in bars 6 and 14 of each verse: with two exceptions, none of their verses have the octave leap downwards, from C to C. Since Turriff and Robertson are both of traveller stock, such resemblances are not surprising. Verbal similarities also appear, including the opening verse (verse 2 of Robertson's) where the girl 'stood up/sat doon an' cried' (instead of 'sighed an' ...said') and the triple reference of each to 'the high road'. A third resemblance is to some kind of 'box' for playing the tune, and the fact that Turriff also takes this literally. At first she thought 'churn-box' referred to part of the butter-churning equipment, but then she realised this could not produce a 'tune' and said the reference might be to a melodion, often called simply 'the box'. In this performance Turriff accompanies herself on guitar, strumming the tonic chord gently throughout the song so that it sounds rather like a pedal-point, or a drone. She lends variety to the verse-ending by rising to high C, or falling to middle C, in alternate verses. The song was learned in childhood, from her mother's singing. Although Jane does not take it as slowly as Sheila, her account is also in her own way unmistakably tragic – the cutting edge in her voice seems to be emphasised – and she is very definite that this should be sung 'in a sad way, it should feel like the real thing'. She finds the reason for the murder hard to understand: 'It's a funny song – I can't make much of it – but it's very tragic...I sing very sad when it is a true sad song.'

Pete Shepheard learned his version from Jane's uncle, old Davie Stewart, 'and conflated it with other versions'. He has heard it sung at many different speeds, from very slow (old Davie) to even faster than his own ('a local Fife singer'). His highly individual conflation is sung to his own lilting, dance-like accordion accompaniment, the whole effect being not only relaxed but almost jolly, and *with gusto*. The tempo is second only to Stanley Robertson's here. (But, although Robertson described the tune as 'pleasant' and chooses a fast pace, he does not sound relaxed or jolly; his fast-driven version has a certain grimness, probably directed against the girl for causing the man to undergo the terrible experience of murdering her!) Shepheard sings most of his songs fast. He is also convinced that the speed and the scale of a melody are unrelated to tragedy, and he is certainly right about the scale or mode. I am not so sure about the speed. (One classic example in art-music is Orpheus' famous lament for Euridice, 'Che faro senza Euridice...' in Act III of Gluck's opera *Orfeo et Euridice*, set in the 'cheerful' key of C major. If sung in a happy manner – which would *include* a faster tempo – it could easily become a song of joyful release: 'She is lost and gone for ever'! as one translation has it.) A tragic song may be sung fast because it was learned in childhood and hence 'gabbled' through without thinking of the meaning. It has been suggested that a fast tempo may either indicate stoicism, or else come into the 'laughing that he may not weep' category. Certainly 'The banks o' red roses' is frequently sung in Pete Shepheard's way by men, but I have never heard, or heard of, a woman singing it thus.

One interpretation of this song is that the girl is not really murdered at all but only lying back exhausted after vigorous lovemaking, the knife and the stabbing 'through and through' being another piece of erotic imagery; and there are versions where this is clearly indicated, including some from Ireland. This underlines the fact that the same words are used in each of these four versions to announce the start of lovemaking and to announce the start of killing, viz. 'he's taen oot' (Sheila), 'Johnny('s) pulled oot' (Stanley) and 'he took (oot)' (Jane and Pete). Going a step further, the connection between murder, and sexual love which is doomed and hopeless, has been made before, perhaps especially in fiction (for example, Tolstoy's Vronsky and Anna Karenina, after the first consummation of their love: 'He felt what a murderer must feel, when he sees the body he has robbed of life.')

I was particularly interested to find that Stanley Robertson and Jane Turriff, the two travellers, should ignore the sexual implications in verse 1 (of music transcription) and wondered at first if this was common in traveller versions generally. But the evidence does not support this. In a recording made by Linda Williamson in 1978, Sissy Johnston and Bella Townsley both sang the words 'tunin' box' in the line referred to. Betsy Whyte of Montrose, who is related to both these women, is quite definite that they would understand this sexually rather than literally. Betsy's childhood was spent in the real travelling life; she often heard the song and says that 'You could see everyone understood this meaning.' She thought the symbolic words were probably used partly to avoid being explicit in front of the children, who were with the grown-ups all the time. She also says she heard it sung, 'He took oot his grinding-box to play his love a tune'; 'grinder' is a name for the penis.

Pete Shepheard comments: 'A beautiful tune that is apparently unique to this song. When I started singing it, the much less interesting Irish version was well known in the revival... On the other hand the Scottish form was widely known by traditional singers, always with variants of the same tune and words. And it had never been published – an excellent survival in oral tradition.' The song is widespread, and Dolina MacLennan suggests that in Skye the literal meaning is generally understood.

We may conclude that this is probably a very old song, and that the symbolic meaning (in verse 1 of the transcription) was suppressed and frowned on at certain times and in certain places.

Johnnie my man

♩ = ± 47

Lizzie Higgins

(V.1)"John-nie my man, dae ye no think o' ri-sin', The nicht it's weel

♪ = ± 80

Stanley Robertson

"John-nie my man, will ye no think o' ri-sin', The night is weel

♩ = ± 94

Cy Lawrie

"John-nie my man, dae ye no think on ri-sin', The day it is

♩ = ± 76

Duncan Williamson

"Oh John-nie ma man, dae ye no think o' ri-sin', For the fire is gaen

spent an' the time's wear-in' on; Yer sil-ler's   a' dene an'yer

spent and the time's wea-rin' on; Yer sil-ler it's a' dene an'yer

spent and the dark's co-min' on; Yer sil-ler's   a' dene an'the

oot   and the bair-nies are home; Our sil-ler it's gaen done, there's nae

stowp's toom be-fore you, A-rise up my John-nie an' come a - wa'

stowp's toom be-fore you, A-rise up my Johnnie an' come a - wa'

a little faster

stowp's toom be-fore ye, Rise up my man John-nie and come a - wa'

faster

meal in the bar-rel, Oh rise up my Johnnie an' come a - wa'

hame". (V.2)'Oh wha is that I hear spea-kin'sae kind-ly, For I

usual speed

hame." "Oh wha's that I hear fa is spea-kin'sae kind-ly, Fine I

usual speed

hame." "Whae is that I hear spea-kin'sae kind-ly, I

hame"."Who is that there at the door there,her voice sounds sae kind-ly, It

ken it's the voice o' my ain wi-fie Jean; Syne **come by me**

ken weel the voice o' my ain wi-fie Jean; Come **sit doon, ma**

ken be   the voice it's ma ain wi-fie Jean;   Come be ma

sounds like the voice o' my wee wi-fie Jean; Oh haud ye a -

dea - rie   an' sit doon be - side me, There is room in this

dea - rie, come sit doon be - side me, There is room in this

dea - rie and sit doon be - side me, There is room in this

- while,   my   bon - ny wee las-sie For you ken I've been

taiv-ren for mair than ene". (V.3)"John-nie my man, oor

a little faster   usual speed

tai -vern for mair than jest ene". "John-nie my man, oor

tai -vern for mair for-bye me". "John-nie my man, your

drin-kin' o' whis-kyan'wine"She said,"Johnnie ma lad-die,that's what I've

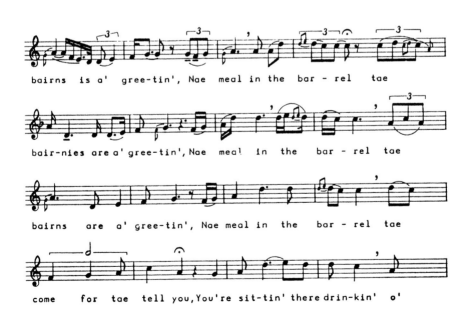

bairns is a' gree-tin', Nae meal in the bar - rel tae

bair-nies are a' gree-tin', Nae meal in the bar - rel tae

bairns are a' gree-tin', Nae meal in the bar - rel tae

come for tae tell you, You're sit-tin' there drin-kin' o'

fill their wee wames; While sit-tin' here drin - kin' ye

fill their wee wame(s);While ye sit   here drin - king you

fill their wee wames; While ye sit   here a-drin - kin' ye

whis-ky an'   wine;   The   fire is gaen oot   an' the

leave me : la - men - tin', A - rise up my John - nie an'

leave me   la - men - tin',A - rise up   my John-nie   and

leave me   la - men - tin', Rise   up my man John-nie and

bair-nies are hun - gry,   Oh rise up my John-nie   an'

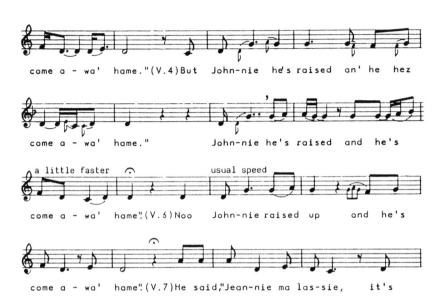

come a - wa' hame."(V.4)But John-nie he's raised an' he hez

come a - wa' hame." John-nie he's raised and he's

a little faster   usual speed

come a - wa' hame".(V.6)Noo John-nie raised up and he's

come a - wa' hame".(V.7)He said,"Jean-nie ma las-sie, it's

got the door o -pen, Say-in',"Cursed be the taiv - ren that's

pushed the door o - pen,Cry-ing,"Cursed be the tai - vern that's

flung the door o - pen, "My curse on the tai - vern that

tak' you ma hand,dear, Oh gie me yer bon - nie wee

e'er let me in; An' cursed be the whis-ky that maks me sae

e'er let me in; And cursed be the whis-ky that maks me sae

first took in; My curse on the whis-ky that mak'd me aye

hand in mine, An' I'll give up drin-kin', oh Jean-nie ma

thir-sty, Fare - weel tae ye whisky for I'll a - wa' home".

thir-sty, Fare - weel tae ye whis-ky for I'm a - wa' home".

thir-sty," Say-in',"Far'thee weel whis-ky for I'm a - wa' home".

las-sie, And I'll go home to that faim'ly o' mine".

Lizzie Higgins. SA 1973/174, Rec. S.S. Aberdeen 1973

1. 'Johnnie my man, dae ye no think o' risin',
    The nicht it's weel spent an' the time's wearin' on;
    Yer siller's a' dene an' yer stowp's toom before you,
    Arise up my Johnnie an' come awa' hame.'

2. 'Oh wha is that I hear speakin' sae kindly,
    For I ken it's the voice o' my ain wifie Jean;
    Syne come by me dearie an' sit doon beside me,
    There is room in this taivren for mair than ene.'

3. 'Johnnie my man, oor bairns is a' greetin',
    Nae meal in the barrel tae fill their wee wames;
    While sittin' here drinkin' ye leave me lamentin',
    Arise up my Johnnie an' come awa' hame.'

4. But Johnnie he's raised an' he hez got the door open,
    Saying, 'Cursed be the taivern that's e'er let me in;
    An' cursed be the whisky that maks me sae thirsty,
    Fareweel tae ye whisky for I'll awa' hame.'

Stanley Robertson. SA 1973/112, Rec. A.M. Kinross 1973

1. 'Johnnie my man, will ye no think o' risin',
    The night is weel spent and the time's wearin' on;
    Yer siller it's a' dene an' yer stowp's toom before you,
    Arise up my Johnnie an' come awa' hame.'

2. 'Oh wha's that I hear fa is speakin' sae kindly,
    Fine I ken weel the voice o' my ain wifie Jean;
    Come sit doon, ma dearie, come sit doon beside me,
    There is room in this taivern for mair than jest ene.'

3. 'Johnnie my man, oor bairnies are a' greetin',
    Nae meal in the barrel tae fill their wee wame(s);
    While ye sit here drinking you leave me lamentin',
    Arise up my Johnnie and come awa' hame.'

4. Johnnie he's raised and he's pushed the door open,
    Crying, 'Cursed be the taivern that's e'er let me in;
    And cursed be the whisky that maks me sae thirsty,
    Fareweel tae ye whisky for I'm awa' hame.'

Cy Laurie. SA 1971/242, Rec. J.P. Kinross 1971

1. 'Johnnie my man, dae ye no think on risin',
    The day it is spent and the dark's comin' on;
    Yer siller's a' dene an' the stowp's toom before ye;
    Rise up my man Johnnie and come awa' hame.'

2.   'Whae is that I hear speakin' sae kindly,
      I ken be the voice it's ma ain wifie Jean;
      Come be ma dearie and sit doon beside me,
      There is room in this taivern for mair forbye me.'

3.   'Johnnie my man, your bairns are a' greetin',
      Nae meal in the barrel tae fill their wee wames;
      While ye sit here a-drinkin ye leave me lamentin',
      Rise up my man Johnny and come awa' hame.'

4.   'Dae ye no remember on the first days we coorted,
      On a bed o' primroses we baith did sit doon
      A-pickin' the floo'ers in each ithers' company,
      We ne'er thocht it lang then nor thocht tae gae hame.'

5.   'Aye weel I remember on the days that ye mention,
      But they are awa' and they'll ne'er come again.
      Just think on the present an' try tae amend it,
      Rise up my man Johnnie and come awa' hame.'

6.   Noo Johnnie raised up and he's flung the door open,
      'My curse on the taivern that first took me in;
      My curse on the whisky that mak'd me aye thirsty,'
      Sayin', 'Far' thee weel whisky for I'm awa' hame.'

Duncan Williamson. SA 1976/29 Rec. L.W. Lochgilphead 1976

1.   'Oh Johnnie ma man, dae ye no think o' risin',
      For the fire is gaen oot an' the bairnies are hame;
      Our siller it's gaen done, ther's nae meal in the barrel,
      Oh rise up my Johnnie an' come awa' hame.'

2.   'Who is that there at the door there, her voice sounds sae kindly,
      It sounds like the voice o' my wee wifie Jean;
      Oh haud ye awhile, my bonny wee lassie,
      For you ken I've been drinkin' o' whisky an' wine.'

3.   She said, 'Johnnie ma laddie, that's what I've come for tae tell you,
      You're sittin' there drinkin' o whisky an' wine;
      The fire is gaen oot an' the bairnies are hungry,
      Oh rise up my Johnnie an' come awa' hame.'

4.   He said, 'Jeannie ma lassie, come sit doon beside me
      There's plenty o' room in this tavern for two,
      For I've been a-drinkin', oh Jeannie ma lassie,
      But I've been a-thinkin', oh ma lassie o' you.'

5.   Oh curse tae the whisky, it's what I've been drinkin',
      An' curse tae the whisky an' curse tae the wine,
      Oh curse tae the whisky, it's what I've been drinkin',
      For it's made me neglect that fine faim'ly o'mine.'

6.   She said, 'Johnnie, my laddie, it's one thing I'll tell you
     You've been sittin' here drinkin' noo since nine,
     The fire is gaen oot an' there's nae meal in the barrel
     An' I'm gettin' worried aboot that faimly o' mine.'

7.   He said 'Jeannie ma lassie, it's tak' you ma hand, dear,
     Oh gie me yer bonny wee hand in mine,
     An' I'll give up drinkin', oh Jeannie ma lassie,
     And I'll go hame to that faim'ly o' mine.'

Versions of these words are to be found in both Ford's and Ord's collections, and also in Greig's *Folk-Song in Buchan*. Ord supplies a tune which is fairly closely related to the four shown above but which differs in lines 2 and 4 of the verse (bars 5-8 and 13-16 above, and bars 3-4 and 7-8 in Ord). All three collectors give six verses corresponding to Cy Laurie's. Ford and Ord add on another three which describe in some detail Johnnie's resolution to 'leave aff the drinking' – or 'the auld deeds' (Ford) – and the happier home of the family thereafter. These three verses, cast in the explicitly moralising vein so popular in Victorian times, have since, it appears, been dropped. Ord's version is the first item under his heading of 'Convivial Songs' – though anything less convivial it would be hard to imagine. Both Ford and Ord state that it was a favourite street song all over Scotland in the 1860s and 1870s, or even earlier, and, Ford adds, 'found ready sale always in penny-sheet form, chiefly among those who required most its pointed lesson'. Greig's remarks in introducing his version of the words, and apropos the 'temperance' lay he has referred to, are profoundly important: 'It does not so much matter what has been the origin or genesis of these lyrics. The fact remains, significant and satisfactory, that they have been adopted by the folk-songist.'

Lizzie Higgins learned 'Johnnie my man' when she was a child, from the singing of her father Donald Higgins. She liked the song, 'because of the tune first and then the words. The message…is to stop drinking and feed his children, and look after his wife, children and his home, and to stop them suffering uncalled-for hardship caused by his drinking. No connection with this song in my life as I never knew hunger or cold, my father always saw we were well fed, and well clothed.' Lizzie always started this song by pitching the opening three words a fifth higher than in the remaining three verses, and a very fine start it makes. Part of her distinctive style is her masterly treatment of grace-notes. There is very little variation in dynamics (which may be defined as change of tone, mainly in volume) and the contrast with the other three singers, particularly Stanley Robertson and Duncan Williamson, is striking. One of her variations in the tune, which although not written here as grace-notes produces the impression of decoration, is in bars 3 and 11 of verse 3. In all the other verses there is an uninterrupted downward leap of a fifth from A to D, and this is found also in the other singers' versions (although not in Williamson's bar 3 of verses 2 to 4, where he has a different tune for the opening line). But in verse 3, where the wife speaks of the children's sufferings and of her own, Lizzie fills in this downward leap with intermediate steps in the scale, in a somewhat wavering and less definite way. It may be fanciful to see in this an attempt to express the intensity of feeling at these points, but it is worth considering. This singer is ex-

tremely sensitive to the meanings in her verbal text, and her artistry in express-
ing these through the music is conscious. (Another version of this song is on
Lizzie Higgins's first record, *Princess of the Thistle* – Topic 12T185.)

Stanley Robertson got his version from his father William Robertson, and
from his great-aunt Maggie Stewart, sister of Maria (Jeannie Robertson's
mother). Here are his introductory remarks to this performance, recorded at
Kinross in the Men's Singing (competition) class: 'I'd like now to do more a lament type – a very, very old song that's been in the family...sometimes when
I'm singing the song I get very emotional so if I greet dinnae take any notice,
just listen to the words o' the song. It's cried "Johnny ma man", it tells the story
of a man who drinks, and I suppose if any of yez have been brought up by a
drunken father ye would understand...what the story is about.' In a letter
replying to questions (1980) he wrote: 'I like this song because it is true to life.
How many basically good men have ruined their homes because of whisky, and
I know personally many "Johnnies"... When the realisation comes to the
drunkard of how much he has deprived his wife and children it leaves a feeling
of deep remorse but to many a reconciliation and resolution. I love the haunting
tune that sends shivers up my spine and I like its beautiful grace-noting. It is a
song that lingers in the mind long after the singer has stopped... Its message is
for fathers to make their homes their castles and their wives queens... It is
against any other organisation that detracts from that home-loving spirit...and
that peace and plenty abide in the homes that have love abundant. It advises
against going to taverns. I am temperant and abhor alcohol taken in large
quantities at any time. I have experience [of] seeing my father drunk many times
and I hated the scenes that took place. [Stanley also said that his father, like
Johnnie, later gave up drinking.] Perhaps for this reason I preferred not to imbibe
myself... I believe it would be an old song because of the verse "Nae meal in the
barrel tae fill their wee wames", because long ago in Scotland folk used only
meal and herring tae live on. Although I only sing four verses I have heard more
verses but I feel that they were added at a much later time. The tune of the longer
version is different and the wording seems more modern, nearer music-hall
period style. My version I believe is from an older version than the longer one
commonly sung in the folk scene.'

I have not found any other tune for this song, but a careful examination of the
various sets of words lends support to Stanley's last point. In comparison with
the succinct 4-stanza version shown above, the two extra verses of 'flowery'
reminiscence lack punch (Cy Laurie's and Greig's verses 4 and 5, Ford's and
Ord's verses 3 and 4), and do not accord with the urgent, minimal 4-verse dialogue, which indeed says everything. As for the last verses in Ford and Ord, they
are embarrassingly *de trop* and sentimental to our taste in a 'nearer music-hall
period style'. (Although one has to admit that the description of subsequent happier conditions does show Johnnie's good resolutions as actually put into practice.)

Stanley Robertson sings this even more slowly than Lizzie, and at less than
half Cy Laurie's fastest pace. I remember well the performance recorded on this
tape; it was one of the most grief-laden I have ever heard, and although the
singer himself didn't greet, a few furtive handkerchiefs appeared amongst the
rest of us. He is the only singer here who regularly (at bars 2 and 10 of the verse)
introduces the minor sixth, B flat, thus placing the melody in the Aeolian mode.

The mid-cadence on C, bar 8, preceded by F and A in bar 7, feels like the dominant note of the relative major, F major. Duncan Williamson does almost the same at these two bars. (The other two also have a mid-cadence on C, but in the bar before they descend only to G and not F: the C therefore sounds more like the third of A, the dominant. The tonic is always a minor mode on D.) At the end of each verse, Robertson arrives at the low tonic note, D, at least a bar before the others, which in this particular instance seems to add to the sombre mood.

Cy Laurie thinks he heard Lizzie Higgins sing this, at Glasgow Folk Centre in the late sixties, at one of her first public appearances. He represents the man as recalling their courtship (verse 4), and the woman replying, whereas in the three printed sources mentioned the order of these speakers is reversed. Although this is taken at the fastest pace of the four it is not at all hurried. It is more relaxed and straightforward but it still has 'the hairt-feeling' as Stanley would say.

Duncan Williamson's words are considerably different from the others, and all seven verses have the same hall-mark of style. Verse 6 seems to repeat verse 3, although in somewhat different words. His opening melody, with its rising fifth in contrast to the more common fourth, has settled by verse 2 into another which he adheres to for the rest of the song. The new 4-bar phrase (bars 1-4 of verse 2 onwards) recalls most hauntingly the opening bars of that powerful and – at least in Scotland – rarely heard Irish song, 'The bold Fenian men'. Williamson first heard 'Johnnie my man' sung by his father's sister, around 1942, at Tarbert in Argyll. He says, 'I like this song because it was sung by a person I respected... I like the theme of the song. A man who was a drunkard all the days of his life had made a promise to his wife and kept it – he is worthy of anybody's respect. It connects with everybody's life who respects that kind of man: those who would like to be like him, who have tried and perhaps failed.' He also says that this song among the travellers is 'as old as the travellers', and that his auntie had said this (i.e. the story in the song) had actually happened to a traveller man and woman.

The words of these four versions contain more Scots words and pronunciations than any of those in the three printed collections, although Greig has rather more than the other two.

Below are names of those who contributed in some way to the 1984 edition, and who have since died. Our debt to them remains.

John Blacking
Morris Blythman
Derek Bowman
Norman Buchan
Alan Bruford
Alex Campbell
Eric Cregeen
Lizzie Higgins
Hamish Imlach
Calum Johnstone
A L (Bert) Lloyd
Ewan MacColl
Josh MacRae
Angus Russell
Willie Scott
Patrick Shuldham-Shaw
J A C Stevenson
Betsy Whyte

Glossary

a'	*all*	ca'	*call*
ablow	*below, under*	callants	*lads*
abuin (abin), abune	*above*	canker	*to fret, become peevish or ill-humoured*
ae	*one; only*	caul', cauld	*cold*
aff	*off*	Ceòl-Beag	*the small music*
afore	*before*	Ceòl-Meanach	*the middle music*
ahint	*behind*	Ceòl-Mór	*the great music (all bagpipe music terms)*
ain	*own*		
aince	*once*	chaumer	*chamber*
alane	*alone*	chiel	*a lad, a man*
alang	*along*	clipe, clype	*to tell tales*
amang	*among*	coniach, conniach	*used to describe the feeling expressed in a performance, vocal or instrumental: an indefinable something which moves the listeners.*
ane	*one*		
aneath	*beneath, under*		
annoled (annealed?)	*Duncan Williamson: 'As if it were moulded from the exact thing'.*		
aroon'	*around*	coorie	*to stoop, bend, crouch*
askit	*asked*	coort	*court*
atween	*between*	couldna(e)	*couldn't*
aucht	*aught*	country hantle	*see* hantle
aul', auld	*old*	cowk	*to retch, vomit*
ava	*at all*	crawin'	*crowing, exulting*
awa'	*away*	cried	*called*
awfa, awfu'	*awful*	crouse	*conceited, arrogant, proud*
ba'	*ball*	cuid	*could*
baith	*both*		
barfit	*barefoot*	dae	*do*
bauld	*bold, courageous*	dang	*to knock, strike, push suddenly*
beggit	*begged*		
ben	*inside, further in*	daur	*to dare*
bide	*to stay, dwell*	deid	*dead*
bield	*shelter, protection*	dene	*done*
birks	*birch trees*	deuk	*duck*
bivvies	*(from bivouac) tents*	dinna(e)	*don't*
bla'	*meal, e.g. oats*	divvies	*(from divot) pieces of turf*
bleezin'	*blazing*		
brae	*hill, hillside*	doon	*down*
brak	*break*	doot	*doubt*
brand	*burning peat, glowing cinder; sword*	doss	*to throw (oneself) down, sit down heavily; to stay, sleep, for the night*
braw	*fine, splendid*		
braxy ham	*salted meat of a sheep that died from the disease 'braxy'; very salty ham (quoted from Chapbook 3, (4))*	dowie	*sad, melancholy, dismal*
		duin (din), dune	*done*
		dule	*grief, misery, suffering*
		dwine	*to pine, waste away*
breist	*breast*	dyke	*low wall or hedge*
brither	*brother*		
brunt	*burnt*	een	*eyes*
bunnet	*bonnet*	eence	*once*

231

fae	*from*
faim'ly	*family*
faur'd	*favoured; (good or bad)-looking*
fause	*false*
feart	*feared, afraid*
fee	*wages; engagement; to hire as a servant*
fit	*foot*
flatties [cant]	*non-travellers*
fly	*knowing, shrewd*
forbye	*besides, in addition*
foumart	*usually ferret, weasel. (Stanley Robertson: 'The travellers always understood it to mean a wolf.')*
fower	*four*
frae	*from*
freends	*friends*
gae, gang	*to go*
gaen, gane; gaun	*gone; going*
gager	*probably guager, i.e. customs official*
gair	*gore*
gallus	*devil-may-care, reckless*
gear	*possessions in general (including money)*
gey	*considerable, or very*
gie	*to give*
gin	*if*
gled	*glad*
Glesgie, Glesca	*Glasgow*
gowd	*gold*
greet	*to cry, weep. Past tense: grat*
guid, gweed	*good*
gyang	*see gang, gae.*
hadna(e)	*hadn't*
hae	*to have*
hairt	*heart*
hale	*whole*
hame	*home*
hanker	*to loiter, linger, hang about expectantly*
hantle [cant]	*people. Country hantle: polite or friendly expression for non-travellers*
haud	*to hold*
haud awa'	*to keep away, keep out or off*
hecht	*promised, engaged*
heelster-goudie	*head over heels*
heid, heid-the-ba'	*head; a football expression*
herry	*to harry*

hert	*see hairt*
heuch (heuk)	*reaping hook, sickle*
hidna	*see hadna*
hie	*to hasten, proceed quickly*
hing	*to hang*
hirple	*to hobble, walk as with a limp*
hoast	*to cough*
howk	*to dig, delve the soil*
hum	*to chew, or to eat greedily*
ilka	*each, every*
ither	*other*
jalouse	*to suspect*
jijimant (jidgimant)	*judgement*
jink	*to frolic, dance; flirt*
jouk, juke	*to dart about; to evade by trickery*
juist	*just*
keel	*red ochre, used especially for marking sheep*
ken, kent	*to know, knew*
kittle	*to whet, sharpen*
lane	*lone, alone*
lee	*lie*
lift	*the air, sky*
loanin's	*lanes, byways*
lo'e	*love*
lowe	*to flame or blaze*
lowp	*to leap*
lyke-wake	*vigil over a corpse until burial*
ma	*my*
mair	*more*
mairry	*marry*
makar	*a poet, a writer of verse*
maun	*must*
Maw	*Ma, mother*
minnie	*mother (diminutive)*
mischanter	*mischance*
mither	*mother*
mony	*many*
mou	*mouth*
muckle	*much, great, big*
muin	*moon*
mun	*see maun*
nae	*no*
nane	*none*
nickum	*scamp, rogue, mischievous boy*

noo	*now*	swack	*pliant, nimble*
nor	*than*	syne	*since; thereupon*
ony	*any*	tae	*to*
oot	*out*	tattie	*potato*
outwith	*outside of*	tent	*to tempt*
ower, owre	*over*	thae	*those*
oxter	*arm-pit*	thon	*that*
		thraw	*to throw; twist*
pairt	*part*	til	*to*
pleisure	*pleasure*	tint, from tinte	*injury, harm, damage*
ploo	*plough*	toom	*empty*
polis	*police*	twa	*two*
puckle, pickle	*a little, a few*	twine	*to separate, part,*
puir	*poor*		*deprive*
redd	*to free*	unco	*unusual, strange;*
reive, rieve	*to plunder, rob*		*remarkable, great*
rickle	*·a loose heap*		
rin	*to run*	wad	*would; to wed*
rive	*to tear asunder, rend*	wadna(e)	*wouldna, wouldn't*
roch	*rough*	wame	*belly*
rottans	*rats*	wan'	*wand*
rowe	*to impel forward, or*	warstle	*to wrestle*
	push	wasna(e),	*wasn't*
		wisna(e)	
saft	*soft*	wean	*child*
sair	*sore*	weel	*well*
samen	*same*	weemen	*women*
sark	*shirt*	weet	*wet*
saut	*salt*	westle	*wrestle*
scaldies [cant]	*non-travellers*	wha	*who*
scoor (scour)	*to rush, run about,*	whaur	*where*
	search hither and	white heather	*refers to TV series of*
	thither		*1960s – Scottish*
shouther	*shoulder*		*dancing and song –*
sic	*such*		*very smooth, re-*
siller (silver)	*money*		*spectable, middle-*
simmer	*summer*		*class, well dressed,*
snaw	*snow*		*etc.*
socht	*sought*	wi'	*with*
sodger	*soldier*	wid	*would*
speir	*to ask, enquire*	windae	*window*
spoliat, or	*despoiled, stolen*	winna	*willna, won't*
spulyeit		wis	*was*
sprog	*crop, usually rye or*	wint	*want*
	barley (Stanley	wuid	*wood*
	Robertson)	wumman	*woman*
spuin	*spoon*	wyte	*to know*
stovies	*a dish made with*	wyn', wynd	*lane, narrow street*
	potatoes		
stowp	*drinking vessel*	yin	*one*
strecht	*straight*	yince	*once*
streitch	*to stretch*	yowes	*ewes*
strucken	*past tense of to strike;*		
	used to mean exact		

Bibliography

Ahlstrom, Sydney E, *A Religious History of the American People*, New Haven, 1972.
Aitken, A J and McArthur, Tom, *The Languages of Scotland*, Edinburgh, 1979.
Allsop, Kenneth, *Hard Travellin'*: *The Hobo and His History*, Harmondsworth, 1972.
Arnot, R Page, *The History of the Scottish Miners*, London, 1955.
Bassin, Ethel, *The Old Songs of Skye: Frances Tolmie and her Circle*, London, 1977.
Benedict, Ruth, *Patterns of Culture*, London, 1935.
Bennett, Margaret, *Scottish Customs: from the Cradle to the Grave*, Edinburgh, 1992.
Blacking, John, *Black Background*, New York and London, 1964.
_____, *How Musical is Man?* London, 1976.
Bohlman, Philip V, *The Study of Folk Music in the Modern World*, Bloomington and Indianapolis, 1988.
Boyes, Georgina, *The imagined village: Culture, ideology and the English Folk Revival*, Manchester and New York, 1993.
Brand, Oscar, *The Ballad Mongers*, Minerva Press, Toronto, 1967.
Briggs, Katherine M, *A Dictionary of British Folk-tales*, 2 vols., London, 1970.
Bronson, Bertrand H, *The Traditional Tunes of the Child Ballads*, 4 vols., Princeton, N J, 1959–72.
Brown, Gordon, *The Red Paper on Scotland*, Edinburgh, 1975.
Brown, Mary Ellen, *Burns and Tradition*, London, 1984.
Buchan, David, *The Ballad and the Folk*, London, 1972.
Buchan, Norman, *101 Scottish Songs*, Glasgow, 1962.
_____ and Hall, Peter, *The Scottish Folksinger*, Glasgow and London, 1978.
Campbell, Duncan, *Reminiscences and Reflections of an Octogenarian Highlander*, published by subscription, Inverness, 1910.
Campbell, Ian, *Kailyard: A New Assessment*, Edinburgh, 1981.
_____, ed., *Nineteenth Century Scottish Fiction*, Manchester, 1979.
Campbell, John Lorne and Collinson, Francis, *Hebridean Folksongs*, 3 vols., Oxford, 1969–81.
Campbell J L and Shaw M F, *Songs Remembered in Exile*, Aberdeen, 1990.
Carter, Sydney, *Dance in the Dark*, London, 1980.
Chambers, Robert, *The Scottish Ballads*, Edinburgh, 1829.
Child, Francis James, *The English and Scottish Popular Ballads*, 5 vols., New York, 1965. First published 1882–94.
Collins, Mal and others, *Big Red Songbook*, London, 1977.
Collinson, Francis, *The Traditional and National Music of Scotland*, London, 1970.
Comunn Gàidhealach Leòdhais, *Eilean Fraoich*, Stornoway, 1982.
Cooke, Peter, *The Fiddle Tradition of the Shetland Isles*, Cambridge, 1986. Accompanying cassette, CUP, 1986.
Cowan, Edward J, ed., *The People's Past*, Edinburgh, 1980.
Craig, David, *Scottish Literature and the Scottish People*, London, 1961.
Crawford, Thomas, *Burns: A Study of the Poems and Songs*, Edinburgh and London, 1960.
Creighton, Helen and MacLeod C I N, *Gaelic Songs in Nova Scotia*, Canada, 1964.
Daiches, David, ed., *A Companion to Scottish Culture*, London, 1981.
Dallas, Karl, *The Cruel Wars*, London, 1972.
Davie, Cedric Thorpe, *Scotland's Music*, Edinburgh, 1980.
Denisoff, R Serge and Peterson, Richard A, *The Sounds of Social Change*, Chicago, 1972.
Ding Dong Dollar: Anti-Polaris Songs, Glasgow 1961-.
Dobash, R E and Dobash R P, *Women, Violence and Social Change*, London, 1992.
Donaldson, Gordon, *Scotland: The Shaping of a Nation*, Newton Abbott, 1974.
_____ and Morpeth, Robert S, *A Dictionary of Scottish History*, Edinburgh, 1977.
Douglas, Sheila, ed., *Sing a Song of Scotland*, Surrey, 1982.
_____, ed., *The King o the Black Art and other folk tales*, Aberdeen, 1987.
_____, ed., *The Sang's the Thing*, Edinburgh, 1992.
Dubofsky, Melvyn, *We shall be all: a history of the Industrial Workers of the World*, Chicago, 1969.
Dunson, Josh, *Freedom in the Air*, New York, 1965.
Elliott, Kenneth and Rimmer, Frederick, *A History of Scottish Music*, London, 1973.
Emmerson, George S, *Rantin' Pipe and Tremblin' String*, London, 1971.

Farmer, Henry G, *A History of Music in Scotland*, London, 1947.
Finnegan, Ruth, *Oral Poetry*, Cambridge, 1979.
_____, *The Penguin Book of Oral Poetry*, London, 1978.
Foner, Philip S, *History of the Labor Movement in the United States*, vol. 4, *The Industrial Workers of the World, 1905-1917*, New York, 1965.
_____, *The Case of Joe Hill*, London, 1966.
Ford, Robert, *Vagabond Songs and Ballads of Scotland*, Paisley, 1904.
Gentleman, Hugh and Swift, Susan, *Scotland's Travelling People: Problems and Solutions*, Edinburgh, 1971.
Gower, Herschel and Porter, James, *Jeannie Robertson and her Songs*, Tennessee, forthcoming.
Grainger, Percy, 'Collecting with the Phonograph', *Journal of the Folk-Song Society no. 12* (vol. 3, no. 3), May 1908. Includes 'Signs and Accents used in this Journal', the notation he devised for his very detailed transcriptions, and 27 songs he collected.
Gramsci, Antonio, *Opere*, Vol. 6 *Letteratura e Vita Nazionale*, Turin, 1950.
_____ 's *Prison Letters* (Lettere dal Carcere), translated and introduced by Hamish Henderson, London and Edinburgh, 1988.
Greenway, John, *American Folksongs of Protest*, Philadelphia, 1953.
Greig, Gavin, *Folk-Song of the North-East*, 2 vols. Peterhead, 1909–14. Reprinted in 1 vol., Pennsylvania, 1963.
Grove, *The New Grove Dictionary of Music and Musicians*, 20 vols., London, 1980.
Guthrie, Woody, *Bound for Glory*, London, 1974.
Hardie, Alastair J, *The Caledonian Companion*, London, 1981.
Harker Dave, *One for the Money: Politics and Popular Song*, London, 1980.
_____, *Fake Song: The Manufacture of British 'folksong' 1700 to the present day*, Milton Keynes, 1985.
Hasted, John, *Alternative Memoirs*, Itchenor, 1992.
Henderson, Hamish, *Ballads of World War II*, Glasgow, [1947].
_____, *Alias MacAlias: Writings on Songs, Folk and Literature*, Edinburgh, 1992.
Henderson, Kathy and others, *My Song is My Own, 100 Women's Songs*, London, 1979.
Herd, David, *Ancient and Modern Scots Songs*, 2 vols., Edinburgh, 1776.
Hunter, Eveline, *Scottish Woman's Place*, Edinburgh, 1978.
_____, *Scottish Women's Handbook*, Edinburgh, 1987.
IWW Songs, 28th edition, known as *The Little Red Songbook*. Industrial Workers of the World, Chicago, more than 30 editions between 1909 and 1980.
International Folk Music Council, Journal of the, vol. 5, 1953.
Jeffreys-Jones, Rhodri, *Violence and Reform in American History*, New York, 1978.
Johnson, David, *Music and Society in Lowland Scotland in the Eighteeenth Century*, London, 1972.
Journal of the Folk Song Society, *One Hundred and Five Songs of Occupation from the Western Isles of Scotland*, London, 1911.
Karpeles, Maud, *Cecil Sharp: his life and work*, London, 1967.
_____, *An Introduction to English Folk Song*, Oxford, 1987.
Kay, Billy, *Odyssey: Voices from Scotland's Recent Past*, Edinburgh, 1980.
Keith, Alexander, *Last Leaves of the Traditional Ballads and Ballad Airs*, Aberdeen, 1925.
Kennedy-Fraser, Marjory and MacLeod, Kenneth, *Songs of the Hebrides*, 3 vols., London, 1909–21.
Kinsley, James, *Burns: Poems and Songs*, London, 1971.
Klein, Joe, *Woody Guthrie: A Life*, London, 1981.
Kornbluh, Joyce L, *Rebel Voices: An IWW Anthology*, Ann Arbor, 1964.
Laing, Dave and others, *The Electric Muse: The Story of Folk into Rock*, London, 1975.
Lampell, Millard, *California to the New York Island*, Guthrie Children's Trust Fund, New York, [1960].
Laslett, Peter, *The World We Have Lost*, London, 1971.
Law, T S and Berwick, Thurso, *Homage to John Maclean*, Edinburgh, 1973.
Leach, Robert and Palmer, Roy, *Folk Music in School*, Cambridge, 1978.
Legman, Gershon, *The Horn Book*, New York, 1966.
Leonard, Tom, *Radical Renfrew*, Edinburgh, 1990.
Lloyd, A L, *Folk Song in England*, London, 1969.
Lomax, Alan, *The Folk Songs of North America*, London, 1960.
Lyle, Emily B, *Andrew Crawfurd's Collection of Ballads and Songs*, Vol. 1, Edinburgh, 1975. Vol. II (forthcoming) Scottish Text Society.

_____, *Scottish Ballads* (Words only), Edinburgh, 1994.
MacColl, Ewan, *Scotland Sings*, Workers' Music Association, Scottish branch, 1953.
_____, *Personal Choice*, Workers' Music Association, London, n.d..
_____, *Folk Songs and Ballads of Scotland*, New York, 1965.
_____, *journeyman: an autobiography*, London, 1990.
_____ and Seeger, Peggy, *Travellers' Songs from England and Scotland*, London, 1977.
_____, *Till doomsday in the afternoon: The folklore of a family of Scots Travellers, the Stewarts of Blairgowrie,* Manchester, 1986.
MacDiarmid, Hugh, *Contemporary Scottish Studies*, Edinburgh, 1976.
MacDonald, Malcolm, *Ronald Stevenson: a musical biography*, Edinburgh, 1989.
MacDougall, Ian, *Essays in Scottish Labour History*, Edinburgh, 1978.
McGinn, Janette, *McGinn of the Calton: The Life and Works of Matt McGinn, with some autobiography and songs,* Glasgow, 1987.
McGinn, Matt, *Scottish Songs of Today*, London, 1964.
_____, *Once Again*, London, 1970.
MacKinnon, Niall, *The British Folk Scene*, Buckingham, 1993.
McLay, Farquhar, ed., *Workers City*, Glasgow, 1988.
_____, ed., *The Reckoning*, Glasgow, 1990.
McLean, Jim, *25 Scottish Rebel Songs*, London, 1968.
McMorland, Alison, *The Funny Family*, plus tape, London, 1975.
_____, ed., *Herd Laddie o' the Glen: Songs of a Border Shepherd*, 1988. Available from School of Scottish Studies, Edinburgh.
McVicar, Ewan, *One Singer One Song*, Glasgow, 1990.
Maver, Robert, *A Collection of Genuine Scottish Melodies*, Glasgow, c. 1866.
Merriam, Alan P, *The Anthropology of Music*, Illinois, 1964.
Mertens, Wim, *American Minimal Music*, London, 1983, pb 1988.
Moffat, Alistair, *The Edinburgh Fringe*, London, 1976.
Morgan, Tom, ed., *New Music 88*, London, 1988.
Morrison, George, *One Man's Lewis*, Stornoway, n.d..
Munro, Ailie, *The Folk Music Revival in Scotland,* London, 1984. Accompanying tape, SSC 076, Scotsoun, Glasgow.
_____, 'The Role of the School of Scottish Studies in the Folk Music Revival', *Folk Music Journal* (vol. 6, no. 2), 1991, pp. 132–68.
Music in Scottish Schools, London, 1978. No. 16 in the Series: Curriculum Papers.
New Edinburgh Review, Festival Issue, 'Folk song and the folk tradition', August 1973.
Newton, Francis, *The Jazz Scene*, Harmondsworth, 1961.
Ó Canainn, Tomás, *Traditional Music in Ireland*, London, 1979.
Opie, Iona and Opie, Peter, *The Lore and Language of School Children*, London, 1959.
Ord, John, *Bothy Songs and Ballads*, Edinburgh, 1990.
Orwell, George, *Decline of the English Murder, and other essays*, Harmondsworth, 1968.
Partridge, Eric, *Dictionary of the Underworld*, London, 1949.
Patriot Songs for Camp and Ceilidh, Bo'ness, W. Lothian, n.d.
Pickering, Michael and Green, Tony, ed., *Everyday Culture: Popular Song and the Vernacular Milieu; Popular Music in Britain Series*, Milton Keynes and Philadelphia, 1987.
Pocket Song Book, Workers' Music Association, London, 1949.
Porter, Gerald, *The English Occupational Song,* University of Umea, Sweden, 1992.
Porter, James, *The Traditional Music of Britain and Ireland: A Research and Information Guide*, New York and London, 1989.
_____, 'Convergence, Divergence and Dialectic in Folksong Parodigms: Critical Directions for Transatlantic Scholarship', *Journal of American Folklore* 106 (419) pp. 61–98, 1993.
_____, (ed. Shields, Hugh), *Problems of Ballad Terminology: Scholars' Explanations and Singers' Epistemics in Ballad Research,* pp. 185–96, Ireland, 1986.
_____ and Gower, Herschel, *Jeannie Robertson: Emergent Singer, Transformative Voice,* Knoxville, 1995.
Previn, André and Hopkins, Antony, *Music Face to Face*, London, 1971.
Purser, John, *Scotland's Music*, Edinburgh, 1992. Double CD, Linn OKD 008.
Rebels Ceilidh Song Book, The, no. [1 and] 2. Bo'ness, West Lothian, [1951], 1965. *Rebel Ceilidh Song Book '67*, Glasgow, 1967.
Reeves, James, *The Idiom of the People*, London, 1958.

_____, *The Everlasting Circle*, London, 1960.
Rehfisch, Farnham, *Gypsies, Tinkers and other Travellers*, London, 1975.
Robertson, Stanley, *Exodus to Alford*, Nairn, 1988.
_____, *Nyakim's Windows*, Nairn, 1989.
_____, *Fish-hoosies*, Nairn, 1990. 2nd printing Nairn, 1992.
_____, *The Land of No Death*, Nairn, 1993.
_____, *Ghosties and Ghoulies*, Nairn, 1994.
Rosenberg, Neil V, ed., *Transforming Tradition: Folk Music Revivals Examined*, Urbana and Chicago, 1993.
Russell, Ian, ed., *Singer, Song and Scholar*, Sheffield, 1986.
Sangs o' the Stane, Glasgow, [c. 1951].
Scotland's Travelling People, 1971–74, 1975–78: six term reports to date, from the Secretary of State's Advisory Committee. The fifth, 1986–88, was January 1989, and the sixth, 1989–91, was 1992. See Chapter VI, notes 16, 17 and 19.
Scottish Arts Council, *The Charter for the arts in Scotland*, Edinburgh, 1993.
_____, *Annual Report 1993–94*.
_____, Arts for a New Century, commissioned discussion papers, nos. 1–26, Edinburgh, 1991.
Scottish Studies, School of Scottish Studies, University of Edinburgh.
Seeger, Peggy, and MacColl, Ewan, *The Singing Island: A Collection of English and Scots Folksongs*, London, 1960.
_____, *Songs for the Sixties*, London, 1961.
Seeger, Pete, *Woody Guthrie Folk Songs*, New York, 1958.
Sharp, Cecil, *English Folk Song: Some Conclusions*, London, 1954.
Shaw, Margaret Fay, *Folksongs and Folklore of South Uist*, Oxford, 1977.
Shuldham-Shaw, Patrick, ed., and Lyle, Emily (general editor), with other editors and with music advisers, *The Greig-Duncan Folk Song Collection*, 8 vols. (1) 1981, (2) 1983, (3) 1987, (4) 1990, Aberdeen; (5) and (6) 1995, Edinburgh. Remaining 2 vols. forthcoming, Edinburgh.
Sing Out! Reprints, New York, 1960–62.
Smout, T C, *A History of the Scottish People 1560-1830*, Glasgow, 1985.
Stavis, Barry, *The Man Who Never Died*, New York, 1954.
_____, and Harmon, Frank, *The Songs of Joe Hill*, New York, 1960.
Stearns, Marshall W, *The Story of Jazz*, London, 1977.
Stevenson, Robert Louis, *Poems*, London, 1914.
Stevenson, Ronald, *Western Music: an introduction*, London, 1971.
Szabolcsi, Bence, *A History of Melody*, Budapest and London, 1965.
Thompson, Fred and Murfin, Patrick, *The IWW: Its First Fifty Years*, Chicago, 1955.
Tocher, School of Scottish Studies, University of Edinburgh.
Van der Merwe, Peter, *Origins of the Popular Style: The Antecedants of Twentieth-Century Popular Music*, Oxford, 1992.
Vansina, Jan, *Oral Tradition*, Harmondsworth, 1973.
Vulliamy, Graham and Lee, Ed, *Pop Music in School*, Cambridge, 1980.
Waters, Edgar and Murray-Smith, S, *Rebel Songs*, Australian Student Labor Federation, 1947.
Watson, Ian, *Song and Democratic Culture in Britain*, London, Canberra and New York, 1983.
Watson, William J, *Bàrdachd Ghàidhlig: Gaelic Poetry 1550–1900*, Inverness, 1959.
Whitman, Walt, *Complete Prose Works*, New York, 1909.
Whyte, Betsy, *The Yellow on the Broom: the early days of a traveller woman*, Edinburgh, 1979.
_____, *Red Rowans and Wild Honey* (sequel to above), Edinburgh, 1990.
Williamson, Duncan, *Fireside Tales of the Traveller Children*, Edinburgh, 1983.
_____, *The Broomie, Silkies and Fairies*, Edinburgh, 1985.
_____, *Tell Me a Story for Christmas*, Edinburgh, 1987.
_____, *A Thorn In The King's Foot*, Harmondsworth, 1987.
_____, *May the Devil Walk Behind Ye!*, Edinburgh, 1989.
_____, *Don't Look Back, Jack!*, Edinburgh 1990.
_____, *The Genie and the Fisherman*, Cambridge, 1991.
_____, *Tales of the Seal People*, Edinburgh, 1992.
_____, *The Horsieman: Memories of a Traveller 1928–1958*, Edinburgh, 1994.
Woods, Fred, *Folk Revival: the rediscovery of a national music*, Poole, Dorset, 1979.
_____, *The Observer's Book of Folk Song in Britain*, London, 1980.
Woolf, Virginia, *A Room of One's Own*, Harmondsworth, 1945.

Song Index

The songs which are *italicised* in this index refer to the songs transcribed in the book; the page number of the transcribed song is indicated with an asterisk.

Index